DATE DUE

DEMCO 38-296

MAKING
THE TURN

MAKING THE TURN

A YEAR INSIDE
THE PGA SENIOR TOUR

Frank Beard

with

John Garrity

MACMILLAN PUBLISHING COMPANY
New York

Maxwell Macmillan Canada
Toronto

Maxwell Macmillan International
New York   Oxford   Singapore   Sydney

Macmillan Publishing Company
866 Third Avenue
New York, NY 10022

Maxwell Macmillan Canada, Inc.
1200 Eglinton Avenue East
Suite 200
Don Mills, Ontario M3C 3N1

Macmillan Publishing Company is part of the Maxwell Communication Group of Companies.

Library of Congress Cataloging-in-Publication Data

Beard, Frank, date.
   Making the turn: a year inside the PGA senior tour/by Frank Beard with John Garrity.
      p.   cm.
   Includes index.
   ISBN   0-02-508060-1
   1. Beard, Frank, date. 2. Golfers—United States—Biography.
3. Senior PGA Tour (Association)   I. Garrity, John.   II. Title.
GV964.B4A3   1992   92-14182   CIP
796.352′092—dc20
[B]

Macmillan books are available at special discounts for bulk purchases for sales promotions, premiums, fund-raising, or educational use. For details contact:

Special Sales Director
Macmillan Publishing Company
866 Third Avenue
New York, NY 10022

Designed by M 'N O Production Services, Inc.

10 9 8 7 6 5 4 3 2 1

Printed in the United States of America

PREFACE

The drama of Frank Beard's comeback as a tournament golfer was muted only by the fact that hardly anybody knew what he was coming back from. He was suddenly *there*, in the hunt, at the 1989 U.S. Senior Open at Laurel Valley Golf Club in Ligonier, Pennsylvania. A second-round 69 gave Beard a one-stroke lead and a seat in the press tent, and he answered reporters' questions with a far-off look in his eyes, as if he were waking from a profound slumber.

Two days later, Beard found himself on national television in a final-round showdown with senior hotshot Orville Moody and somewhat unsure whether his nerves could stand the test thrust upon him so abruptly. Playing in only his eighth tournament as a member of the Senior PGA Tour, the fifty-year-old Beard stood over the shot so long at times that he seemed certain to shank or skull the ball.

"I felt his fear," said his wife, Susan, who walked the course with their children, Bridget, then seven, and Michael, nine. "Those who knew him—they could all see it."

That Beard held himself together in spite of the stares and speculation made his final-round 72 at Laurel Valley perhaps his biggest achievement as a golfer—bigger, certainly, than the eleven PGA Tour wins he had between 1963 and 1971. Time after time, when it seemed that his composure might crack, he drew the club back with a smooth motion that drew murmurs from the gallery and then applause for the ball's classic flight, a low, climbing draw. Beard didn't win the Senior Open—he finished second to Moody—but he evoked the admiration of all who watched his performance and tears from a few of them.

"There's nobody on earth that tries as hard as he does," Susan Beard said when the tournament was over. "God, to watch him struggle the way he does. I think I'd kill myself."

I had never met Frank Beard before Laurel Valley. I knew him only through his book, *Pro: Frank Beard on the Golf Tour*, published in 1970. Written with author–TV commentator Dick Schaap, *Pro* was a revealing, if less ribald, golf counterpart to Jim Bouton's classic baseball book, *Ball Four*, published the same year. Beard depicted professional golf as a two-tiered traveling show, 10 percent glamour and 90 percent grind. Superstars like Arnold Palmer and Jack Nicklaus toured by Learjet and dined with captains of industry, while journeyman pros drove hundreds of miles between stops, stayed at cheap motels, and prayed that enough putts would drop to meet expenses. "The tour's not what most people seem to think," Beard wrote. "It's not all sunshine and pretty girls and cheering crowds. It's a life without roots. It's a potentially rewarding life, but also a frustrating life. There's no real opponent except your own stupid mental and physical mistakes."

Some of Beard's remarks were taken as sour grapes. On the golf course, the purposeful, tight-lipped Beard saw large crowds only when he was paired with gallery favorites like Palmer, Gary Player, or the flamboyant Doug Sanders. Even in 1969 (the year covered in *Pro*), when Beard outplayed all the glamour boys and was the tour's leading money winner, he inspired mostly yawns. Comedian Don Rickles said, "He looks like a bad doctor from Elko, Nevada, whose chemistry set blew up and he's golfing for penance." Beard's game was so conservative, so calculated, that observers saw in him the golfer as businessman—the pro with the briefcase, reading the *Times* and waiting for the 6:18 to Pine Valley.

They thought so, anyway, until the publication of *Pro*. Beard's journal of a year on the golf tour revealed that the gray man with the grooved swing had a technicolor psyche. Fretful and pessimistic—"I'm a chronic worrier," he admitted—Beard nonetheless proved to be a keen and witty observer of tour life. For example:

- On Arnie's Army: "They run and stampede to see Arnie. They knock you down. They know nothing about golf etiquette. . . . If he pees in the fairway, they're happy."
- On charisma and his lack of it: "As I was leaving the clubhouse today I passed Lee Trevino packing up his car, wearing his cowboy hat and cowboy boots. I couldn't help but notice that he had a bigger crowd watching him load his car than I'd had watching me shoot 66."
- On golfers' vanity: "Lionel Hebert works so hard on his game he always looks amazed when he makes a mechanical mistake. The other day, I heard, he took a two-iron, stepped up and hit the ball so fat he tore up the turf and splattered mud all over himself. His shot was right on line, but the ball fell 30 yards short of the green. With mud dripping from him and from his two-iron, Lionel shook his head. 'I'll never learn to take the right club,' he said."

Of course, a lot has changed in twenty years. The biggest change in golf is an institution that did not even exist when Beard and Schaap wrote *Pro*—the Senior PGA Tour. From its germination a dozen or so years ago in a nostalgic exhibition series called "The Legends of Golf," the senior tour has grown to rival the regular PGA Tour in popularity. In 1991, the year covered in these pages, the circuit for pro golfers fifty years and older put on forty-two tournaments and paid out over $24 million in prize money. Twenty-four of the tournaments were televised, nine by the networks and fifteen by ESPN. *Golf World* recently called the PGA Senior Tour "the sports marketing success of the 1980s." It hasn't hurt, either, that

Jack Nicklaus and Lee Trevino, two of the biggest drawing cards in the history of tournament golf, have turned fifty and lent their prestige to the seniors.

The concept for *Making the Turn*, therefore, could not be more obvious: a sequel to *Pro*, a week-by-week journal of a golfer's life on the PGA Senior Tour. Each night, Beard spoke into a hand-held tape recorder, giving his impressions of the day just completed: the rounds of golf, the locker room conversations, the little crises of tour life. The tapes have been transcribed and edited into book form, but I have tried to preserve the spontaneity of the original entries. Part of the pleasure in reading any journal is seeing how rarely events conform to our expectations, how Monday's certainties become Sunday's doubts.

As the title implies, *Making the Turn* is about life's back nine. Most of the men Beard competes with today were in their competitive prime twenty years ago: Palmer, Player, Trevino, Gene Littler, Al Geiberger, Orville Moody, Chi Chi Rodriguez, Bob Charles. Their swings are not so long and supple now, their drives land twenty yards or so shorter than those of their big-tour counterparts, and some seniors suffer from the yips. But their pleasure in playing the game seems, if anything, enhanced. Beard's diary shows us how these athletes have changed with the years and how the game itself has changed.

Making the Turn is also an apt metaphor for Beard's own story: his comeback from alcoholism. Beard is blunt and unsparing of himself in relating how he drank away his golf game, his first family, and his self-respect. More than most senior golfers, he appreciates the second chance that the senior tour represents. More than most, he savors the simple joy of playing the game well again.

In his introduction to *Pro*, Dick Schaap noted an interesting phenomenon about the tapes he received from Beard: "I was fascinated by the way his spirits soared and sank in direct relationship to his play. If he had never mentioned a daily score, I could have guessed, strictly from his remarks and his tone, within a stroke or two."

I found that to be true of my own collaboration with Beard. There were times when he tried to trick me—leading off with some It's-great-to-be-alive anecdote before confessing that he'd shot 78 in the wind—but his voice always gave him away.

Happily, the perfectionism that makes Beard his own harshest critic also makes him a compelling observer of the golf scene. A hundred years from now, when golf historians sift the twentieth century for insights, I suspect that Frank Beard's tour journals will be quoted the way Tocqueville's diaries are quoted by students of democracy.

And they'll be a lot more fun to read.

John Garrity
Kansas City, Missouri
November 1991

ONE

JANUARY 1, TUESDAY/PASADENA, CALIFORNIA

The pressures I put on myself sometimes are unbelievable. Unbelievable! At fifty-two, I've got no reason to feel pressure at all. My house is paid for, my car is paid for, I've got my insurance done, I can take care of my kids' education. I'm not rich by any stretch of the imagination, but I've got nothing to worry about. I've got the PGA Senior Tour that pays us money no matter what we shoot. And if you can play a little bit—not great, just a little bit—you can earn a whole bunch more. I've got a great wife and kids, and the children from my first marriage are coming around. There's just nothing to worry about.

So why, when I go to the golf course, do I always feel like I have to prove I can play? I proved twenty-five years ago that I can play. I won eleven tournaments on the PGA Tour, and I was the leading money winner in 1969. I've earned half a million dollars in less than two years on the Senior Tour. I won a tournament last year, the Murata Reunion Pro-Am in Dallas. I finished second at the 1989 U.S. Senior Open. Everybody knows I can play.

And still, for reasons that are beyond me, I put this pressure on myself every time I play a tournament round. There's a little voice that says, "Today, you must prove to somebody—to yourself, to humanity, to God—that you can play golf."

1

It's been that way as long as I can remember, since I was
ten or eleven years old. I've always had to prove that I was
the best, that I could do it all—make straight As, serve Mass
every day, please my parents, and win golf tournaments. I
need to do these things to prove that I'm okay and to get
people to accept me and love me. Basically, that is the pressure I've lived under for most of my life.

Even in 1969, when I was winning all that money, I wasn't
a real confident person. I was always worried about finishing
in the top forty on the money list, that sort of thing. When I
began to go downhill in the seventies, my lack of confidence
turned into terror. Real fear. Never mind winning or making
the cut. I was only into saving face. I would have given $200
just to shoot a 74 and not embarrass myself.

My goal for 1991, then, is to shed some of the pressure.
Call it a New Year's resolution, a promise to myself, whatever . . . but this year I'm going to be nicer to Frank Beard.

I've got nothing to prove.

Tomorrow, my wife, Susan, and my nine-year-old daughter,
Bridget, will join me in San Diego for the Infiniti Senior Tournament of Champions, the first tournament of 1991. Yesterday, my eleven-year-old son, Michael, and I drove over the
mountains from our home in Palm Desert, California, played
a quick practice round on the tournament course at the La
Costa Resort, and then drove up to Pasadena for the Rose
Bowl Game. The game was nothing special—Washington beat
Iowa handily—and my mind kept wandering. It wandered
where it often wanders: to thoughts of my next tournament.

The Tournament of Champions has always been very special to me, and not just because I won it a couple of times
on the big tour, back in 1967 and 1970. The T of C brings
together all the tournament winners from the previous year,
so it's the most elite field of the year. It's also the smallest
field of the year, which means the money will be good. Fifteen
of us seniors qualified this year—sixteen if you count Jack
Nicklaus, who turned down his invitation—and we'll split a

purse of $350,000. First prize is $80,000, and even last place gets $11,000. And they treat you like kings—free rooms, free food, no thirty-six-hole cut. Our wives get the run of the place, including the La Costa Spa, where a mud pack normally costs fifty dollars and the therapy pools go for twenty dollars a day. It makes for a pretty easygoing week.

There's pressure, though. It's a tournament within a tournament, and we'll be playing the same golf course alongside the young pros. And it's the first big television tournament of the year, so all the snowbound golfers will be home, huddled around their sets.

I'm getting nervous already.

JANUARY 2, WEDNESDAY/CARLSBAD, CALIFORNIA

Mike Hill was talking in the locker room this morning. He thinks the golf course is too long for us, even at 6,814 yards. "They'll set the pins for the young guys," he said, "the big hitters like Norman and Couples. They'll be hitting 7-irons and 8-irons to the greens, so the pins'll be tucked. But we'll be hitting 3-irons and 4-irons, and some of us will need woods to reach some of the par-4s."

You hear that kind of talk occasionally on our tour. It's the senior's lament: "Where did my distance go?"

None of us will cry for Mike, though. He won the million-dollar tournament we had down in Puerto Rico just before Christmas. He took home $150,000, and for that kind of money he'd hit a fairway wood on every hole.

I looked around while I changed into my golf shoes, and there weren't many seniors in view. That's because there aren't that many seniors in the tournament—just thirteen now. Jack Nicklaus, who doesn't play many senior events, is skipping this one, and Gary Player and Bob Charles elected not to leave their homes in South Africa and New Zealand for this one tournament. The locker room is mostly full of the regular tour guys. They've got a thirty-one-man field, and that's without the Europeans, Nick Faldo and Jose Maria Olazabal—two guys I would love to have seen.

I did see Lee Trevino. SuperMex was grinning and wise-cracking, as usual. "I can tell I'm not in a Senior Tour locker room," he said, sniffing the air. "You walk into one of our locker rooms, it smells like a hospital."

Lee stopped to say hi. He's got a house in Palm Springs, and we have four or five common friends that we gamble with when we're home. They're all chiselers and they've got good handicaps, and Lee and I laugh about how they try to hustle us.

He gave my shoulder a slap and then wandered off between the lockers. A minute later, I heard him yell. "Hey, Chi Chi, I can't bum a cigarette off any of these kids! I bet they drink orange juice for breakfast instead of scotch!"

I just listened. My role in the locker room, as it is too often in life, is that of audience.

This La Costa golf course has changed some. I last played here in April of '72, so we're talking nineteen years. When the tour first came here, back in the sixties, there was very little development around—a house here, a house there. The course was pretty stark looking. All we had was the clubhouse and eighteen holes.

The trees, of course, have grown. The brown hills—the mountains, whatever you want to call them—are now covered with houses and condos and high-power transmission lines. There's eighteen new holes, too, and the greens are a little different. But basically it's the course as I remember it, only easier. I say easier because there's not much rough. La Costa used to have rough up to your butt. You used to show up at a tee shaking, because you knew if you hit it into the rough it was a sure bogey.

Susan and the kids spent the day horsing around while I played in the pro-am, so my companion most of the day was my caddy, Gary Colvin. Gary's name will come up a lot in the coming months. He's about four years older than me, and he's my very best friend. He's the food and beverage director at the Palm Springs Hilton, but he used to be my starter when I was head pro at the Canyon Hotel. He's going to come out and caddy for me some this season, when he can get away.

Caddying for the seniors is a lot of fun. First of all, you can use a golf cart, which takes away the back-breaking labor. Second, there's a teeny bit less pressure. Senior golf is serious business, but it's a little more relaxed than the regular tour was. It's easier for a friend to step in and caddy. Gary won't club me or read greens for me—he shoots about 95—but he'll get the cart down the fairway, clean the clubs, rake the traps, and keep me company. It's just another way to make tournament golf more pleasurable, less of a grind.

I saw a few of the younger players on the practice range, the regular-tour guys that Trevino calls "flatbellies." Some of them were knocking practice balls over the high wire fence at the far end of the range. Tom Kite asked me how my family was. Lanny Wadkins stopped to chat. These are guys I played a little golf with toward the end of my regular tour career, so we're friendly.

Everybody was talking about the little string of tragedies we've had this week. Dale Douglass's mother died and Jim Dent's brother died, and now it's in the paper that Tim Simpson's brother-in-law got stabbed to death in Atlanta. Simpson is one of the good young players on the big tour, and I wonder how this will affect him. He's not here, of course. He's back in Atlanta, trying to make some sense of things.

Jim Dent was in the locker room. He's a big, powerful man, and for years he played golf as if it were a test of strength, driving the ball longer than anybody else on the tour. I've known him for twenty-five years, and I don't think we've exchanged more than fifteen words at a time. We're friends, I think, but we've never talked in a meaningful way. I don't think it has anything to do with the fact that he's black and I'm white. We've just never been close.

Today was a little different. I said, "Gee, Jim, I'm sorry

about your brother." And he started talking to me about it. He told me his brother had been on dialysis but didn't like the treatments and didn't feel he wanted to live like that. Jim said his brother, as he neared death, gathered his sons around him and told them, "Take care of the women, they're weak." That old chauvinist stuff.

My gut feeling, as I listened to Jim, was that this was a man who needed to grieve. I could be wrong. Maybe he goes behind his bathroom door and cries his eyes out. But I think he was trying to be strong.

I don't know what I could have done—given him a hug?—but he obviously needed something more than somebody shaking his hand. Some men go through life and never shed a tear over a parent's death, a divorce—any pain at all. And they carry that pain around with them.

Nobody seems to be talking about Jack Nicklaus this week. Last year, Jack got criticized because he showed so little interest in playing in our tournaments. Dave Hill, in particular, got upset when Jack made some caustic remarks about the quality of competition on the Senior Tour.

Of course, Jack always backs up what he says. He played in only four senior events last year, but he won two of them and finished second in the other two. He'll probably play in the same four this year, but it's no longer an issue. "More money for us," is the prevailing attitude.

"Personally, I don't think we ever have to worry about Nicklaus," Rives McBee said recently. "He's not going to lower himself to play in the two pro-ams, which he would have to do each week."

It might be different if we didn't have Lee Trevino. Lee turned fifty a few weeks before Nicklaus, but unlike Jack he embraced the idea of the Senior Tour and played a full schedule last year.

People make jokes about Trevino's swing, but I don't think there's anybody who hits the ball as well as he does. Maybe his putting is not quite as good as some of the other guys', and he has foibles that can get in the way of winning sometimes, but nobody hits the ball better. And I include Nicklaus and the young guys on the regular tour. Trevino would still be winning tournaments on the big tour if he hadn't devoted so much of his time in his forties to television commentary.

Trevino, of course, is favored to win this week. Only a fool would bet against him after what he did on our tour last year: seven victories and over a million dollars in official prize money. He earned more prize money last year than Greg Norman, the leader on the big tour.

Lee jokes about it: "Whatever I made, it's not enough." I don't know his financial status, but he's been up and down the last twenty years, a published bankrupt once or twice, married three times. He's definitely chasing the buck right now.

That doesn't mean I'm conceding the Tournament of Champions to Trevino or to anybody else. I want to win the tournament. If I can't win it, I want to finish second. If I can't do that, I want to finish third. If I can't finish third . . .

But there I go again, putting pressure on myself.

JANUARY 3, THURSDAY/CARLSBAD

As I get older, I try to think of the bad things that happen to me on the golf course as "tests." They're not hurdles, they're not bad marks or punishments. They're things I need in my life, things that bring me back to reality. Today, in the first round of the Tournament of Champions, my test came in the form of a triple bogey on the third hole.

It was a gray day, cool, with occasional light showers. British Open weather. I had birdied No. 1 and parred No. 2, but on the third hole, a par-3, I hit a bad iron and the ball plugged under the lip of a sand bunker. I really had no chance, I couldn't get out. I barely dislodged the ball with my first attempt. Then I stopped thinking and didn't get out with my second, either. I barely escaped with my third.

This sort of thing has happened to me fairly often in my year and two-thirds on the Senior Tour, and it happened a fair amount in my declining years on the regular tour, when I played through a haze, a kind of funk. It's almost as if I'm outside my body, looking at myself and saying, "I don't believe this is happening." I'm not saying I'm two people, but I was down in that bunker today, and a voice was saying, "Back off, collect yourself."

But I didn't back off, I kept going. The voice said, "Stop! Stop!" I heard the voice, and I thought, "Why don't I stop?" But I took the club back, and before I knew it, it had taken me three to get out of the sand.

Is this part of the game when you get to be fifty-two? Is it normal for your mind to just go blank like that? I wonder, because I see the same thing happening to the other senior golfers. We miss the green and flub a chip shot and realize we're not going to make par, and we get so distraught and distracted that we make a 6 instead of a 5. Conventional wisdom would probably say, "Well, these guys are over fifty now, they're wise beyond their years. That's not going to happen anymore."

I'm telling you, it does happen. The things I was taught at sixteen and learned at twenty-five, I'm having to relearn at fifty-two.

Once I got out of the bunker, I made a nice little chip and a putt for my 6. And then I was back in the game. Actually, I felt as if the pressure had been lifted off me. The effcct of the triple bogey was, "Okay, okay, we're not going to shoot a 63 today, we're probably not going to win the tournament. We've got a little hurdle to jump now. But we can do it."

It probably made a difference that my little boy, Mikey, was there, watching. He's learning from me.

After that, I played good, solid golf. I birdied the next hole, almost birdied the next, and birdied the one after that. I wound up with a 69, and tonight I'm leading the tournament by a stroke.

Trevino, meanwhile, ran afoul of the cold, damp weather and had to withdraw from the tournament with a bad back. As I understand it, he hurt himself eight days ago in the desert, but he's been playing so well he didn't want to quit. He was off to a great start today—4-under on the front side—but then he aggravated his back and played the rest of the way in real pain. I ran into his caddy, Herman Mitchell, who said, "I tried to get him to leave the golf course, but he wanted to finish the round. He thought he might be better tomorrow."

I don't know much about kinesiology and what goes on in our muscles, but I'm sure this cold, misty weather doesn't do us any good.

After my round, I was summoned to the interview room, which at La Costa is in a movie theater inside the hotel. It's always a neat feeling to go to the press room. For one thing, it means you've done something worth talking about. They only bring in the tournament leaders.

I didn't used to get along with the press too well. I got burned a few times, got misquoted or had things I'd said quoted out of context or sensationalized in headlines. Even now, there's a part of me looking for a fight when I sit behind the microphones, a piece of me just hoping that somebody will say something that I can tee off on. But that's just nonsense from twenty years ago. The questions today were fun. The guys asked me about my round, about how I'd been, about Trevino's withdrawal, that sort of thing. I enjoyed it thoroughly.

The other night, in South Carolina, someone asked me a question at dinner, something about how I felt coming back to tournament golf. I said, "It's taking time, but I'm starting to get in touch with the little boy in me, the part of me that has fun on a golf course. I haven't been in touch with that little boy for a long, long time, but I feel him coming back."

Susie brought that up tonight. She followed me around today, and she said she had enjoyed our little conversations between holes, my banter with Gary, the way I kept my composure after the triple bogey.

She said, "Beardsy, it's good to see you making room for that little boy."

JANUARY 4, FRIDAY/CARLSBAD

Trevino was on a table in the fitness trailer this morning, trying to get his back in shape. "You know what I think it's from?" he said. "I been riding carts down in Palm Springs, and I just don't stretch those muscles out like I do when I walk."

Lee's had some serious back problems going back to the time he was struck by lightning at the 1975 Western Open. "This is different," he said. "Just a muscle pull. But damn, it hurt when I yanked it yesterday. I've had two back operations, and this thing was a *lot* worse."

My playing partner yesterday and again today was Bruce Crampton. Bruce is a very fine golfer, but he's difficult to play with. Every move, every flutter bothers him. Today, he was about to tee off on one hole when he got distracted by a marshal kneeling inside the ropes. The marshal was perfectly still, but Bruce's paranoia convinced him that the guy would stand up during his swing. So Bruce stepped away and asked the guy to move.

I think Bruce takes it a little too far. I mean, I've played on public golf courses and I've played college golf, and the only thing that bothers me is if you scream on my backswing. If you're moving off behind the tee somewhere or blowing your nose on the next green, I'm not aware of it. In fact, I wonder how Bruce can even see those things. He must have incredible peripheral vision.

Otherwise, I guess he's a pretty good guy to play with. He's very quiet, never says anything except "Good shot," moves along, and is very competitive. He wants to cut your balls off, so to speak. That makes you want to do the same to him. It's pleasantly combative.

Today's round was practically the reverse of yesterday's. I played solid golf for nine holes and was 2-under, and I could have been 3- or 4-under if I hadn't missed a couple of birdie putts. I was fine, I was rolling.

All of a sudden, I went into one of those funks. If I had hit a terrible shot or if something had happened, I could explain it. Nothing like that happened. I pushed my drive on No. 10 and made bogey. Okay, that's a tough hole; I'm still 1-under for the day and 4-under for the tournament. But that's when the funk began. The next hole, I took a 6-iron when I should have taken a 7, quit on it, and pulled it. But it was still just in the fringe, and I hit a beautiful chip, ran it three feet past the hole, only to miss the putt. Left it short, if you can believe it.

Okay, so I made two bogeys. I'm not down on myself. I don't like it, but I'm saying, "Let's go, let's get it back." On the next hole, I'm twenty-five feet from the hole, putting for birdie, and I hit it too hard. It's part of this thing where I'm going, "I *told* you not to hit it too hard, and you just did it!" I say, "Don't do it," and before I can finish the sentence, I've done it. It's weird.

The putt back was three or four feet, not a hard putt, but I missed it and made another bogey. After that, I wasn't into it. I had lost the rhythm, I had lost my flow. When things are going good, the flow is good. When things go a little askew, I'm lost. I don't get back in the game real quick.

Old man? I don't know. Maybe a year and a half of competition isn't enough. Maybe it's going to take me four years to relearn the lessons I mastered when I was twenty-one.

Anyway, I really lost it. I hit the next tee ball too quick— my tempo was bad—and hooked it into the woods for another bogey. The next hole, the par-3, was just a blank. Blocked an iron and buried it in the trap. I was lucky to make 4.

I don't know how you get it back together. I gave myself

the same pep talk going to the fifteenth tee that I'd given myself the last four holes. I hit a good tee ball there, hit an iron about six feet behind the hole. But even playing the hole correctly I was still in a funk, and I missed the birdie putt. Same thing on the next hole.

On No. 17, I left a wedge short of the green and was lucky to make par. But you know, if anything's going to keep me in the game this week, it's that par: seventeenth hole, second round. I made about a six-footer. I had dropped all the way back to even par for the tournament, and if I'd missed that one . . . well, I wouldn't have gone looking for a gun or anything, but it felt good to make one. I told Gary, "That's the hardest shot I've had in two days."

Even with my collapse, I'm not that far behind. My 75 leaves me in second place, five shots behind Crampton. Bruce shot a 69 today and was so happy that he smiled once.

But I wish I knew what causes my lapses in concentration. My mind is cluttered, for one thing. Mikey, my eleven-year-old, goes out to play, and you know what's on his mind? Nothing! His best friend could have just stolen his little girlfriend an hour before, but do you think Michael's going to think about it? No, his mind's on his golf shot. But as we get older, our minds get cluttered. We've got marriage, divorce, spirituality, money, depressions, investments, taxes, more marriage, more divorce, kids coming along. It's not all bad stuff, but it's clutter. All day long, my mind kept wandering: Am I going to win? How much money are we playing for?

I mentioned this to Susan this afternoon. She said, "You just need to talk back to yourself and say, 'Frank, thanks for sharing your thoughts with me, but I've got things to do.' Send yourself packing and get back to the game."

Then she got the kids, loaded their things in the car, and drove them back to Palm Desert. Michael has a soccer game tomorrow and Bridget has dance lessons, so they had to get home. But Susan will be back in time for my round tomorrow.

I'm glad of that. I want my baby by my side.

JANUARY 5, SATURDAY/CARLSBAD

Money is a big thing with me. It always has been. I get that from my mother, and it's been a driving force in my life. I can think of nobody better to win the lottery than me. I don't really need the money—I don't buy boats, I'm not obsessed with fast cars, I don't want to change my wardrobe—but I'm always afraid I won't have enough. It's crazy. I've been dead broke three times, but even during those periods I had everything I needed. I never lost a house, I never went hungry, I never slept in a flophouse. Nothing in my life gives credence to these fears.

I mention this because I was talking to Mikey on the phone a while ago. He said, "Good round, Dad. Four back, huh? What's second place?"

I said, "Fifty thousand dollars."

"Boy, that's almost like winning. You can still beat him, Dad. But if you can't, that second-place money will sure help a lot."

What have I done to him? He's not even eleven years old and he's thinking about the money. I've made a conscious attempt to shield him from that kind of awareness, but somehow he's gotten it from me. He doesn't get it from Susan.

He's right, though. Fifty thousand dollars, that's almost like winning.

After two days of rain and mist, we finally got some sunshine today. Warming up this morning, I watched some of the young guys hit balls—Bob Tway, Chip Beck, Lanny Wadkins. I enjoy seeing the young guys hit. They don't hit it any better than we do, but they hit it more consistently. Out of ten shots, Bob Tway might hit eight or nine, and I might hit six or seven.

I try not to compare myself to the fellows on the big tour. That's a mistake the women of the LPGA used to make, and it's a mistake some of the seniors make. The truth is, there's no comparison. Athletes are better today. I mean, the hundred-yard dash hasn't gotten any shorter, but they're taking less time to run it than they did when I was young. The athletes are better, the equipment is better, the coaching, training, and conditioning are better. To win here in 1970, I shot a 273, a very nice golf score. But I doubt that the Frank Beard of 1970 was as good as the Greg Norman or Tom Kite of today.

I have to say, the senior scores here have shocked me. After today's round, I'm four shots behind Crampton, who shot his second straight 69. George Archer and Mike Hill are six shots behind me. The other guys have put up numbers that would make a professional bowler happy.

I don't know where these scores are coming from. The course is playing relatively easy. As I mentioned before, there isn't much rough, and we play the course at 6,814 yards, a couple of hundred yards shorter than it measures from the championship tees. Even the rainy weather, to some degree, lends itself to low scores. The rain's not fun, but it makes the course softer. The greens are receptive, not hard and flaky looking. I just thought we would play better as a group. Nicklaus isn't here and Trevino had to pull out, but we're still talking George Archer, Dave Hill, Chi Chi Rodriguez, Jim Dent, Charlie Coody. Those are heavy-duty golfers.

With all those guys having problems, I guess I was lucky to be playing with Bruce for the third straight day. Part of me would like a change, but there's another side of me that says, "If it works, don't fix it." Crampton's playing nice, solid golf, and you'd rather be playing with a guy like that than with one of the fellows having problems. Bruce and I will be paired again tomorrow because we have the two lowest scores. That means we'll have played all four rounds together. I don't think that's ever happened to me before.

Gary, my caddy, hates Crampton right now. Not personally. He just looks at him as our enemy. "I know we can beat him," Gary keeps saying, "I know we can beat him." Gary is nervous as hell, and I think the fact that Crampton is so finicky makes him more nervous out of fear. With Crampton, you have the feeling at any given time that he's going to look at you for some insignificant thing and then miss his shot. You just never relax with Bruce.

Today, for example, I got into a funny exchange with him over a rules matter. It started on the twelfth hole, when I got a little quick with my tee shot and hit a horrible duck hook toward some houses and out-of-bounds stakes on the left. Upon landing, the ball hit something and ricocheted all the way back across the fairway on the fly. The way it bounded, it had to have hit a rope hold, one of those metal things that supports the fairway ropes.

It wasn't until I got to the green after my second shot that I noticed my ball had a cut in the cover. The rule book says I can mark the damaged ball and exchange it for a new one, as long as I announce my intention to my scorer—in this case, Crampton—and get his okay. It's the same rule that applies if you want to repair a ball mark on the green. You call your scorer over and say, "This is a ball mark," and then you fix it.

Now, I discovered a long time ago, maybe around 1965, that I was playing with about three hundred guys and I could trust them all. One or two cheaters turned up every year, but they were gone real quick. So if a man is behind the grandstand and he says, "Frank, I've got some cans of water here," I just say, "Fine, take a drop." Same thing with a ball change. All the guy has to do is hold up the ball for me, and I'll say, "Fine."

Most of the touring pros are just like me, and we extend each other a certain measure of trust. I can't remember the last time I asked somebody if I could fix a ball mark. I just fix ball marks. And when I have a ball to take out, usually I'll wave it at somebody. The usual response is, "Fine."

But Crampton is such a stickler in life that if you didn't show it to him, he might call a penalty on you. Not out of spite, not out of resentment—that's just the kind of person he is. So when I wanted to change that ball today, I took it over and showed it to him. He took it from me. And he *studied* it!

It kind of tickled me. He finally said "Okay," but as I walked away I said to myself, "Beard, you did the right thing." The exchange was no big deal, but it illustrates how stressful playing with Crampton can be.

As for my round today, I played very well. My only mishap came early, on the par-5 second hole. I've got it in my mind that I can hit a 3-wood onto or close to this green, so I haven't laid up on this hole. Water runs all the way down the right side, and a lot of the guys lay up or bail out to the left. I felt I was so far behind Crampton that I needed to make something happen, so I went for the green, came off the ball a little, and watched helplessly as the ball carried the water, hit the bank, and bounced back into the drink. I wound up making a 7.

Just as I did Thursday after the triple bogey, I kind of relaxed after that. "There's only a pinhole in the balloon," I told myself. "No 60 today. No no-hitter." All the standard clichés. In my case, they usually work. I came back with seven birdies and only one bogey, and I finished with a 68, the best round of the day. To be in the place I am with a double and triple bogey is almost insane, but it's a nice lesson. It's a lesson I'd like to print and hand out to kids, just to show them it can be done.

I can still win this tournament. Crampton has a four-shot lead and he's playing very good golf, but I can still win. My position is very good. I'm close enough to win, but not close enough to lose any sleep tonight. I guess that's the ideal position for me to be in, going into the final round.

Pressure has never been one of my friends. I've been able to use it and respond to it over the years, and my record would indicate that I am not prone to crumpling when the heat is on. But sometimes, when I am leading or close to leading and I go out and birdie the first two or three holes, I feel the pressure doubling on me. It's like, "Oh, Christ, here I am right in the middle of it now." Whereas, if I make a double bogey right off the bat, I feel the pressure slide away. I don't quit on myself, but I don't feel so much the burden of expectations.

I know that's not the ideal attitude for a professional golfer, and I don't imagine Jack Nicklaus has these thoughts. But that's how my mind works.

JANUARY 6, SUNDAY/CARLSBAD

I had no reason to be nervous this morning, but I was. I couldn't eat breakfast. Susan and Gary were on me to eat my waffle, eat my carbos, eat some fruit, do this and that. I just couldn't get anything down. That's not new for me. I've played many times with nothing in my stomach, with only my adrenaline to carry me.

We had a 9:30 tee time, and that may have contributed to my nervousness. Normally the tournament leaders tee off last, at around 12:30 or 1:00, but the television people wanted us to finish up while the regular-tour boys were turning nine. That way, they could get the seniors battle on TV before Tom Kite and Lanny Wadkins got into camera range.

At least I think that's what they had in mind. I was supposed to do an interview with ABC, but they didn't realize we were teeing off so early and nobody showed up. So I was out there and ready to go a lot earlier than I meant to be. That didn't help my nervousness any. I hit balls and practiced putting, and I kept asking Gary, "How much time do we have left?" I didn't have enough sense to go back to the locker room and take off my shoes, maybe watch some of the football game.

We finally got to the first tee, and my nervousness subsided a bit. I don't know why. I tried to get outside my nerves and talk to myself. "Beard, there's no reason to be nervous. There's plenty of money and plenty of titles to go around. Whatever happens, you've played well."

It must have worked because I felt halfway decent and hit a pretty good tee ball. Then I hit a good iron to about six feet and almost made birdie. I was pretty disappointed that I didn't, but boy, that's a good start. Usually, when I'm that nervous, I struggle on the first hole.

For Bruce and me, this was the fourth straight day cramped on that plane together. As I said before, I'm ambivalent. I've always liked to play with somebody different, just for the sake of variety, and there are friends I'm comfortable playing with. But Bruce and I were the only two in the field who were playing well, and you play a lot better when you play with somebody who is on his game. I'd rather be with Crampton than some guy who is struggling to break 80. That kind of play can rub off on you.

I was four behind, but I knew I could catch Bruce. He is a wonderful player and a great competitor, but he's not infallible. Anybody can stumble, particularly if you throw a couple of birdies on the board. That's what I was thinking on the second hole, the par-5. Yesterday, I knocked it in the water trying to reach the green in two, and I could have laid up today. Instead, I decided to try it again. Gary gave me a questioning look, but I took the wood for my second shot, hit it flush, and carried the water right up to the front of the green. From there, I wedged up and made birdie. Bruce, who had laid up with an iron, made par.

On the third hole, I hit a 5-iron to about six feet and made another birdie. Just like that, I had cut the lead in half, and it felt good. I hit the ball great on the next four holes and just missed birdie three times. Meanwhile, Bruce was kind of struggling. He was hitting some funny-looking iron shots and two-putting from thirty and forty feet. I said to myself: "Beard, you may have a shot at this."

On the eighth hole, he missed the green to the right and made bogey, and suddenly his lead was one.

The ninth hole is a par-5 back toward the clubhouse with water guarding the green. I hit over the water on my second, but Bruce had to lay up. He hit his third maybe twenty-five feet from the hole. I hit a nice pitch to about ten feet, and I had a further advantage: My putt was on roughly the same line as Bruce's. He missed his birdie putt, and I got to watch his ball roll. It went right.

I had a chance to tie the tournament right there, but I guess

I'm not smart enough to believe my own eyes. I played the putt to go straight, and it went right and missed the hole. Just like his.

Even so, I'm feeling good at the turn. One down and going to the back nine. I mean, that's a pretty enviable position. There's not a player in the world who wouldn't take one down at the turn on Sunday. I'm still feeling good on the next hole, even though I hit a pretty funky iron to the green. But I missed a two-foot putt for par, which I hadn't done all week. Bruce made par, and that kind of gave him a breath of fresh air.

Through all this, Gary was trying to be the perfect caddy, worrying that something might upset me or throw me off my game on the TV holes. On No. 13, I hit a squirrelly duck hook off the tee. An old fellow following me yelled, "Good shot, Frank! Good shot!"

Gary kind of looked back at the guy. A duck hook into the rough and behind a tree is not a good shot. He thought the guy was being sarcastic.

I walked down to my ball and studied the shot. I had about 180 yards to the hole, assuming I could bend it around the tree. I grabbed a 7-iron from Gary, took a whack at the ball, and watched with some pleasure as the ball curved around the tree, bounced between two sand traps, and rolled to within four feet of the hole.

The old guy yelled, "Good shot, Frank! Good shot!"

This time, Gary and I looked at each other.

As Gary was driving the cart to the next tee, the old guy came up to him. I was walking ahead. When Gary joined me on the tee, I said, "What'd the old fellow want?"

"He wanted to know what club you used. I told him, and then he said he's always loved you as a golfer. He followed you around when you won the Tournament of Champions here in 1970. He's not heckling you, he's cheering you on."

I teed up and then looked back at Gary. "Well, if I hit it in the trees here, we know there's one guy who'll think it was a great shot."

After I hit my tee ball—"Great shot, Frank!"—I walked over to the ropes and said hello to the old guy. He got a big kick out of it, and it also helped Gary to relax a little. I think he was more uptight than I was.

Getting back to the play-by-play, Crampton and I both parred No. 11, and we both had six-footers for birdie on twelve. I missed and he made his, and the lead was back to three shots going to thirteen. On that hole, as I mentioned, I hit a great 7-iron out of trouble to about four feet. Bruce left his iron in a bunker in a spot where even Bruce Crampton, the great bunker player, couldn't expect to get up and down. He didn't hit that great a bunker shot, and he wound up twelve feet back of the hole. I was thinking, "Maybe I can get those two strokes back right here."

Instead, he made his putt and I missed mine. We both made pars.

That pretty much finished me off. You don't ever give up, but at some point you buckle—the straw that breaks the camel's back, something like that. The next hole, I missed a par putt from six feet and Bruce had his four-stroke lead back. That's how it ended: Crampton 279, Beard 283. George Archer and Mike Hill finished third at 287.

I didn't win, but I was very proud of my play. I got a nice ovation when I holed out on eighteen, and Susie hugged me when I came out of the scorer's tent. Gary had a big smile on his face.

But I have to be honest. I have played enough golf and won enough tournaments that I am not exhilarated with a second-place finish and a $50,000 check. Don't get me wrong—when the week started, I would have taken this and run with it. But there was a tinge of disappointment because I had come so close to catching Crampton. I really wanted to win.

So while we packed the car for the drive back over the mountain to Palm Desert, my mind worked on the positives. One: This big second-place check gets me off and running on the money list. That's important because we get certain perks for finishing high on the money list. Two: A good start means that I won't have to play such a rigorous schedule through the year. One more early finish like this and I'll be able to spend more time with my family.

And it's such a neat feeling to know that I can still compete. I played poorly the last five months of 1990, so this was a wonderful shot in the arm. The Tournament of Champions has a small field, but it's the cream of the crop, our very best players. This tournament said to me, "Hey, Beard, you can still play. You really do belong out here."

But I'm thinking. Should tournaments still be talking to me, at my age?

TWO

JANUARY 7, MONDAY/PALM DESERT, CALIFORNIA

It didn't take me long this morning to get down to my AA meeting and see my guys. Alcoholics Anonymous meets every day of the year in a room at Fellowship Hall, a church building a few blocks from our old house in Palm Desert.

This valley is a haven for alcoholics. There's no place in the world that has the meetings and the fellowship we have here. Five meetings a day, seven days a week. You go in and realize that you're not a three-headed goat, because you're sitting next to a chairman of the board, a laborer, a golf pro, you name it. We all have the same problems.

I like my AA meetings, and when I'm home I attend from one to three a week, depending on how I feel. It's sort of like having a second family to come home to, a very diverse family. They're my friends. They're the ones who, along with Susie, help me keep my head level and keep my priorities where they're supposed to be.

They'd all heard about my good finish at La Costa and were happy for me, but once the meeting started we were into our sickness. Frank Beard, the "celebrity," is never present in the meetings. The fact that I play golf and play it well is fun for them, but they look at me as a recovering alcoholic, somebody

22

who is serious about doing something with his life on a level that matters.

After the meeting, I went home and piddled around the house, paid some bills, tried to use the time constructively. I don't have a home office. I just go into the bedroom and close the door, or I spread stuff out on the kitchen table. Today, I went through a pile of mail, and then I worked on my schedule for the next few months.

So far, I've got two outings lined up for the year. That's what we call these one-day pro-ams and corporate events that have become so popular. The producers and promoters of these events beat the bushes early, so I'm not surprised when I get approached in the locker room or coming off the range. They offer you anywhere from $2,500 to $7,500 for an outing, and some of the stars get more than that. My normal fee is $4,000 to $5,000 plus air fare and expenses. One of those I've lined up, with the National Football League players, is a repeat from last year. The other is a one-day charity pro-am that Bob Murphy hosts the week after the Royal Caribbean Classic. There will be others as the year goes by, and I'm not including the ones I do under my contracts with Hillerich & Bradsby and Mazda.

Some of the players have managers to handle this stuff, but I've kind of had it with managers. They take a cut, and for me, at least, they've never done a whole lot. I think I do better on my own.

I wish I wasn't home, to be honest. No, let me put that a different way. I wish I had a *tournament* this week. The first regular tournament on the seniors' 1991 schedule isn't until the first of February, so I'm looking at a three-week layoff. That's great if you're in a slump or need a rest, but I played very good golf at La Costa and would like to keep it going. I can't make any money hitting good golf shots at home.

When I'm home, I try to get the kids breakfast, fix their lunch, take them to school. Those aren't duties, it's just something I like to do.

The other essential part of my routine is my physical workout, which takes about an hour. I don't do anything special, just ride a stationary bike and do some stretching. My weight averages around 180 pounds now, but I weighed as much as 205 on the big tour. I was *round*. Now I'm more health-conscious, as are most of the seniors. I get high blood pressure when my weight goes over 190, so I have to watch that. And I've become very conscious of cholesterol. Fortunately, I married a woman who is very, very health-conscious. No matter how many times I slip off to McDonald's with the kids, I know I'm getting at least one meal a day that's good for me.

Blame it on the trendy California lifestyle, I don't care. I like the way I look in clothes again and I feel halfway decent.

What else? Maybe once a week I'll answer some letters or pay some bills while Susan does her yoga, and then we'll have lunch, either here or at a restaurant, and spend the afternoon together.

Most other days, I go right to the golf course. I usually practice at the Citrus Course, which is one of the La Quinta Hotel golf courses, because the practice area there is so nice. But I also play the hotel's other courses, the Mountain and the Dunes. The Landmark Development people, Ernie Vossler and his crew, have always made me feel very welcome, and I've been able to play and practice there for years. I'll always be grateful to them for that. I'm almost a member without being a member.

When I practice at the Citrus Course, I beat balls for a while on the range and then go over to the practice green and work with the wedges and putter. I'll stand there chipping, and some of the regular crowd will come over to shoot the bull. They're all golf nuts, and they've played in a lot of pro-ams. They smoke their cigarettes, and we just visit. "What do you hear about this new Cobra driver? . . . I'm playing with Brad Faxon in the Hope, what do you know about him, Frank? . . . That long putter you're using, you got the yips, or what?"

There always seems to be somebody to talk to, so I guess I'm not the only guy who doesn't have an office to go to.

JANUARY 11, FRIDAY/PALM DESERT

My check arrived today, the $50,000 I won for finishing second at the Tournament of Champions. There's two ways you can get your money these days. Merrill Lynch has worked a deal with the PGA Tour where they plug your earnings into a money-market account on Monday morning. You draw interest on it, you can write checks against it, whatever you want. I haven't availed myself of that. I just have the tour mail me the check. It usually leaves Florida on Wednesday morning and reaches me by the weekend.

On the old tour, they used to give you your check the next week at the tournament site. A tour official would walk around with a hundred thousand dollars' worth of checks in a briefcase. If he missed you early in the week, he'd have the check waiting for you on the first tee on Thursday.

I won the Tournament of Champions one year, when it was still in Las Vegas, and they had twenty thousand silver dollars stacked up for me to take home. It made a good picture for the newspapers, but I didn't want to have to carry my winnings off in a wheelbarrow. I asked for a check instead.

JANUARY 12, SATURDAY/PALM DESERT

I've been thinking about the problems I continue to have with pressure, the fears I carry with me during a round. I've learned in my AA meetings that a lot of people have the same feelings and problems. They just don't show it.

The golfers I play with aren't any different. I've talked to Harold Henning and Larry Mowry, and both of them, without admitting to feelings of terror, have fears that I would not have thought they had. Golf fears—worries about trouble to the right or left, fear of pulling the ball, that sort of thing. And I see guys laying up on certain holes, when they should be going for it. Like that second hole at La Costa, the par-5 where I hit the ball in the water and made double bogey in the third round. Bruce Crampton laid up on that hole all four days. It shocks me that a guy who hits the ball as well as he does, a guy with so much control, would lay up there.

Was Bruce afraid? I don't know. I haven't asked him, and Crampton probably wouldn't tell me if I did.

Fear is a tough word and certainly a label no one wants to own. Maybe I should say we're more conservative than we were on the regular tour, less confident. Our edges aren't holding as tightly as they did before.

At least I'm aware of the problem. I'm still going to therapy, I go to my AA meetings, and I pray a lot. I feel that somewhere down the line I'm going to beat this thing.

JANUARY 14, MONDAY/PALM DESERT

I got started on my taxes this morning. Spread everything on the kitchen table and started sorting and adding and subtracting. I have an accountant here in town, a dear friend named Dennis Godecke, who does the actual tax returns, but I have to give him everything he needs. I suppose it takes me only four or five hours to do, but I spread it over two or three months.

My taxes used to be very complicated, back when I was trying to invest and be a big mucky-muck. They aren't that complicated now. My life is basically income/expenses. All I have to do for Dennis is keep track of my income, which comes right off my deposit slips, and my expenses. The income is easy. Every time I win money in a tournament, the check from the Tournament Players Division comes with a computer printout, which is cumulative for the year. The expenses are a little trickier, because I have to keep track of hotel bills, entry fees, caddy fees, car rentals, plane fares, and meals. Dennis has me on a computer here, and he keeps a running tab.

What complicates the tax picture for a professional golfer is the requirement that we file state income tax estimates and returns. We've kind of come full circle on that. When I was on the regular tour, we had to file tax returns in all the states that had income taxes, all the states where we made money. It was a big pain in the neck, and we in the Tournament Players Division fought it.

Then we went through a period where we didn't have to file all those returns, we just filed in our home states. That was nice.

Now the states want their money again. It's not just golfers. Apparently they're going after ballplayers, too. If Jose Canseco of the Oakland Athletics plays five games in New York, then New York wants its share—whatever 5 is to 162, the number of games in a season. It has nothing to do with where you live; it's a question of where the money is generated.

This has really opened a can of worms. Last year, I had to file in thirteen other states. If I win $2,000 in Kansas City, the state of Missouri will hear about it. If the Wigwam Hotel pays me five grand for an outing in Arizona, that's five grand I have to account for in Arizona. I don't lose any money paying these taxes—I'll get a credit in California—but it's a lot of trouble. Dennis figures the state returns off the federal returns, and he prorates everything. He even prorates his accounting fee. If he charges me $1,000 for something, I get a prorated deduction from all the states. It's a mess. And if you don't pay, they'll come and get you. They'll attach your money!

I know, nobody likes to pay taxes.

JANUARY 17, THURSDAY/PALM DESERT

This week, I've been working a lot on tempo in my golf swing. Like most pros, when I miss a shot it's usually because I get anxious. I get quick. That duck hook I hit in the third round at La Costa, the one that hit the rope holder and ricocheted across the fairway—that was the result of a too-quick swing.

So now my battle is to work on tempo. Which is really hard to do. Hank Haney, the teaching pro, told me something four or five years ago. He said, "There is no way you can *make* yourself swing with tempo. You have to be mechanically correct, and that creates tempo."

That kind of makes sense to me. If you try to create tempo, you tend to swing slow, and you can't swing slow. You want to swing hard and fast, but correctly. Otherwise, you're like the little kid trying to draw a straight line. The kid tries to be so careful—he goes *soooo* slow—and he gets this wavy line.

So I think Hank is right: Good mechanics correct tempo. But for me, the mechanics are there. My tempo is thrown off by these dark images. I get up on the tee and there's a creek snaking along the right side of the fairway, and it's, "Oh, jeez, I don't want it to go over there." Once you start that, you're dead. Almost invariably, your swing gets fast. What happens is, your back and leg muscles won't work. Your body basically stays still and you end up hitting with your hands and arms, which is a very fast, incorrect move in any sport. Try throwing a ball or hitting a tennis ball with just your hands and arms. Try throwing a discus. It just won't work.

That pretty much tells the story of almost every shot I miss.

JANUARY 19, SATURDAY/PALM DESERT

Ten days till the start of the 1991 season. Two weeks since I last played a competitive round. Any momentum I might have had coming off the Tournament of Champions is gone.

It occurs to me—as it has before—that my golf swing is pretty sound. In fact, my golf swing is about as good as it ever was. It will work, if I can just get my head screwed on right. For a golfer of my ability, the mental side is much more important than the physical side. You learn to hit the ball when you're eighteen years old, but then you have to learn to use your brain effectively. For the young guys, the mental side is learning how to play golf—course management, temperament, that sort of thing. For those of us who are older, the mental side is trying to recapture some of the concentration and confidence we had at our peak.

That's why I've been working with a sports psychologist, a little gal named Dr. Deborah Graham. She works with some of the other fellows on both tours, so she's pretty familiar with the golfer's mind. We've been trying to improve my imagery on the golf course as a way to keep focused on the moment. She likens it to a light switch I can flick on and off— charging warrior on the golf course, placid family man at home. If the imagery works, it should bring me right to the moment, ready to execute my golf shot with intensity and with nothing else on my mind.

Our work at this time is new and certainly hasn't shown any results yet, but I have confidence in Dr. Graham and where we're going. I think it will show some dividends if I can stick with it.

JANUARY 20, SUNDAY/PALM DESERT

I watched a little of the Hawaiian Open on TV this evening. It was on during prime time because of the time difference.

I don't watch as much golf as I used to, and I don't enjoy watching the seniors at all. It means I'm not playing well or I'm not there, and I don't want to see them making all that money. But I enjoy watching the other tour, if for no other reason than they're better players. I like to watch golf swings, and I love to see the young guys play the holes I played when I was on the big tour. I like to see where they hit their drives and how they manage the course.

Lanny Wadkins was today's winner, which tickled me. Lanny is almost a good friend of mine. I'm older than he is, so we've never traveled in the same circles, but we played a lot of golf together and we get along well.

If there's one connection I have with the junior tour, it's the older players. And I pull for 'em. The Ray Floyds and the Hale Irwins, they're my guys. Tom Watson. Even Nicklaus, when he goes back over there. I follow the names I know.

I don't know if I have joined the battle of old against young. I don't dwell on age. I don't fall into the stream of old men who say they feel old. I don't *feel* old; I feel the same as I did twenty years ago. But neither do I fool myself into thinking I can play with the young guys anymore. It just does my heart good to follow the older players.

Okay. Maybe 1 percent of me says, "You can still do it out there."

JANUARY 25, FRIDAY/PALM DESERT

Well, I'm a published writer again. The latest issue of *Golf World* came in the mail today, and I turned right to the last page. There it was—"Opinion from the Tour"—with old Beardsy as the guest columnist.

This is something I worked out last summer with the *Golf Digest* people, who publish *Golf World*. I used to write a column for *Golf Digest* when I was one of their "playing editors," back before I fell off the world. Last year, they asked if I'd like to renew the relationship, and I did some exploratory interviews at the Players Championship with Geoff Russell, one of their good young writers. Then, at the U.S. Senior Open, I hammered out an agreement with Terry Galvin, *Golf World*'s editor. The contract calls for me to do six columns this year in rotation with Paul Azinger and Amy Alcott, who will comment on the regular tour and the LPGA.

Geoff called with some more questions shortly before Christmas, and he's put together two or three columns based on last year's interview. In this first one, I draw a comparison between Lee Trevino and Jack Nicklaus. Lee decided a few years ago that he was going to play the Senior Tour, and he really set his mind to it, while Jack sees senior golf as pretty humdrum. But I explain in the article that Jack doesn't need the money, while Lee does. Unlike Jack, Lee was never able to build the money he earned from golf into a personal fortune, so winning a million dollars out here gives him some breathing room financially.

I also point out that hitting a golf ball interests Lee more than it does Jack. When we were in Scottsdale last year for the Tradition, and Lee wasn't playing well, he was hitting five hundred to six hundred golf balls a day. He loves to play golf, and he thinks he can only add to his reputation by playing senior events. Jack, who is probably the greatest golfer to ever play the game, doesn't think he can add any more luster to his career by winning on our tour. But playing poorly on the Senior Tour—*losing* on the Senior Tour—might tarnish his image.

Anyway, Mikey read the column, my first in ten years. He didn't have anything to say about the content, but he liked that they ran my picture over the words. Susan had some nice things to say about it. And Bridget didn't care at all.

Maybe I need to write something more controversial, stir things up a little.

JANUARY 26, SATURDAY/PALM DESERT

I broke one of my rules and watched some senior golf on TV today—that's how anxious I am to get back to work. The Senior Skins Game was on, and I watched it. That's as close as I'll ever get to that cash cow, unless I buy a ticket to Hawaii and show up as a spectator.

I'm not jealous. I don't feel deprived. The TV Skins Games are television shows, and Frank Beard has never been magic on the small screen. The guys who are playing this year—

Nicklaus, Palmer, Trevino, Gary Player, and Chi Chi Rodriguez—
will draw the viewers. The way I look at it, that's got to
help me. Those guys make our sponsors feel more secure
about the tour, they give us credibility. And that adds to *my*
security.

Twenty years ago, I felt the same way. I didn't complain when
we'd go to an outing and I'd get $1,500 and Palmer would get
$7,500. I said, "That's what he's worth, compared to me."

Nothing has changed. I could have a ten-times-better record than Chi Chi and Nicklaus combined this year, and I
still wouldn't be invited to the Skins Game. That's fine. I
understand.

But the Skins Game, for me, doesn't have near the validity
it would have if the guys had to pony up a couple of hundred
thousand dollars to take part. There's still no pressure like
playing for your own money. I suppose that Nicklaus and
Palmer could shrug off $200,000, but still, if they had to write
the check . . . yeah, it would make a difference.

I can say that because I've played for a little more money
than I had in my pocket. I never played with a Dr Pepper
bottle, the way Trevino did down in Texas, but I bet on myself
on occasion in high school and college. That's pressure. When
I went out on tour, playing for twenty-dollar nassaus in practice rounds, I was spitting the bit. I'm kind of a tightwad, and
it just irritates me to take money out of my pocket.

Tournaments are different. I was telling Susie the other
day, "I don't think I ever choke in a tournament, because I
know I'm always going to get some money."

That's how I feel. There's a guy standing over there, and if
you play good he gives you *this* check. If you don't play good,
he gives you *that* check. I'd rather have the big check, but I
know I'm going to get one. You can't lose.

That's not to say there's no pressure in these big Skins
Games. The fear is that you'll get shut out, that you'll get
embarrassed. Today, for instance, Gary Player's golf was as
good as anybody's, but he didn't make a cent. So he'll be a
little desperate for a skin tomorrow. There isn't a guy who's

been shut out in a Skins Game that wouldn't have *given* $25,000 to win a skin.

JANUARY 27, SUNDAY/PALM DESERT

Gary Player was all set to win $285,000 today, but he forgot who he was for a moment and left Hawaii with nothing but a tan. He and Nicklaus were playing for the last carryover, the other three players having bowed out on the first playoff hole. Nicklaus tried to exploit his strength on the hole, a reachable par-5, but drove his ball way right into the lava rocks and had to take a drop. He was in the rough, 265 yards from home, with a bunch of palm trees in his way. Player, figuring that par would win the hole, played short with his second, but then hit an awful chip that didn't even reach the green.

Nicklaus, meanwhile, hit an incredible hook around the trees and made it to the front edge. Both guys made par, and Player had to be kicking himself. One hole later, Nicklaus putted in from the fringe for an eagle and the $285,000 payoff.

I'm sure Don Ohlmeyer, who created and produces the Skins Games, was pleased. His ratings rise and fall with Nicklaus and Palmer. The playoff format, in fact, all but gives Jack the money before he even tees off. Instead of starting the playoff at No. 15 or No. 1, Ohlmeyer sets it up so only two holes are used—ten and eighteen. Both those holes are par-5s, giving Jack, with his tremendous length off the tee, a leg up on everybody else.

Now, Ohlmeyer's going to say that it's easier logistically to move the crowds around those two holes, and I'm sure that's part of it. But television producers are somewhere between insidious and totally ingenious. Ohlmeyer knows that if Nicklaus wins, Nicklaus will be back next year. So Ohlmeyer gives him every chance he can.

I have to confess, I didn't see Jack's last putt. By that time, I was out at La Quinta working on my own game.

I'm tired of watching other people make money at golf. I can't wait to get down to Miami and get this season rolling.

JANUARY 28, MONDAY/PALM DESERT

Nolan Henke won the Phoenix Open yesterday. First prize was $180,000—more than I made for all of 1969, the year I was leading money winner.

Do I feel gypped? Not at all. I came along just after Arnold Palmer and television made their nice marriage, and I made good money. I was into the $100,000 years pretty quick. That's not a lot by today's standards, but it was a *whole* lot by the standards of the time. I had a good career, and I think most of the seniors would say the same thing.

Maybe we'd feel different if we didn't have the Senior Tour. Then we'd be like old ballplayers, sitting around on benches in the sun and grumbling about the money the young punks are making. We're lucky. We've got a tour. And it's not just an old-timers' game. We've got a lot of money and competition.

But someone like Henke wins a tournament, and the guys at La Quinta come up to me and say, "Frank, who *is* this guy?"

I don't know Henke, but I can generalize about the young guys who are starting to win tournaments. They're kids who grew up playing golf and went to college and hit balls until their hands bled. Just like I did. Tom Kite was their model, just like Ken Venturi was mine. I remember when I first went on tour. Venturi and Cary Middlecoff were standing there, and I went, "Oh, my God. I'm actually gonna play with them!"

So the kids today aren't any different. They're just better athletes now. And I have to tell you, I like to watch them swing. There's a youthful arrogance about them that I feel I had at one time.

It didn't take me long to pack tonight. I've been doing this so long, Jesus Christ, I ought to know what goes where in a suitcase. Tomorrow I fly to Miami and start a new season on the Senior Tour. I'm taking ten or twelve pairs of slacks, a dozen Mazda shirts, my Power-Bilt visors, and some socks and underwear. My most important possession is my little coffeemaker, but I also take a travel iron. I pack pretty much like an old lady. The suitcase is one of those old grasshoppers, the kind that puffs up at either end. It seems like you can always get something else in it.

Everything has to go in the suitcase and in my golf bag. I don't carry a briefcase. The most you'll ever see me with in the airport is a newspaper or a book to read on the plane.

Bridget is all in an uproar about my leaving. We were driving around before dinner, the kids in the back seat, and Susie and I were talking about the trip—"What time do you have to be at the airport? Have you got what you need?"—the stuff we've been talking about for days. Bridget wasn't really listening, but suddenly something we said sunk in. She screamed, "Nobody told me Daddy was leaving tomorrow!" She started crying.

It was pretty dramatic. When we got home, I tried to explain to her that I'd never be gone more than two weeks at a time this year, and that we'd talk every day. "I'll call every night," I said, "and sometimes in the morning before you go to school. Daddy will be home pretty quick. And remember, you're going ice skating next Thursday, and Betty's birthday is coming up the Friday after . . ."

She was pretty much inconsolable. Michael, who's more tuned in to adult talk, knew exactly when I was leaving and when I'll be back.

I don't remember my kids from my first marriage crying like Bridget did tonight, but they grew up with my travel and got used to it. I mean, Danny went to Hawaii with us when he was seven months old, he practically grew up in motel rooms. He thought all daddies came home just to change clothes.

That doesn't mean they liked it. I've since learned that my leaving was very, very sad for them and left some lingering wounds. But they didn't cry and carry on. Daddy leaving? It was just a fact of life.

THREE

JANUARY 29, TUESDAY/KEY BISCAYNE, FLORIDA

When I got off the plane at Miami International Airport this afternoon, I didn't have to scramble to catch a cab or lug my bags out to the curb to wait for a rental-car shuttle. At every airport there's a tournament transportation desk near the bag claim area, and all we have to do is check in with them. They give us a folder full of maps and a directory of recommended restaurants, tourist attractions, local doctors, twenty-four-hour pharmacies, and convenient shopping sites. The minute my bags were off the carousel, I was on my way to the golf course in a car driven by a tournament volunteer. At the golf course, I was given the keys to a new Cadillac, which is mine for the week. There's a parking space by the clubhouse that has my name on it.

We didn't always get the star treatment. When I was a family man on the big tour, I drove from tournament to tournament in a station wagon full of kids, toys, diapers, laundry bags, suitcases, golf clubs, and headaches. When I began to make some noise as a player, I sometimes managed to get a courtesy car for a few weeks at a time, usually a Buick. But it was no sure thing. I had to hustle for it.

Now I have to laugh when I drive around in one of these big white Cadillacs. The sticker price for one of these babies is more

36

than the total purse of a typical tournament in 1962, the year I joined the tour. That says something about how far professional golf has come. Or about inflation, I don't know which.

The tournament headquarters hotel this week is the Sheraton Key Biscayne. The tour gets us a rate wherever we go, so I stay at the Sheratons, Marriotts, and Hyatts. It's expensive by my standards—sixty-five or seventy-five dollars a night—but a lot of guys traveling on business would love to get rooms for that.

It's nice that we get the rate, but I stay at better hotels because I've changed. I used to cut corners on the regular tour, living two or three to a room at the cheapest Ramada Inn or Holiday Inn I could find. My first year on tour, I spent $11,000 on travel, lodging, and food. That was my *total*. My original sponsors, ten guys who were bankrolling me, finally took me aside and said, "Beard, it's time to start eating some T-bone steaks and staying at better places. You're playing good now, but if you keep eating McDonald's you're going to turn into McDonald's."

It was good advice. I made myself eat the occasional T-bone and I stopped sharing a room. But I was still cheap. For five straight years, beginning in 1967, I earned more than $100,000 in official prize money, but I continued to stay in hotels that cost about twenty dollars a night. And I hated to spend *that*.

Anyway, when I started back on the Senior Tour, I said, "Hey, we're playing for a lot of money and I'm going to be making a lot of money. I'm going to live nicely. Not in penthouses and suites, but I'm not going to look at the cost."

Another thing I promised myself on the Senior Tour: no more penny-pinching on caddy fees. On the old tour, I was notorious for paying a caddy what he was worth to me, not what *he* thought he was worth to me, and certainly not the going standard, which was not necessarily my standard. There was a story in *Pro* about my winning the Westchester Classic, the biggest-money tournament on the tour in 1969, and paying my caddy $750, which was a lot more than I thought he was worth. He looked at the check as if I'd handed him a roll of wet toilet paper and said, "Are you kidding?" He thought he was worth twice that.

What I didn't write was that my coauthor, Dick Schaap, had to talk me into giving the guy that much. I was writing out a check for about $250, and Schaap said, "Frank, you can't! They're gonna crucify you!" So I gave the caddy three times more than I was going to, and they *still* crucified me— "they" being the caddies and the press.

So that's another thing. I've done my arithmetic, and I figure paying the going rate will cost me $4,000 or $5,000 a year more than I would gladly pay. But it's no longer worth it to me to save that money. It's not worth it to have these caddies sitting there saying, "There goes old cheap Beard."

So the word is out: Frank Beard pays $350 a week and 5 percent of what he earns. Some caddies actually smile at me now when I walk by.

That may explain why I had no sooner gotten out of the car today when Seemore the caddy trapped me.

"How are you, Frank? You got somebody this week?"

Seemore's real name is Melvin Johnson, but he goes by the name of Seemore because he claims he can "see more" on the greens. Which he can't. He's just a little fellow, a slightly built black man about my age or older with gray hair and a lot of miles on him. I guess I've known Seemore for thirty years. He caddied for me off and on back on the old tour, and I always liked him.

I said, "Let me see, Seemore."

It's not that I don't want him. I just don't want to rush into it. I decided last week that I would wait until the last minute to pick a caddy here. It's a complete departure for me. I want to see what happens if I don't plan and measure everything down to the last centimeter. I find that when I don't rush into things, when I wait and let the plan unfold in front of me, good things happen.

So I said, "Check with me tomorrow, Seemore. I'm going to sleep on it and decide tomorrow."

This is the new Frank Beard.

JANUARY 30, WEDNESDAY/KEY BISCAYNE

Today started on a sad note. When I got out to the Links at Key Biscayne, the tournament course, I learned that Charlie Coody's dad died during our layoff. I can't remember when a death in another person's family has affected me so much. Mr. Coody was a dear friend of mine, so I feel the loss personally. But more than that, I feel for Charlie, who was so close to his dad. Charlie broke the news to me in the locker room, and I could see the pain in his eyes.

We, the senior golfers, are reaching the age now where this sort of thing happens more frequently. I have to remind myself to pay more attention to what kind of day it is, to put aside more time for people, to stop and smell the roses, all that cliché stuff. This has been tough for me. I've been a perfectionist and a workaholic all my life, and I have not stopped enough to enjoy what's going on.

Later, I ran into Lloyd Moody, Orville's brother. Lloyd's playing his first tournament since winning a spot in the qualifying school, and he looked like a kid on his first day at a new school. It's hard to believe that a golfer can be nervous at age fifty, but God, can we get nervous. You wonder if something happened to your golf game while you were home. You wonder if your body will give out. All these crazy thoughts come into your mind. I don't care if you won five tournaments last year and were leading money winner—you're back at zero now.

Orville was with Lloyd, and we talked a little bit about the off-year he had last year. The Sarge won't admit it, but I think he had some physical problems. He missed a few tournaments in '89 because of his blood pressure, and I just don't think he was up to snuff last year. And that affects you psychologically. He played enough—he was there, he wasn't walking around with a cast on his leg—but he didn't come close to the great year he had in '89, when he won the Senior TPC and the Senior Open and made about $650,000.

After talking to Orville, I walked over to the caddy tent and selected a caddy. As I mentioned, this is a departure for me, picking a caddy thirty minutes before I tee off in a pro-am.

I'm not going to have a regular caddy this year. I had Steve McGee all last year and Sam Bateups the year before, and while they both were very good friends and excellent caddies, I found that I had begun to give them too much responsibility. They hadn't *taken* it, they'd not made any mistakes—no fingers pointed at them—but as I began to let them read greens and help me select clubs, I found myself losing intensity.

The Japanese have a word for "the moment"—they call it *satori*. When I should have been in the moment, totally burning in the moment, I would turn to Steve and say, "A little 6, a big 7 . . . what do you think, Steve?" And as he would cogitate and give me input, I would briefly lose contact with what I was trying to do. I was out of *satori*. It may not seem like much, but over eighteen holes it was happening too often. I was giving my caddy part of my energy.

So I've decided this year that I'm going to get a different caddy each week, or maybe the same one for a couple of weeks, but not much more. He's going to clean the clubs, carry the bag, maybe get a few yardages, but I'll pick my own clubs, do my own putting, and read my own greens. I feel comfortable about this. I think this is going to work very, very well for me.

The caddy I selected was Seemore.

So Seemore and I went out and played in the pro-am. This tournament, the Royal Caribbean Classic, is a regular Senior PGA Tour event, which means we play two days of pro-am before the individual tournament gets started on Friday. Each pro plays with a team of four amateurs who pay about $2,500 each for a round of golf, cocktails, a pairings party—usually held in the hotel on Tuesday evening—and an awards party on Thursday or Friday. Typically, you're paired with business executives, real estate developers, politicians . . . guys who are successful in life. There is prize money for the pros who shoot the lowest daily scores and more prize money for the pros whose teams turn in the lowest best-ball scores. It's only a few hundred bucks, but it's enough to keep it from being just a practice round for the pro.

I should confess at the outset that I never liked pro-ams when I played the regular tour. I was obliged to play in them every Wednesday, but I moaned and groaned about it, as did many of my peers. We were full of oats and wanted to prove we were the best golfers in the world. You couldn't prove that on Wednesday, nursemaiding a bunch of hackers.

It's different now. For one thing, it's sunk in that the pro-ams are where a lot of our prize money comes from. If four guys pony up $10,000 for the dubious privilege of playing golf with us, we figure they're entitled to a golf lesson and some fellowship along with the round of golf. So we make an effort to be friendly. We help them with their golf swings and their course management, and we try to make the tournament as much fun as we can for them. You've got your quiet guys like Coody, who's just very natural and low-key with his pro-am partners, and you've got your rah-rah guys like Kenny Still, who gives Knute Rockne–type speeches and practically jumps in your arms when you make a putt. But everybody's out to have a good time.

Am I saying there are no horse's asses playing the Senior Tour? No, there are a few. There's one guy out here who used to be famous on the old tour for his rudeness to pro-am partners. One time, this pro came to the eighteenth green of a pro-am. His amateur partners, as usual, were sick of him. For seventeen holes he hadn't cracked a smile or said a word. But they had played pretty well, and when the pro looked up at the leader board he saw that his team had a chance to win the pro-am if one of the amateurs could make a short putt.

Talk about a change in attitude! The pro plumb-bobbed the

putt for the amateur, checked the line from three directions, told the guy where to aim, and gave him all kinds of encouragement.

The amateur, who almost couldn't breath for all the attention he was suddenly getting, looked up from his putt and glared. "If I make this, how much do you make?"

The pro said, "Oh, I'll win about four or five hundred dollars."

The amateur gave it a moment's thought, turned around, and knocked the ball into the parking lot.

True story.

JANUARY 31, THURSDAY/KEY BISCAYNE

Did I mention that I don't like Florida?

That's a bit strong. I don't like playing *golf* in Florida. Never have. Which is curious, because I played my college golf at the University of Florida. I played five or six tournaments a year in Florida from 1963 to 1980, and I spent a couple of winters in Ocala with my first wife. You'd think I'd eat it up.

But I've never played well here. Last year, I finished fifth in this particular tournament, the Royal Caribbean, and I think that's the highest finish I've had in Florida since 1963. It's usually early in the year when we come to Florida, which means my game isn't sharp yet. Throw in the wind, the strange grasses and everything, and I'm not much use as a golfer.

The wind is the single biggest terror in my life. I've gotten a little better, but through the years the wind has cost me a whole lot more money than it's made me. I get my mechanics screwed up.

Actually, the wind has very little effect on a well-struck golf shot. Dr. Cary Middlecoff told me that in about 1963, and I've found it to be true.

Doug Ford had the most wonderful philosophy about wind and bad weather. "When we start," he said, "90 percent of the guys are gonna quit before they go out there. So I've only got 10 percent to beat, and I think I can beat half of them anyway. So I'm almost pumped up when we have bad weather."

I've seen enough to agree with him, but I still dig a hole for myself when I see the wind blowing.

As you can probably gather, my game is not sharp. On the practice tee today, I talked to Bob Murphy, who's passed me a few tips since we played together on the big tour. "Frank, I could be wrong," he said, "but I think your stance is too narrow."

He wasn't saying that to stick some new idea in my head; he actually *remembers* that twenty-five years ago I had a wider stance. So I tried widening it, and immediately I felt better. The wider stance helps me get my legs into the shot a little more.

These are not rocket-scientist-type insights, but a tip like I got from Murphy can be very helpful. I particularly like to talk to fellows who knew what I looked like when I played well. Murphy was there. I trust him.

I'm still trying to put the mental and physical together. I lie on my bed at night and try to visualize myself in certain golf situations. First I try to see myself as being very aggressive, and then I see myself as very relaxed. The idea is to stay relaxed but to become intense in the moment and escape the outside thoughts that disturb me.

I brought along some additional reading that Dr. Graham prescribed for me. To be honest, it's kind of confusing me. My mind is too busy right now, and I'm not real happy with that. I'm not knocking Dr. Graham's ideas or questioning their validity, but at this moment I am very, very confused and overwhelmed. Golf is difficult enough without all this stuff going through your mind.

I checked the first-round pairings, and for the first time this year I won't be playing with Bruce Crampton. Instead, I've got Jim Ferree, who's a great guy, and my old buddy Larry Mowry. I ran into Larry today and he was yippy, kind of hyper. He said he quit smoking on New Year's Day and he hasn't been his calm, peaceful self since. I noticed that he's also picked up some weight, which smokers who quit seem to do.

We talked about the cigarettes and how it was pretty much the same as our drinking, and we almost had a little AA meeting going. That's my special bond with Larry, our alcoholism and our recovery. The second week I was on tour, in March of 1989, I walked into the dining room of the Philadelphia Marriott, where we were staying. Larry was at a table with some people, and he called me over. He said, "We just sat down. Would you like to have dinner?"

I said, "I'd love to."

For the next half-hour, Larry made me feel very welcome. Nobody had done that. Not that they needed to; I'd only been out there ten days. But we had a great time, sharing our common histories of drinking and nondrinking.

Since then, we've been good friends. There's times when we're jumpy and fidgety, and we know it's not golf. It's just the compulsive-obsessive situations that recovering alcoholics run into. This smoking thing, for instance. I've never smoked myself, but I know from my meetings and from friends that Larry's in a tough, tough spot right now, trying to quit. To cheer him up, I told him how much I was looking forward to our playing together in the Legends of Golf down in Texas this spring. We sort of cemented our relationship with our partnership at last year's Legends.

Speaking of relationships, Seemore and I are getting along fine. He knows what he's about out there, and I kind of enjoyed being with a caddy from the old days.

When I think of Seemore, I always think of Las Vegas and the fifty-dollar chip. This goes way back, and we've had a lot of fun with it over the years. Seemore caught me drunk one year at the Sahara Hotel. I was wobbling across the casino floor, and Seemore caught me and said, "I need fifty dollars, give me fifty dollars." I had a handful of chips, so I gave him a fifty-dollar chip. Smiled, waved, and went my merry way.

Time passed, and I wanted my money. Every week I'd see him, it'd be, "Where's my fifty dollars, Seemore?" And he'd go, "Well, I uh, uh, uh . . ."

The caddies never have it. If you give them money, the only way you can get it back is to have them work it out. But I had another caddy then, so I had to ask for the money. And it became a real joke between Seemore and me and the other caddies. Seemore and the fifty-dollar chip.

This went on for a few years until Miller Barber won the Kaiser International tournament at Silverado in 1969. Seemore caddied for Miller at that time, so I knew Seemore had a pocketful of money.

The day after Miller's victory, I'm at the Los Angeles Open and Seemore comes around the corner and nearly runs into me. He's got a woman on each arm, he's got his sport jacket on, he looks prosperous.

"Just the man I want to see! Where's my fifty dollars?"

Seemore gives me this big toothless grin. He says, "Yessir, Frank. You know, after all these years I *could* pay you that. I've got the money. But you know, if I paid you that right now, you and me wouldn't have nothin' between us. We wouldn't have nothin' to laugh about anymore!"

And with that, he and the women just took off. Left me there with my mouth open.

To this day, Seemore hasn't paid me that fifty dollars.

FEBRUARY 1, FRIDAY/KEY BISCAYNE

I had a really interesting occurrence today. I have been very nervous all week, and I know my nervousness comes from low self-esteem and not keeping things in perspective. I'd like to be able to go out and play and enjoy life, and if the golf comes, it just comes.

Anyway, I saw a fellow in the pro-am yesterday who played in a stand-up wheelchair. He's a paraplegic, paralyzed from the hips down, but he can stand up. They strap him in something that looks like a furniture mover's dolly.

So here's this poor guy who can only swing with his hands and arms and shoulders, and he's continually smiling. I'm thinking, here's a guy who probably wouldn't even want to leave the house, and he's out in front of all these people playing golf and he has absolutely the most wonderful look on his face. He looks like he has what I want.

I wanted to talk to him yesterday, but I couldn't do it. I don't know why, I just held back. But I was on the putting green today, over in the corner by myself, and I turned around, and there he was, standing alone. I walked over and said, "I can't believe you're standing here all by yourself. I want to talk with you."

He said, "You do? What about?"

And I went through the whole thing, told him how much I admired his attitude and how he really has what I want; that I get so intense with my golf, as if it was the most important thing in the world. "You don't seem to feel that way. It looks like you really enjoy life and are grateful for whatever chance you have."

He laughed, and then he told me the whole story. About how he had wanted to kill himself after his car accident, and how he had finally learned about life and what was important, and how fun it is to live, and how grateful he is to have a chance, and so on. He was smiling through all this, and it was absolutely the most wonderful experience I've had in a long time. I went out on the course after that, and even though I didn't play well I felt grateful just for being able to play. I carried an image of that fellow all the way around.

I wish I could have shared my attitude with Larry Mowry. Larry shot a 74, and he was hyper all day. He just wasn't the same Larry. And I know it's the cigarettes. I felt sorry for him. He actually hit the ball well, but he just wasn't in the game. There wasn't the calmness and peacefulness I usually see in him.

As I said before, I played poorly myself and shot 73, seven strokes behind the leaders, Bruce Crampton and Chi Chi Rodriguez. It was kind of windy, as Florida always is, but that's no excuse. Heck, Jim Ferree shot 70. Jim has just a marvelous golf swing and I'm surprised that he doesn't shoot 60 every time out. I've known him for thirty years. He's very pleasant, he never gets upset, and his swing is almost infectious. While I don't think I swung like Jim Ferree today, I'm sure whatever I did I did better for having played with him.

After my round, I went to the practice tee again and saw Bobby Brue and Bob Murphy. "I can't believe it," I said. "I have no idea where the ball's going."

I meant it literally. I make a swing, I look up, and wherever the ball goes I'm surprised. I know that sounds weird, that a golfer with my experience could say he has no idea, but I tell you, on Friday of this tournament I have no idea where the ball's going.

I'm really into swing thoughts right now, and that's usually what leads me to disaster. Swing thoughts are for the practice tee. Once you get to the first tee of a tournament, you should get away from swing thoughts and get into playing golf. I have not been able to do that the last couple of days. At the Tournament of Champions I had a little gimmick that I used, something to do with keeping my head still. And it worked. But I tried it here earlier in the week, and it was gone. Absolutely 100 percent gone, nothing left.

So now I'm kind of between old swing and new swing, no confidence and some confidence, and 73 is what I came up with.

Can you imagine Michael Jordan going out tonight and trying to shoot a jump shot, and just as he gets the ball, he says, "I'm going to plant my right foot, push off, jump up, release the ball on the count of three. . . ."

It's not going to work for him, and it's not going to work for me in the middle of a tournament round.

I'm looking forward to tomorrow. Maybe I'll do a little better.

FEBRUARY 2, SATURDAY/KEY BISCAYNE

Another 73. Again, I played very poorly. My swing and my confidence are in shambles at this point. It's hard for me to believe I can play as well as I did at the Tournament of Champions and then come here three weeks later and have no idea where the ball's going.

I played with Lee Elder today, and Lee doesn't speak to me when we play. He hasn't spoken to me in twenty-five years. I'm not sure what happened between us; I don't remember any fights or anything. But it's okay. He goes his way and I go mine.

Jimmy Powell was our third, and I love Jimmy. He's the king of the practice tee. Jimmy hits more practice balls than any five guys, he's out there from sunup till sundown. We all think he practices too much for a guy his age, but that's the way he does it. He shot 74 today.

After the round, I talked to Phil Rodgers on the practice tee. He really understood. He gave me a few tips, but he agreed with me that swing thoughts absolutely will not work out on the course.

I don't know what it is, but there's been a lot of damage to my golf game over the years—to my thoughts, to my processes. It used to be so easy. When I was at the top of my game, when I was winning tournaments and lots of money back in the sixties, I never fooled with swing thoughts. I just hit the ball whichever way felt good. It was mostly "feel." And I used to have more fun with it, I didn't worry about it as much.

What's most important for me right now is trying to separate my golf results from my self-esteem. When I play badly, I see myself as a bad person. When I play well, I see myself as a good person. Well, I don't care how good a golfer you are, you never play quite as well as you want to. That's why I rarely feel that I'm as good a person as I want to be.

This is anathema to me.

As I ramble on here, you can easily see where my mind is. It's going eighty-eight different ways: self-esteem, sports psychology, golf swings, stances, scores, back again. I'm like a cat chasing his tail. I need to be quieter. I need to get away from the swing thoughts and psychology and more into the inside of me.

Easy to say right now. It's been very hard to do.

FEBRUARY 3, SUNDAY/KEY BISCAYNE

Al Geiberger told a cute story in the locker room today. Al's known as "Mr. 59" because he's the only player who's ever broken 60 in an official tour event. He shot a 59 in the 1977 Memphis Classic, and everybody's been trying to duplicate the feat ever since. Nobody's really come close, but Al said he got a scare a couple of years ago when he picked up the paper and saw the headline BAIRD SHOOTS 58.

It turned out that Butch had shot a 58 for sixteen holes— two holes of the course were closed because they were muddy. The subhead said, ". . . for 16 holes."

Al said, "I covered up the little headline with my finger and showed it to my wife. I sighed and said, 'Well, it finally happened.' She was really upset until I moved my finger."

Geiberger's 59 will probably be a topic of conversation all year. We've got a new contract with the Hilton Hotel people: If anybody shoots a tournament round of 59 or better on either tour, Hilton will give half a million dollars to the new "Mr. 59" and half a million more to charity.

"The way I see it," Al said, "the million dollars practically insures that nobody will shoot 59. The pressure will just be too much."

The wind really blew today, and when it's windy, swing thoughts don't work. *Swings* don't work. You've got to keep the ball on the ground, play trick shots, do whatever it takes to get the ball up and down.

That's what I did today, and I played much better. It wasn't pretty, it wasn't beautiful, but I shot 71.

Maybe there's a lesson here. I always tell my kids, "Play golf on the golf course, swing golf on the practice tee." I might play better if I practiced what I preach.

My 71 left me thirteen strokes behind Gary Player, who won the tournament, but at least it kept me out of the 500 Club. That's what we call the guys who finish low each week—the 500 Club. Everybody who finishes is guaranteed $500, the amount you get for fiftieth place right on down to seventy-eighth. There's kind of a stigma attached to membership in the 500 Club. We don't look down our noses at one another, but it's one of those deals where you say, "Boy, did I play bad this week." I haven't seen the results, but I probably made two, three, maybe four thousand dollars.

Larry Mowry finished with an 80. He's 500 Club for sure.

How did things go for me this week? Overall, good. I shot a couple over par for the week and I've got the blahs, but it's no big deal. On sports psychology, I'll give myself a C-plus for the week. My playing golf, *playing* golf, was a C-minus. It just didn't work out. But I give myself an A-minus for my attitude—my general outlook, my reading, my readiness to play. I kept a good attitude all week long. I stayed with it. I didn't get down on myself. And I feel good about that.

After dinner, I'm driving up to Delray Beach. We've got a pro-am tomorrow, one of those outings, and I'm looking forward to a nice relaxed day and making a few more bucks. Then it's on to Tampa and probably more wind. I know it's going to blow again in Tampa.

Oh, I paid Seemore after the round. I told him he'd done a good job for me and I might be able to use him again later this year. He was tickled and promised to stay in touch.

And no, I didn't take the fifty dollars he owes me out of his check. If I had, we wouldn't have nothin' between us.

FEBRUARY 4, MONDAY/POMPANO BEACH, FLORIDA

I really miss my family. I've only been gone a week, but the more I'm away from them, the more I realize how important they are for me. I call home every night, and sometimes I call in the morning, early. It's expensive, but there's some things that even tight people like me don't worry about, and one of them's calling home.

I noticed in the paper this morning that I won about $3,000 in Miami. I'm still feeling a little bit down about last week, but Sunday was a good round in the wind. This is where you shrug and say, "So what?" Whether you make three bucks or you make $3,000, you've always got another week coming up. That's the neat thing about golf. There's always tomorrow.

I had a nice relaxed time at Murphy's pro-am, which he's been putting on for a local hospital for years. I worked on my swing a little during the round, but mostly I tried to get to know the guys I was playing with, help them with their golf, that sort of thing.

There was some talk about the contract Trevino signed with Cadillac last week. Lee's contract will reportedly pay him more than $700,000 a year to appear in commercials, show up at a few functions, and wear the Cadillac logo on his shirt.

Isn't that unbelievable? And Spalding gave him the same amount! I hear he's getting a million and a half from those two companies, and that doesn't count the bonuses he gets from them every time he wins a tournament. I don't know how much bonus money Lee gets—$25,000 or $30,000, I can't say—but if he wins six tournaments a year, that's another $150,000 or so.

I'm not saying he's not worth it, but we're talking *big* money here. And it's only twenty-two years since George Forrester started paying golf pros to wear hats and visors with "Amana" printed on them.

I was one of the pioneers, you know. In 1969, the year I was leading money winner on the tour, I got paid fifty bucks a week to wear the Amana visor. I thought that was phenomenal! As the years went by, Forrester gave me additional work as payment for wearing the thing—outings and stuff—and toward the end they gave me an airline credit card to travel the tour with my family. That was in the late seventies.

The Amana thing ended for me because I don't like hats much. I didn't want to wear them, and sometimes I conveniently forgot. They'd say, "You gotta wear it," and I'd say, "All right." Then they'd catch me without it. Finally, they decided to go in some other direction. I just shrugged and said, "Hey, I've got plenty of money." I didn't put two and two together.

But what's happening now—the bidding wars over hats and shirts and golf bags—is just insane. We're getting hundreds of times what we got in 1969. Some guys are getting *thousands* of times more.

I don't have illusions that I'm a big star, but last year Mazda and Hillerich & Bradsby got into what you might call a bidding war over the right to advertise on my forehead. Mazda actually had the right to the visor, the right of first refusal, but H&B really wanted it because I've been with them for thirty years. So Mazda made an offer, H&B made a counteroffer, and Mazda couldn't match it. As simple as that.

H&B doesn't mind that I wear a shirt with the Mazda logo. The hat is the only thing they're really interested in, because the TV people won't show anything else. Frank Chirkinian, who produces golf for CBS, told me that. He said, "We won't show your bag and we won't show your shirt, but your visor? We can't keep it out of the picture."

I'm wearing the Mazda shirt because I wanted to do something for them. Phil Armbruster, the rep at H&B, said, "We don't require the shirt. We'd love to have it, but we don't require it. Never have."

I said, "What if I offer it to Mazda? They've been good friends of mine since I started in '89." So Mazda agreed to give me a lesser amount to wear the shirt.

As I said, I've been with H&B for thirty years, I've played with Power-Bilt clubs my whole career. We're talking family. I don't let an agent handle that contract because it's more than a money thing with me. They stuck with me when my game fell apart, so I feel a real loyalty to them.

Susan says, "Hey, you're a good guy, you're good for the company."

I guess I am. But I'm also realistic enough to know that I

get this money basically because I'm a good player and I'm gonna be on TV.

They don't give the money to a good guy who's never going to be on TV.

FEBRUARY 6, TUESDAY/TAMPA, FLORIDA

Some of the guys were talking in the locker room this morning, just hanging around and eating sweet rolls. "Wasn't like the Crosby of old," somebody said. "It's not the Crosby unless you've got icicles hanging from your shaft and a fifty-mile-an-hour wind in your face."

They were talking about the AT&T National Pro-Am at Pebble Beach, which is what they now call the tournament that Bing Crosby created for his Hollywood friends. Paul Azinger won it Sunday, and I think they were showing highlights on the locker room TV.

It brought back some memories. The year I was the leading money winner, I went to Bing and said, "I've been pretty loyal. I played with Donald O'Connor, and he was so drunk he never got a ball into the hole. We played fifty-four holes, and I bet he didn't finish four of them. Then I played with Mr. Magoo and his cronies—what's his name, Jim Backus—and they were fine, I loved 'em. But I really want to bring in a guy I know."

Bing said, "Sure, why not? You deserve it."

So I brought a good friend from Louisville. We played the Crosby together for three years and had a marvelous time. I'll never forget the first time we drove in on 16 Mile Drive. You kind of wind down through the forest, so you can't see the ocean through the trees. I parked behind the Del Monte Lodge, took Bill in and registered. I knew what room we were getting, one that looked right out on the eighteenth green. We walked down the hall and into the room, and I threw back the curtains. And there was the postcard that we've all seen: the big cypress tree overhanging the eighteenth green, the cliffs in the distance, the waves crashing, a couple of seals on the rocks. Bill couldn't believe it.

So he's going to play golf. And God bless him, he's so nervous he can hardly walk straight. We play with Bobby Nichols, who was an H&B guy like me, and Glen Campbell, who was Bobby's regular Crosby partner. We play Spyglass Hill, we play Cypress Point, and Bill is starstruck. He's spinning around every time he catches a glimpse of Bob Hope or Phil Harris or Dean Martin. And he's shaky because he's got five thousand people lining the fairway. Can't hit a lick.

Come Saturday, we're playing Pebble Beach and we're on national TV because of Glen Campbell. It's the eighteenth hole, the most famous par-5 in the world. The bleachers around the green are packed with people; the fairway down the right side is lined two and three deep with spectators; the ocean is crying "feed me" on the left; and half the country, not to mention everybody Bill knows in Louisville, is watching on TV. And there's Bill in the fairway. He's got a 4-iron for his third shot, and he gets a stroke on the hole.

It was incredible. Bill hit his 4-iron two inches from the hole. The only shot he hit in three days, but he saved it for just the right moment. I remember saying, "Bill, that's a memory you'll have for the rest of your life."

That's the wonderful thing about golf. You can't play quarterback for the Detroit Lions, I don't care what George Plimpton says. And you can't face Nolan Ryan's fastball in Yankee Stadium in front of a standing-room-only crowd. But even an amateur, a 12-handicapper, can get lucky in a pro-am and experience the thrill of a lifetime.

After hanging around the locker room for a while, I headed out to the range and got to work. I've got pro-ams tomorrow and Thursday, so I decided to devote today to practice. I haven't done that in a long time. At the Tournament of Champions I didn't think practice was it, I was trying to shore up the mental side. Now I'm going to try the other. I'm going to beat a lot of balls this morning. This afternoon, I'll go back to my room and work on my priorities.

I feel like I'm sixteen again, quite honestly. When I was sixteen I had to go sit down and prioritize everything. I had to see where I was with my golf swing and my life. Now I'm fifty-two, and I'm still not comfortable with myself as a person and I'm not comfortable with myself as a golfer. Either of those alone would be a tough task to unravel, and I'm trying to unravel both at a tournament site.

FEBRUARY 6, WEDNESDAY/TAMPA

I have another caddy this week, a guy named Alan. He's a fellow I've tried to get with for a long time. He caddies regularly for Jim Ferree and a couple of other guys, but he caught me in Miami and said, "How about next week?"

I didn't have anybody lined up, so I said, "You got it, pal." He's a nice guy, he'll do a good job for me. He doesn't owe me any money, either.

I played early this morning in the pro-am and shot a very respectable 71. Tampa Palms is an Arthur Hills golf course, and it's one of our better courses. There are no parallel fairways, and it's so tight you simply must hit the ball straight to score.

The seventeenth hole is the signature hole, a 549-yard par-5 with swamp, pines, water, alligators, snakes, and birds on both sides. You have to respect this hole. Most of us hit a 3-wood off the tee because you can't get home in two. And it seems like the wind is always in your face. I've hit a 1-iron or 2-iron off the tee on occasion, and then used the same club to lay up. You have to respect your third shot, as well. The green is pretty severe; it slopes down and away from you. And when it gets hard, the ball just bounces. If the pin is to the left, you just don't go for it because the water is right there. Dave Hill lost the tournament two years ago when his ball landed on the seventeenth green and then hopped into the water. He wound up making triple, I think.

The tournament is moving next year because it's hard to move the galleries between some of the holes—too much water and wild areas. I sure hate to see us leave Tampa Palms, because next year's site is the new Tournament Players Club at Cheval. Mike Fetchick has played over there, and he didn't like what he saw of the greens. Typical TPC greens—hard and undulating.

Let me confess. As soon as I hear the initials "TPC," I'm not ready. I don't like the original TPC at Sawgrass, I don't like the ones Nicklaus has built, I don't like any of them. And the ones in Florida are the worst, because you're playing in the wind. You've got no chance.

Maybe I'm a traditionalist, or maybe I'm just an old man who can't play anymore. I played a Gary Player course in Florida last year, the first Player course I'd ever played on, and it was marvelous. I've played Tom Fazio's stuff, and I love it. But these TPCs all seem to have the same look, the "stadium course" look. Railroad ties everywhere, tabletop greens . . . and if you miss a fairway or green, you can't recover. You can't get up and down.

I just feel like, through the years, we've given too many jobs to the Nicklauses and Pete Dyes. It's almost as if we, the tournament players, endorse their work. I would prefer to spread the work around to Fazio and Hills and some of the guys who aren't as well known.

Following my round, I drove seventy-five miles to Ocala to work with Jim Yancey, Bert Yancey's brother. Jim has helped me with my golf game off and on for twenty-five years, and he's one of my dearest friends. He looked at my swing, and we talked. He didn't see anything wrong with my golf swing structurally, but he thought it looked a little fast. That got us to talking about where I was emotionally, because a fast swing is usually a product of anxiety.

Afterward, I had dinner with Jim and his wife and some of their friends, and it was a real nice evening. Just a wonderful way to get away from it all and still keep a little focus on the game. Susie and the kids are on my mind more than ever, but we're getting short-term now. I'll be home Sunday night.

Looking ahead, Trevino's the pretournament favorite again. He finished second at Miami, although his body is still bothering him some. I didn't get a chance to talk to him about it, but apparently the trouble is under his shoulder blade, not really in his back at all. He was only two behind Player, so it must be nearly healed.

Personally, I'd pick Player to win, and not just because he won last week. The harder the golf course, the better chance he has, and these Florida courses just play into Gary's hands. There's a lot of sand down here, and nobody's better out of bunkers. He's a good putter, great around the greens, terrific in wind. He's not long off the tee, but that's not what it takes to play well in wind. It takes patience and a real gutty approach, which Player has. And confidence. Gary has unbelievable confidence.

Where does he get that confidence? I wish I knew. It's said that little people think they have something to prove. The Ian Woosnams, they live on guts, they're out to show the world. And that's what I see in Player. He's not obnoxious with it, but sometimes he looks like one of those little dogs running around yipping at people's legs. It was always Arnie "the King" Palmer and Jack "the Golden Bear" Nicklaus and maybe a pretender to the throne—Billy Casper or Tom Watson—and there's Player running around thinking, "My record is as good as anybody's, and nobody notices me!"

That's how I see Player. He's a likeable player, the fans respect him, but there's never that recognition of greatness that Hogan, Snead, Palmer, Nicklaus, and even Trevino get. You watch: This week, the crowds will be following Trevino, not Player.

FEBRUARY 7, THURSDAY/TAMPA

Gay Brewer, the old Masters champ, was walking up and down the practice tee today, sticking his nose into everybody's bag. Jesus Christ, he hasn't changed a bit. He's a golf club collector, and he always wants one of your clubs. He must have a hundred thousand clubs by now.

When he got to me, he let his eyes linger for a second on my old Wilson R-90 sand wedge that's been in my bag for two hundred years. He said, "Still considering my proposition, Frank?"

I smiled and shook my head. Gay came up to me years ago, back on the old tour, and tried to con me out of my little brown club. He said, "I tell you what I'll do, Beard. You see this dirty old club in your bag? I'll give you five brand new wedges for it."

We've laughed about it for years, but he's like Wile E. Coyote after the Roadrunner—he never gives up. Today, I just shook my head and said, "I'll remember you in my will, Gay."

Not much else happening today. One of those petitions was going around the locker room. There's a group of guys—senior golfers, names you wouldn't recognize—who want to change the structure of our tour so more spots are available for the better golfers. By "better" golfers they mean unknown players who shoot better scores than our older stars like Arnold Palmer, Doug Sanders, Dow Finsterwald, and Doug Ford. The petitioners feel that their rights are being violated by our current rules, which exempt from qualifying those players who were successful years ago on the regular tour. One guy, Art Silvestrone, actually sued the PGA Tour a couple of years ago.

I didn't sign the petition because I think these guys are completely off-base. Our tour is built on nostalgia. The public wants another chance to see Sam Snead and Billy Casper and Gene Littler, and the fact that they can still play golf is just icing on the cake. Competitiveness, while important, isn't the foundation of the Senior Tour.

Unlike the PGA Tour, where the pecking order is based strictly on how well you play, the Senior PGA Tour rewards players who have made a reputation for themselves. Most weeks, thirty-one places are reserved for players on the all-time money list, which combines a player's career earnings from both the regular and Senior tours. Due to withdrawals and overlaps with other exemption lists, a player from as far down as seventieth on the list can get a spot in a tournament. For instance, I currently rank twenty-sixth, about $4 million behind Jack Nicklaus, who ranks first. Gene Littler is seventh, Arnold Palmer eighth, Julius Boros thirty-sixth, Art Wall forty-first, Sam Snead fifty-second, and Dow Finsterwald sixty-third.

Are we being too generous to the older guys? I don't think so. I talked about this with Geoff Russell of *Golf World*, and I used the example of an old-timers' game at Yankee Stadium. You could have Mickey Mantle, Whitey Ford, and a bunch of their old fat teammates throwing the ball around, and I could easily find an American Legion team in Hackensack that could beat them. But no one is going to pay to see the guys from Hackensack, even though they can play baseball better than Mantle, Ford, and the rest of the Yankees.

It's the same with us. Sure, I can find a bunch of fifty-year-olds who can beat Fred Hawkins, Doug Ford, and Gardner Dickinson. But nobody wants to see them. *Nobody*. Maybe Julius Boros can't play well enough to win anymore, but he could go off the first tee today as a onesome and take a thousand people with him. A threesome of Ben Smith, DeRay Simon, and Gordon Jones wouldn't sell fifty tickets.

Guys like Art Silvestrone argue that they have a *right* to play the Senior Tour. If the Senior Tour was built with tax dollars, or if it was a public instituion, or if the primary reason for having it was a person's ability to play, then—and only then—would they have a right to be out there. But they don't, because when they were younger and tried to play the regular tour, they couldn't hit it a lick.

The bottom line is, they have no more "right" to play the Senior Tour than Betsy King does. By right, I mean *ini-*

tial birthright. That belongs solely to the guys who played the PGA Tour in the fifties and sixties, before million-dollar purses, multimillion-dollar endorsement contracts, and constant television exposure. In relative obscurity, they laid the groundwork for the circuit the young guys play today. That's why they deserve first shot at the spots in our tournaments.

It's not as if we shut the door on the good players. We have a qualifying school every fall. The top eight finishers get cards and the next eight become alternates. Each Monday there's a qualifying tournament for four spots in that week's tournament. In addition, each sponsor gets to grant four exemptions. So in a given week as many as twenty of the seventy-eight players—a fourth of the field—can be relative unknowns. That's enough. That's more than enough.

Walt Zembriski? Larry Mowry? Rives McBee? John Paul Cain? Fine. The fact that those guys made it is great. It gives the cabdriver a chance to say, "Hey, I could have done that." But they made it through the system, and if these new guys are as good as they think they are, they'll make it, too.

FEBRUARY 8, FRIDAY/TAMPA

I don't know where it came from, but I played really good golf today. I putted good, thought good, and I got away from my golf swing. (The wind was only at half-gale force. That helped, too.) Whatever is was, I shot a 4-under-par 68, and that puts me in the tournament lead with Bob Charles and Bob Brue.

My pairing today had to help. I played with Dale Douglass, who shot a 70, and Tom Shaw, who shot 74. Two good friends, great guys to be with. Pairings are very important. When you're with guys like Douglass and Shaw, it's easier to relax. I don't mean that we're buddy-buddy or funny-funny all day long, but we've had fun together over the years and there's a real feeling of camaraderie.

Tom, in particular, is so cheerful that I used to think he was faking it. Twenty years ago I said, "Nobody can be that up, that smiley all the time." But he's still smiling, so I guess it's genuine.

Parenthetically, I still lack confidence. When I came off the eighteenth green, my thoughts went to, "How did I do that?" I wasn't really sure how I pulled it off.

Once I'd signed my card, a tour official ushered me to a golf cart and drove me to the press center, where I did my best to keep the golf writers from nodding off. If you read my first book, you know I vowed once never to talk to a reporter again except to say, "Driver, 8-iron, two putts." I just got sick of being misquoted or having things I said taken out of context. I'd make a joke in the interview room, something like, "Jack must be slipping, he only leads the tournament by two," and I'd wake up the next morning to headlines: BEARD SAYS NICKLAUS SLIPPING. I was also appalled at the frequency with which reporters just plain got their facts wrong.

I didn't stick to my vow of silence, of course. For one thing, I love to talk. My ego's too big to pass up the chance to show people how smart I am. When the writers want me, they don't have to hunt me down with a gun.

But I've gotten much more careful about what I say and how I say it. Sometimes I'm explicit: "I'm getting ready to say something about Gary Player, and I want you to understand that this is tongue in cheek . . ." And I repeat myself until I'm certain that everyone present understands my point completely.

This is what I've learned to do in my three short years on the Senior Tour, and you know what? In three years I have not been misquoted once.

After my press conference I went to the locker room, where I spotted Ralph Terry with a couple of guys I didn't know. Ralph used to be a star pitcher for the New York Yankees, and now he plays on our tour. He's got a foot in each game, so to speak, so when you see him with strangers they're likely to be old ballplayers. I'm a big sports fan, so I insinuated myself into the conversation and got to meet Clete Boyer, the old Yankee third baseman, and big-league catcher Mike Heath.

I've met a lot of sports stars through the years, and they're neat guys. Regular guys. You look at a fellow like Clete Boyer—I mean, if you ever watched him play third base, you'd think the good Lord himself threw him down—and he's sitting there, a little pot gut on him, having a drink and laughing. He was kidding Terry about all the ballgames he'd saved for him at third, and Ralph looked lost and said, "You did?" And then they needled Ralph about some kid who just signed a baseball contract for a million a year, a pitcher who was 4-9 last year with a 4.90 earned run average. It was fun watching them jibber-jabber.

I don't know why it shocks me that these guys are so normal. I'm just a regular guy myself, but some people look at me as if I hung the moon because I can hit a golf ball straight.

Anyway, I had a great time. As I mentioned before, when guys are talking I just sort of sit down with them and listen. I'll answer a question or throw in an occasional remark, but I'm more of a gleaner than an entertainer.

I could be wrong, but I think the guys hang around the locker room more than they used to. There's always somebody holding court, whether it's Trevino or Chi Chi. Guys talk about their rounds, their crazy pro-am partners, about Michael Jordan and the Bulls. Most locker rooms have a little food out now, and that will always draw somebody's attention. There's also the long-distance phones that MCI installs in every locker room for our free use. There's three of them, and they're in constant use; sometimes you have to stand in line.

Maybe we just have more time for one another these days because we're old farts. You come in from a round, you're a little pooped. You sit down, there's a little finger food there and a few guys watching a basketball game on TV. It's just a nice place to unwind and talk.

And where else can you get the Chi Chi and Lee Show, in person, for nothin'?

FEBRUARY 9, SATURDAY/TAMPA

I don't want to talk about it. Seventy-nine. Seventy-nine! I shot a 79, for God's sake!

I look back over it, and it was just one of those days. The snowball started downhill and it just got away from me. Honestly, I hit only three bad shots the whole day, and I almost made par with those. But didn't. I made a double bogey on the last hole with a really, really great iron shot. It was one foot short of carrying the water. Two more feet and it might have been in the hole.

It was that kind of day. The wind blew like crazy, I putted bad, played bad, got into my swing again and got away from playing golf. Absolutely nothing went right. The wind dried the greens out . . . what can I say, it was just a miserable day.

I never give up, it wasn't that. The one commitment I made when I came back out here in '89 was that when I finished each round of golf I was going to be able to say, "That's the best I had." I think I kept my promise today. There were no backhand putts, there wasn't even a hole where I can say, "Wait a minute, you just didn't try as hard as you could have." But it's hard to get your heart into some rounds. I just couldn't.

That last hole, the par-3. I hit an 8-iron and I thought it was in the hole. It landed one foot short, hit the wood pilings, and went into the water.

That's golf. Yesterday the ball carries a foot farther and I shoot 68. Today it doesn't, and I'm a dog. That one hole didn't give me a 79, it was just a double bogey. But I had two or three holes like that.

I just don't play well in the wind. If I get off in the wind, I can't get back. And it doesn't help to know that seventy-seven other guys were playing exactly the same course today, and that a few of them shot in the 80s. If I'd just shot a 75, I'd be in third place.

I don't know what's going to happen tomorrow, but I'm going to cut this short. This is a day I want to forget. I just have had enough.

FEBRUARY 10, SUNDAY/TAMPA

Play was delayed two hours this morning by fog, so we started off on the first and tenth tees at 9:45. The sun finally came out, but it was still windy. I won't say anything more about the wind.

I played with Terry Dill and Dick Rhyan, nice guys. I don't know that much about them. I shot a 74, birdied the last hole, made about $5,000. But it really was not a good way to finish up. Yesterday's round just left me . . . I don't know.

I don't think I ever realized how much confidence I had on the old tour. I used to worry a lot and I got nervous, but I don't think I ever had a fear about pulling a shot off. I always thought I could do it.

Now I find myself wondering if I can still do it. There are times when I hit shots with as much ease and freedom as I used to, but my golf game is just not where it was in '69 and '70. I don't think there's any mystery why that is so. I finished up badly on the big tour, from '75 to '81. I didn't play much after that. The clubs sat in the garage.

So there's definitely been some damage to my golf. When I tried to play again, after I quit drinking, I couldn't make it from a foot. I couldn't chip a ball on the green. I mean, it was terrible. I was probably the best putter that ever lived in 1969, but in 1982 I was shaking over the ball.

That's part of the problem. When I came back to tournament golf, my recent memories were of playing badly.

I'm not going to dwell on it anymore, not now. I'll be home in a few hours, and I can't wait to see Susie and the kids. I gave Alan, my caddy, $550 for the week—$350 plus a percentage of what I'd won. I didn't have time to visit, but I told him he'd done a good job and maybe we'll get together again somewhere. He didn't say much, so I guess he was disappointed with my finish.

I can't say I blame him.

FOUR

FEBRUARY 11, MONDAY/PALM DESERT, CALIFORNIA

According to the morning paper, the seventeenth hole at Tampa Palms struck again. I didn't wait around yesterday, but Bob Charles wound up the winner when Trevino triple bogeyed No. 17. Talk about déjà vu—Charles won the tournament two years ago in a playoff after Dave Hill tripled the same hole. Bob is going to miss old No. 17 when we move to the TPC next year.

What Lee did shocks me. He was tied with Charles on the seventeenth tee, and for some reason he didn't hit his 3-wood. He took out his driver and sliced the damn thing into the swamp. After that, he got desperate and went for the pin with his approach. He put *that* in the water and wound up with an 8. Charles won easily, by four strokes.

I'm just glad to be home. I went to my AA meeting this morning, and it did me some good. I haven't had a drink since December 10, 1981, but I need the meetings the way a diabetic needs insulin. I have to go to meetings, I have to read, and I have to pray. If I don't, I gradually work myself into what we call a "dry drunk." I feel this tightness in my chest. I get upset with you and with myself. I jump on everybody. That's when I know I have to treat my disease. And it's daily.

I will be an alcoholic till the day I die, but I'm always in a state of recovery as long as I do two things: don't drink and treat it. It's as simple as that.

The term we use is compulsive-obsessive. Gamblers, drinkers, compulsive shoppers, overeaters, shoplifters—we all have the same disease. The average person thinks drinking is the cause of the problems. That's wrong. The problems cause the drinking. I drank because I couldn't stand sobriety. The person who doesn't drink has the same problems I do, the same pain—but that person *deals* with it. "Hey, I've got a problem. What am I going to do about it?"

I didn't deal with my pain. I drank it away. I anesthetized myself.

People ask me when I became an alcoholic. Well, I never drank till I got out of college. I drank a little when I was in the service and I drank some when I started the tour—beer with pizza, that sort of thing. Things didn't get rolling till 1964 or '65. I remember playing in the Crosby one year. It was cold, wet—typical Crosby weather—and one of my playing partners invited me up to his room for a drink. When he asked what I wanted, I said, "I'll have a scotch and water." I'd never had one before. I just wanted a taste.

That clicks in my mind because that's when I began to drink scotch. Which is what I drank, mostly.

But the problem is deeper-rooted than that. I've never been able to relax. Before I drank, my compulsiveness expressed itself in a punishing perfectionism. I got it in my head that I had to be a good altar boy and make straight As and win golf tournaments and work very hard and get all my ducks in a row, or no one would love me. The Beards were a wonderful loving family, but my subconscious somehow picked up the idea that love was conditional. I wanted so much to succeed for my parents that I couldn't accept striking out in baseball or getting less than the best grades in school. Whenever I was unsuccessful, I was devastated. Devastated! That's why, to this day, I can't cope with a score like I shot Saturday in Tampa.

It's interesting that it was a 79, because another 79 caused one of my worst times in golf. It was at the 1957 Kentucky high school championship. I was the favorite to win the tournament, but I went out the first day and shot a 79.

I can't begin to describe the pall that hung over the Beard household. My mother took me to church that evening, and we sat there and said the rosary. I felt like I'd let down God, the pope, my parents, Father Burns, right on down the line. I went out and won the tournament the next day, but can you imagine?

That was my compulsiveness. Right to the end of my tour career, I called Louisville every Friday night to tell my parents whether or not I had made the cut. When I missed the cut, I dreaded making the call. And I was forty years old.

The real unknown killer of drinking is that it stunts your emotional growth. We grow out of pain, but alcohol kills the pain. We stay in the same place. I tell people that when I quit drinking, at age forty-two, I was an emotional twenty-year-old. Through all those years, when I should have been maturing and learning how to deal with the fears and anxieties that were normal for guys my age, I just drank it away. That's why I say that I've learned more about myself in the last nine years than I learned in the first forty-two.

But all alcoholics are masters of denial. To this day, I get smug; I think I can go without my meetings. That's when the dry drunk comes back, the anger, the resentment.

This may not have much to do with golf, but it has a lot to do with how I play.

FEBRUARY 13, WEDNESDAY/PALM DESERT

I hear that Brian Henning, our tournament director, has gotten thirty-seven player responses to his recent invitation to name the Senior PGA Tour's slowest players. If we're ticked off about a specific player, we can turn in his name anonymously. Henning says, "There are about ten senior players who need to be told to pick up their pace, and they will be told."

This so-called crackdown on slow play has been going on

so long that most of us have given up hope. We're still four hours plus, no matter where we go, and it's up to five hours on some golf courses. Somebody got penalized for slow play three or four weeks ago—was it Butch Baird?—but it was a slap on the wrist.

A while back, the tour distributed a survey in which all of us rated one another on our speed of play. When I got mine back, I learned that my colleagues think I'm about average. Sixty players commented on me. Forty-eight said I was just average, six said I was fast, and six said I was slow.

Actually, I'm a very fast player. But after twenty-five years of playing with these slow guys, I've learned to pace myself. What good does it do to run up to the ball when the guys on the green haven't even made their first putts? I would love to play an hour faster. I would love it! But if you look at me and don't know the story, I look average. There's a lot of guys like that.

We had a tour official, who will go nameless. I went to him a while back to complain about the slow play, especially in the pro-ams. I had played with the lead group in some pro-am, and I told this official how fast we had played, how much fun we had had, and how low we had shot. He agreed the tour had a problem. But then he spent thirty minutes telling me why we couldn't solve the problem.

This is a guy I pay!

I don't want to make this an indictment of the tour officials, because to some degree their hands *are* tied by tour policy. When we wrote the speed-of-play rules, we set them up too easy. The lead group has to play each hole in thirteen and a half minutes. If that goal is met, there is no penalty.

But it's too *slow*. In my opinion, it should have been twelve and a half minutes. After all, each of us gets to use a golf cart, if we can't drag our butts down the fairway.

The guys that are slow say, "Beard's a crazy man. He wants to play like Doug Ford."

Well, they're right. I do!

So you start with the fact that the time limit is too lenient. On top of that, enforcement is a joke. You've got to be a complete screw-up to get penalized. They come out and time you, and if you get three bad times, you know what happens? They *warn* you! You get three warnings, and only then do you get a fine.

George Archer was talking about that the other day. He said, "If you fall behind in Japan, a yellow flag goes up and you're penalized two shots on the spot. No questions asked. Here, you see a group fall three holes behind and they say, 'Well, they're playing in the allotted time.' What the hell is that? You should have to keep up and play golf."

I agree. Set a twelve-minute limit and let's go on down the road. End of sermon.

FEBRUARY 17, SUNDAY/PALM DESERT

Somebody, some senior, won a lot of money down in Naples this afternoon. I don't know who, because I didn't watch it on ESPN.

I did watch the final round of the San Diego Open. Jay Don Blake, a good-looking kid with a mustache and more hair than all the seniors put together, got his first tournament win. What amazed me was his score for four rounds. He was 20 under par! That is unbelievable golf. When I used to play in that tournament, 8-under was a winning score. And it's the same golf course—they haven't done a thing to Torrey Pines.

You have to give some credit to technological innovations, the new balls and clubs and shafts and stuff. But not that much. These guys are just much better athletes than we were. They get exposed to the game at a more sophisticated level at a younger age.

And there's more of them. That's what really gets me. When I started on the tour, if you finished third in a tournament you might finish third by yourself. Today, there's a five-way tie for third. The scores are lower, the cuts are lower. When I made a bogey in 1966, five guys went by me. You make a bogey today, the whole *field* goes by you.

On another matter, I read that Dave Hill says the contributions of Nicklaus and Trevino have been overrated. "The Senior Tour had it made before Trevino and Nicklaus ever got here," he told reporters in Tampa. "The man who put this tour on the map was Arnold Palmer, not Trevino and Nicklaus."

What Davey says is true; he just says things in a bellicose way. Palmer *did* put us on the map. Had Trevino come ten years ago and Palmer now, Trevino would have put us on the map and Palmer would have increased our popularity. So what's the point? For Dave to insinuate that we don't need Nicklaus and Trevino is a crock. Palmer's sixty-two now, he's not going to last forever.

I think Dave's still teed off by some remarks that Nicklaus made last year when he turned fifty. Jack made some caustic remarks in a *Golf Digest* interview, something along the lines of, "Why should I look forward to playing a bunch of guys I've been able to beat all my life?" Meaning the senior golfers. A lot of us took umbrage, not just Davey. I was hoping Jack would say he was misquoted, but he never did. They were not classy statements. They didn't need to be made, tongue in cheek or any other way.

To Jack's credit, he's come out and done what he said he'd do—beat the living tar out of us.

As for Davey, I think it's fair to say he's not mellowed as a senior. Not one iota. Frank Beard, he loves. He's not mad at me. He's not mad at you, either, or the guys he plays with every day. It's Nicklaus he wants to take on. It's the golf course architects, the corporations, the government, the world in general. Somebody once dubbed him "the last angry man," and I guess that's true—since his brother Mike has calmed down.

FEBRUARY 19, TUESDAY/PALM DESERT

This is one of the few weeks I don't get to play in a seniors event I'd like to play in: the Chrysler Cup, down in Sarasota, Florida. It's set up like the Ryder Cup series, with a team of American seniors playing a team of International seniors.

I'm not there because I don't qualify for it. If you don't finish in the top seven or eight on the money list, you don't play.

I don't know why the Chrysler Cup doesn't get more attention. The money is great—$50,000 for each member of the winning team, $25,000 for the losers. It's always been televised, it has a good sponsor, and it has the top senior players in the world. Part of the trouble may be that the International team is mostly made up of guys that play regularly on our Senior Tour. This year, only Brian Waites and Roberto de Vicenzo are guys you can't see at a run-of-the-mill tour stop. I mean, the average golf fan might have trouble figuring out which guys are supposed to be the foreigners. Gary Player? Bob Charles? Bruce Crampton?

The other negative may be the golf course. The Chrysler Cup is played at the TPC in Prestancia, and I understand it's your typical TPC—stark, humped up with ugly spectator mounds, and not much fun to play.

The only thing that concerns me about these specialty events is if they take the spot of a legitimate cosponsored tournament with a full field. It would disturb me greatly to find out that some city was told, "We don't have a date for you," and this was one of the dates they could use. Our specialty things should run when nobody wants a tournament.

FEBRUARY 21, THURSDAY/PALM DESERT

I have to know everything. My wife will call a guy in to fix the light. I don't know how to fix the light, but it tees me off that she doesn't say, "Frank, fix the light, will you please?" At least give me a chance to bump around and work at it until I give up and say, "I can't do it, call the guy." For her to *assume* that I can't do it irritates me no end.

After all, I'm the man of the house.

FEBRUARY 26, TUESDAY/OJAI, CALIFORNIA

The drive from Palm Desert took about three and a half hours. Susie and I got in a little late, but there was still time to hit a few balls after check-in. We're staying at the tournament site, the Ojai Valley Inn and Country Club. It's a resort like La Costa, one of those places where your room is practically on a fairway. We love it.

I walked by the caddy tent and saw a bunch of familiar faces—Golf Ball, Seemore, Fast Eddie, Winston, and so on. The all-time mystery is how they get from Point A to Point B so quick. You can pay them on Sunday night in Miami, and they'll be in New York on Tuesday morning. All of them. I guess they put five or six in a car and drive all night or until the beer runs out. Greyhound can't get them there that quick, but they get there.

I just stopped for a minute to chat. "My wife's caddying for me this week, fellas." They didn't tease me. They know Susan played on the LPGA tour and they respect her knowledge of the game.

As I was walking away, I ran into Alan, who caddied for me in Tampa. He looked at me kind of funny and said, "Frank, did you pay me what you meant to pay me down in Florida?" He made it sound as if I'd shortchanged him or something.

I said, "I paid you what I paid you, Alan," and started to walk away.

He came after me. "Hey, I didn't mean to get you upset." But it really ticked me off. I can't stand it when caddies challenge what you pay them. And it's not like we had an agreement. We hadn't discussed money in advance. If I had paid him $350 plus 5 percent, I think it would have come to fifty dollars more.

He's lucky. I could have given him $200.

On the practice range, the guys were kidding Gary Player and Bob Charles for playing the wrong balls in the Chrysler Cup last week. They were partners Friday in the alternate-ball matches, and they didn't realize till they got to their balls in the second fairway that they had forgotten to play each other's balls on No. 1. Al Geiberger and Mike Hill won the match by disqualification. The next day, when Player and Charles were introduced on the first tee, Miller Barber and Chi Chi Rodriguez jumped in to present each of them with a brightly colored ball with his name on it. Pretty good gag.

"I never played that format in my life," Charles said. "I thought you hit two shots and then rotated. It was my mistake." The U.S. team wound up winning the Cup, 58½ to 41½.

The forecast is for rain tomorrow.

FEBRUARY 27, WEDNESDAY/OJAI

I thought I was supposed to play in today's pro-am, but they didn't have me down. That bothered me a little. I didn't play a practice round yesterday because I thought I was playing today.

As it turned out, nobody played today. The rain came, as predicted, and we spent most of the day hanging around the clubhouse. I ran into Larry Mowry, who I hadn't seen since Tampa, and he was smoking again. "I just couldn't take it," he said. "I shot a 79 the first round at Naples, ran into the men's room, locked myself in a stall, and smoked three cigarettes as fast as I could."

It must have calmed him down, because he shot 65 and 69 the last two rounds down there.

It poured all afternoon, and it's still pouring tonight. We had dinner with Larry and with Kenny Still and his wife. Kenny, of course, is the all-time sports nut, the trivia king. They still tell the story about Julius Boros trying to sleep the night before a tournament round. There was this terrible racket coming from the next room at the motel, and Julius figured it had to be a pretty wild party. So he pulled on his pants, went out in the hall, and pounded on the door. The door opened, and it was Kenny. "Julius, pal! Come on in, we're having a great time!" It was just Kenny in the room. He had two radios going—a baseball game on one, a football game on the other—and a fight on the TV.

Tonight we talked about Sandy Koufax and the Dodgers and the old-time players, and it was just a great evening, the kind I enjoy. It brought back a lot of nice memories of the old tour, which was mostly couples and kids. I haven't been able to do much of that on the Senior Tour, what with Susie being home most of the time. To be out with another couple, some guys and gals—well, it made a nice cap to a lost day.

FEBRUARY 28, THURSDAY/OJAI

Rained out again, before we could even bat an eye.

Rainouts are tough for everybody. I always feel bad for the sponsors, who have worked for a solid year to get their tournament ready. Of course, I'm also thinking of me and my buddies. We're here to put on a good show, but we're trying to make a living, too

There's also the guys we play with in the pro-am, the amateurs who put up their 2500 bucks to play a round of golf with us. We had a clinic for them at the inn this afternoon, while the rain came down. We told jokes and stories, gave lessons—whatever we could do to keep them amused. We do that on occasion. One year in Philadelphia, they rented the hotel's ballroom and set up a three-hole mini golf course, the damndest thing you ever saw. It had sand traps, water hazards—I mean, it was *big*. And we took our pro-am groups through it. It wasn't the same as playing eighteen holes in the sunshine, but it was the best we could do, and some of the amateurs had so much fun they said they were *glad* they were rained out.

Today's clinic wasn't as elaborate as the one in Philadelphia, but there was plenty of food and the guys had a good time.

Susie and I spent the rest of the afternoon at a metaphysical bookstore, where we bought about a hundred dollars' worth of books. I'm not sure the books will do much for my golf game or my life, but they're fun to read. Actually, I got mine together pretty quick and went out to the car to start reading. Susie took about an hour to pick hers out.

After that, we somehow ended up buying a couple of antiques. I had put my foot down very solidly that we weren't going to buy them, but she tricked me. She read me some cards over hot tea in this little store with Johnny Mathis playing in the background. I'm not sure what happened, but all of a sudden I bought these antiques for her.

You could say that these two days together were sort of an anniversary gift. Our real anniversary got rained out, in a manner of speaking, and our time together here partially made up for it. Without Susie, the rain would have driven me crazy.

Even so, we're both anxious to get out on the course. I turned to her at dinner tonight and said, "Are you nervous about tomorrow?"

She gave me a puzzled look and said, "No-ooooo . . ." As if she had to rack her brain to think: Nervous about what? I don't know why I thought she'd be nervous about caddying. After all, she spent years inside the ropes as a player.

I hope the weather forecast is wrong. It says, "More rain."

MARCH 1, FRIDAY/OJAI

It quit raining this morning, although it was sopping, and it actually looked like we might get the first round in. They moved the tee times back an hour and a half, and everything was ready to go by nine o'clock. All of a sudden, at about 9:15, it started raining again. Thirty minutes later, they canceled the round.

It's just a tough situation. Our rules say that if one day is canceled we just have a two-day tournament. The sponsors here say they'll play even if we get rained out to one day.

It would be an unofficial event and wouldn't count on the money list, but they'd still pay the purse. In all fairness to them, we're hoping for a beautiful weekend and two rounds of tournament golf.

While Susie did some yoga in the room, I had breakfast with Bobby Nichols, the 1964 PGA champion. Bobby and I go way back. He's about four years older than I am, but he's from Louisville and we've been good friends for years, pulling for the Kentucky Wildcats, talking about the Kentucky Derby . . . anything Kentucky. At one time, we also shared the same attorney-manager, who I'll call John Smith. Smith was Bobby's friend and manager when I joined the PGA Tour, and he became my friend and manager, too—in fact, he became my closest friend and next-door neighbor and handled all my affairs until 1980. We're still good friends, even though we don't see each other often.

Unfortunately, Bobby says he has begun to have some serious problems with Smith. He says that Smith has been stealing his pension money and mishandling some investments. There's some fraud involved, some forging of signatures. I don't know how deep it goes, but the FBI's into it. Bobby has filed a big, big lawsuit, and the commonwealth attorney in Louisville may file criminal charges.

It's one of the saddest things I've ever had to deal with because Smith is a good friend. He's got a problem I can relate to—heavy drinking—and a gambling habit, too. Bobby and I have had discussions about it for about six months. We were in some common deals together, and he's trying to glean information from me about other people who were connected—anything that might help him. I've also called Smith and tried to give him some support. It's a tough hat to wear, trying to comfort Bobby and comfort Smith, when actually they're becoming archenemies. It's a terrible situation.

After breakfast, I talked on the phone with Jim Yancey, who I just visited down in Ocala. Jim's a dear friend of a lot of the fellows on the tour, and he's facing surgery for throat cancer. I had a great talk with him, but his situation added to the overall pallor of the day. The cancellation of the round seems trivial when I consider that one good friend is about to have a cancer operation and another good friend is looking at jail time.

Yes, professional golfers have to deal with life, just like everybody else.

I did manage to get out to the practice range this afternoon, when the rain finally let up. Susie gave me a lesson or two, which shows me she is getting more and more into it. She's got the cart and the caddy bib—she really looks the part. All we need now is some decent weather, and the weather report is very good for the weekend.

MARCH 2, SATURDAY/OJAI

It was a clear, beautiful day, and we finally got to play some golf. I had a 10:30 tee time with Larry Mowry and Lee Trevino. Lee is a good friend, but I don't ever welcome playing with him. I feel the same way about Jack Nicklaus and Arnold Palmer, and I felt that way when we played together on the old tour. Their personalities tend to usurp everything around them. Lee attracts a gallery that is unruly and shows little respect for lesser-known players, which makes it a little like trying to play in the eye of a hurricane.

The crowd wasn't bad today, a little unsettled. Trevino shot a 2-under-par 68 after kind of a funny start. He was out there hitting fat iron shots and spraying mud everywhere and talking about how he wasn't going to play in this tournament ever again, how the marshals were this and the marshals were that. He looked like he had gone stir crazy after sitting around for three days. He was really dogging it.

When we got to the eighth tee, he was 2 over par and Larry and I were 1-under. Lee turned to his caddy and said, "Well, Herman, I looked at the board and I'm four back, and that's far enough back."

He played 4-under from there, really good golf. In fact, he

had several putts lip out or he would have shot a really low round. It just proves to me that golf is mind over matter. That's especially true for a guy like Trevino, because his golf swing is almost never out of kilter. When he's playing bad, it's because his head goes screwy for some reason.

Larry's round was just the opposite. He was going along pretty well and then he got this crick in his neck that he's had since Puerto Rico last year, and he kind of limped in, bogeying three of the last five holes for a 72. "What burns your fanny," he whispered as we watched Lee hit a shot, "is there's three or four players who *never* seem to have a bad week. A bad week for them is twelfth place."

I bogeyed two of the last four myself and also shot 72. My golf game was pretty bad. To be honest, I don't have much confidence right now, and I didn't need to go out in front of a couple of thousand people—Lee's fans—and hit golf balls all over the place.

Susie didn't like my attitude, and she called my hand on it. She said if we were going to have a good round and have some fun together, then I would have to change my attitude. She didn't wring me out, but she laid the law down.

I think that's why I want her to caddy for me—so she can come inside the ropes and see what a jerk I can be. I've thought about it, and maybe I'm kind of like a kid with his hand in the cookie jar—hoping that his parents will catch him, punish him, and get it over with. Subconsciously, I want Susie to come in and hop on my neck.

As my first step toward a better attitude, I'm putting the driver back in my bag. I've been driving with my 2-wood, but I've got to show more confidence in myself, and that means the driver. I'm six strokes behind Bruce Crampton with just one round to play, but you never know. I could put together a good round and earn a big check tomorrow.

One little postscript. There was a big crowd following us because of Trevino, and Susan had to maneuver the cart through a lot of people between the greens and tees. The professional caddies just yell, "Carts! Carts!" and barrel on through, making everybody scramble off the cart path. Susan kept saying, "Excuse me . . . excuse me . . ." kind of poking along. On the fourth hole, Herman finally looked back and said, "Mrs. Beard, you're too nice. You gotta yell *'Carts!'* "

So she's going to work on that, and I'm going to work on my attitude.

MARCH 3, SUNDAY/OJAI

I shot a 68! My attitude, according to Susie, was not much better, but I played better. I stayed more into the game today, I kept trying to shoot a score. And it helped, although my mind was still on my swing some.

I used my driver and the results weren't very good, but I made a good swing on the final hole, a tight par-5, and hit a wonderful drive. I was real pleased with that, and I'm glad that it came on the last hole. It's something I can take away with me.

I played with Dale Douglass and Ben Smith. Dale was his usual steady self and shot 68, while Ben shot 70. Ben is a great story. As I understand it, he was a car mechanic somewhere down in south Texas—no tour experience, no pro experience, not even any tournament experience. He was just a car mechanic who hustled golf on the side. The Senior Tour came along, and five or six years ago Ben came out and got his card. He's kept it ever since and has made $700,000 or $800,000. He's already exempt off the all-time money list, and last year he made the top thirty-one for the fifth time.

Ben was 3-under today, but he played like an old man for two or three holes, which we all do, and made a double bogey and a bogey. Right behind us was Larry Mowry, smoking his cigarettes and cricking his neck, and he shot 66. I was real happy for him, and I was reasonably happy for myself. I'll probably make about $3,000.

The sponsors have to be happy, too. The weekend weather

was good and the crowds were wonderful, so everyone is relieved. It was a good week.

We're heading home now to get our kids. Susie reiterated that she enjoys caddying for me, and that really tickles me. In fact, she surprised me by offering to do it every time she comes to a tournament, and that tickled me even more. There's nobody I'd rather have inside the ropes with me. And she's a good caddy! I tricked her into reading the greens with me a little bit. We had a bit of a battle over that, but I think she saw the value of getting in there and helping the old fart read the greens.

So it looks like something we're going to do again. For Susie to be able to share with me the thing that's most important to me—after the most obvious things like family and God—is a wonderful, enriching experience.

I only wish I could have played a little better.

MARCH 4, MONDAY/PALM DESERT, CALIFORNIA

The newspaper this morning didn't have much on Ojai. Just that Chi Chi Rodriguez won it with a two-round score of 132.

What do I say about Chi Chi? Chi Chi is what you see. He's one of the warmest, gentlest people I've ever met. He's admired for his work with children and his charities, and if he tells the truth there must be twenty-five family members that he takes care of in Puerto Rico.

No one remembers what he was like before he became the showman and developed his crowd-pleasing routines. When he first came over in 1960, you couldn't get a word out of him. He was just this little Puerto Rican who showed up with Kenny Still one day. I remember Kenny telling me what a great player he was going to be, but it was hard to believe because Chi Chi was so quiet and shy. But then he got going, and I don't know whether show biz got hold of him, or he had that in him all the time, or his manager said, "Let's try some shtick and make some bucks with it," but suddenly Chi

Chi was throwing his hat over the hole when he made putts and wiping blood off an imaginary sword before sliding it into an imaginary scabbard. There can't be a player who is more beloved on our tour than Chi Chi Rodriguez.

What gets overshadowed is the fact that Chi Chi is a marvelous ball striker. He really has extraordinary control of the golf ball—more so, perhaps, than Trevino. And this is not always to his benefit. If Chi Chi has a failing as a golfer, it's that he sometimes gets in his own way. He'll try these tricky little shots, when a straightforward shot would do just as well. He'll try to fit the ball into tight places when he doesn't have to. And he's got about thirteen ways to hit a chip shot.

But that's totally overshadowed by his abilities as a golfer. He had some lean years in the seventies when he played the big tour, but his Senior Tour record is enviable. It's only when I play with Chi Chi or Trevino that I get the full impact. I almost don't want to play with them because they're that much better than I am. They have marvelous, marvelous control of the golf ball.

The other thing that deserves mention this week is Paul Azinger's controversial disqualification from a PGA Tour event down in Florida. Azinger was playing in the Doral Ryder Open on Friday when he hit his ball into a lateral water hazard on the eighteenth hole. The ball was sitting cleanly on some pebbles, so Azinger elected to play the ball out of the hazard, which he can do. Unfortunately, while taking his stance, he sort of wiggled his feet to get settled in, and in so doing he inadvertently dislodged a couple of small stones. Not realizing that he had moved some loose impediments in a hazard—a rules infraction calling for a two-stroke penalty— he hit a superb recovery shot, parred the hole, and finished his round a stroke out of the lead.

Here's where the controversy comes in. Azinger learned Saturday, when he was about to tee off, that someone watching TV at home had called tour officials and reported the infraction. No one on the golf course had seen the pebbles

move—not Azinger, not his playing partner, none of the caddies, nobody in the gallery, and no tournament officials—but
the long lens in a TV camera had homed in on his feet and
beamed the violation from coast to coast. The officials reluc-
tantly informed Azinger that he was not simply out two
strokes because of the infraction—he was out of the tournament for signing an incorrect scorecard!

This is not going to go down well. And I don't just mean
with the players; those who follow golf aren't going to like it
either. No one disputes that he broke the rule. I've seen the
replay several times, and the pebbles move. Azinger has seen
the replay, he says the same thing: "It's a violation, there's no
doubt about it."

But who enforces the rules? Certainly not TV! Certainly
not some guy sitting at home with his popcorn and his beer.
Television should have no role whatsoever in the conduct of
our tournaments, any more than I should be able to call in
and get the key play in the Super Bowl reversed.

I can't quote the rules of golf from memory, but the feeling
I get from reading the rules as they were set down in Scotland
250 years ago is basically this: You and I, as playing partners,
bear the burden of policing ourselves and each other. The
integrity of the game is in our hands.

Now granted, the game has changed; the presence on the
course of ropes and galleries and TV towers has created a
need for officials to make some on-course rulings. But basically, the integrity of the game demands—*screams*—that rules
enforcement be kept totally in-house. To me, that means the
three guys playing as a group, with help and interpretation
from the officials as needed. And never, ever, should a player
be disqualified after the fact. The injustice of it is self-evident.

And what could be more arbitrary than a TV penalty? Only
a few players are ever shown on TV. It's only by happenstance
that the cameras were peering at Azinger's feet. Mark
Calcavecchia or Payne Stewart could be doing the same thing
on another hole, but it's not shown on TV and they aren't
penalized.

I feel the same way, incidentally, about instant replays in baseball and football. Games are played by humans, and humans will always be imperfect. Let's officiate the best we can and get on with it.

MARCH 6, WEDNESDAY/PALM DESERT

"I'm going to live till I'm 120," Chi Chi said the other day. He added, "If I'm off five years one way or the other I'm not going to sweat it."

I guess that was Chi Chi's latest shot in his battle of one-liners with Lee Trevino. Lee's latest came recently when somebody asked him why he didn't use a teaching pro or a "swing guru" like David Leadbetter. He said, "When I find a swing guru that can beat me, I'll take some lessons from him."

I don't know how they come up with their material. Some of that stuff sounds like it was written in Hollywood. To me, though, Chi Chi is the funnier of the two because so much of his stuff is off the cuff. You tell him he shouldn't be eating red meat because of the cholesterol, and he comes back with, "I never saw a lion with heart problems."

Where does that come from? It blows my mind. Sometimes he just turns numbers upside down and makes Yogi Berra–type remarks like, "He can't beat four-thirds of the field." Or he says, "I'm on a grapefruit diet. I eat everything but grapefruit."

Trevino's is more of a straight-on, biting kind of humor. He'll pick somebody or something and go after it in a humorous way. Example: "I was gonna buy one of them Johnny Miller leisure suits, but the dude said the fire marshal took 'em off the racks." Or, "When I retire, I'm going to get a pair of gray slacks, a white shirt, a striped tie, a blue blazer, and a case of dandruff and go stand on the first tee so I can be a USGA official."

He's more of a needler, whereas Chi Chi's stuff is just off the wall.

MARCH 9, SATURDAY/PALM DESERT

I watched some of the Honda Classic this afternoon. I even listened some. The TV analysts, in my opinion, say very little, but I like what Johnny Miller's been doing. Without being caustic or slam-bang, he calls it the way it is. Another guy I like is Peter Allis, the British announcer. He's got a very dry, sarcastic way of telling you what's going on. Ben Wright gets off some good ones, too.

My fight with most golf analysts is, they never say anything. I don't need somebody to tell me the ball is close to the hole; I want somebody to tell me if Smith is in the fairway browning his pants because it's the Masters. I want to hear that Jones won't go for the pin because he's got no confidence in his fade.

Swing analysis? These TV guys haven't got a clue. Peter Kostis is pretty good and Allis knows what he's looking at, but it's pitiful the nonsense some of these guys put out. I can't tell you the number of times I've heard the color guy say, "He really spun out on that one, that's why he hit it in the water." And the swing looks *exactly* like the swing before, the one that almost went in the hole.

I speak with a spoonful of authority because I spent some time behind the microphone in the seventies, when my game was going to pieces. I broke in with an outfit called People and Properties, doing color. I worked for the old Hughes Network, did one tournament for NBC, and seven or eight for CBS. My reviews were good, and it looked like color commentary might be my calling.

Not many people know this, but I was considered for the job Lee Trevino did for NBC in the eighties. Vin Scully came to me in about 1983—I had worked with him once or twice at CBS—and Vin said, "Frank, we're gonna do fifteen tournaments or so a year for the next few years, and we need a color man. Quite honestly, they want Trevino, but we don't know if we can get him. If you don't mind, I'd like to put your name in the hat."

I said, "I'd love it. I'm very flattered."

Vin was honest. "Don't even begin to think about it," he said, "because if Trevino nibbles, he'll get it."

Trevino nibbled, and that was the end of that.

So my most visible work was on CBS. Frank Chirkinian, who produces golf for CBS, was very clear in his directions to me. He said, "Frank, we want you to *say* something. That's why you're here."

So I said things. If Tom Watson hit a bad shot, I *said* it was a bad shot. Then I said *why* it was a bad shot. I didn't gloss over anything, but I didn't feel it was hardball, either. You can tell it like it is without playing hardball.

Truth time: I loved it. I'm a talker, a BS-er. And when you're talking about something you love, it shows. I think I was pretty good.

The only time I got in over my head was the time People and Properties asked me to anchor a hole for them. It was much more difficult than I had anticipated. When you're doing color, you just answer questions or interject a comment when you have something to say, but to anchor you need a pro, someone smooth like Scully or Jack Whitaker. The anchor has to open and close the segments and go in and out of commercials. The anchor has to say, "We're here at the fourteenth hole at historic Pinehurst No. 2, where violent afternoon thundershowers have interrupted Hale Irwin's dogged pursuit of his first PGA championship and left a soggy field of golfers mired in muck and dwindling hopes."

I found out real quick: I ain't no Whitaker.

MARCH 18, MONDAY/INDIAN WELLS, CALIFORNIA

Lee Trevino told me today that the shot he hit on the last hole yesterday to win in San Antonio was one of the greatest shots he ever hit in his life. He said he had about 250 to the hole and he took a 5-wood. You'd have to know the hole. It's a weird par-5 and there's a lake on the left, trees on the right, and a little opening between two or three yawning fairway bunkers. You usually just lay up and then wedge on. But Lee took his 5-wood and he hooked it around this tree that's in the middle of the fairway, landed it short and ran it up about five feet from the hole. "That was some shot," he said. "I'm real proud of that shot."

How much of it is luck and how much of it is Trevino? I don't know. Why do the Jack Nicklauses and Lee Trevinos of the world hit these shots, and not the Rocky Thompsons and Frank Beards? That I can answer. They're better players.

I have *never* hit the golf ball like Lee Trevino. I can't even carry his shoes. And basically, I've never been as good a golfer as he is.

I always make that distinction. There's two sides to golf: one is hitting the golf ball and the other is playing golf. The playing part, the only part that really counts, demands that you know who you are and what you can do, and that you stick with it. You don't try shots you can't possibly make. You try to be the general of your own army—your army being your total resources, only one of which is hitting the golf ball. At one time, let's say 1969, I was probably as good a golfer as Lee was, but only because I was a better general of my army back then. I knew what I could do, I knew my limitations, and I had more patience, maybe.

But I could never hit a golf ball like Lee Trevino. Never have been able to.

MARCH 19, TUESDAY, INDIAN WELLS

Rocky Thompson is shaking his head over what happened to him Sunday. "The bad-luck fairy got me," he says. "I've played six hundred tournaments, and I'd never led one coming into the last hole until Sunday. I just can't believe I'm that unlucky."

You hear guys talking like that all the time, but apparently Rocky's got a right to feel star-crossed. "Rocky got one of the worst breaks I've ever seen," Charlie Coody said. "We got to the eighteenth hole, the par-5, and Rocky had a one-stroke lead on me and Lee and Mike Hill. And Rocky hit a tremendous ball off the tee, just a great shot. I mean, he turned away from it, he didn't even watch it. And the ball hit something in the fairway, kicked straight left, and rolled up against a tree trunk. All he could do was chip out, and he wound up making bogey and losing the tournament."

Rocky's one of the tour's characters, and not just because he believes in fairies. For some years he's been the mayor of Toco, Texas, wherever the hell that is. I've never been to Toco, maybe Rocky has. It's only got about a hundred people, and it's supposedly named Toco for Rocky's father's business, the Thompson Oil Company. We're always asking Rocky what his responsibilities are as mayor, and he says, "When there's a sewer break, I'm the guy who calls the plumber."

Rocky has always been a little different. He's not weird, but he's always had this look on his face, like the whole thing was a goddamn joke and he was the only guy that knew it. Maybe it's that little red mustache. The caddies call him "King Rabbit" because he's played the tours his whole life and never been exempt till a couple of years ago. He's never won a golf tournament.

I don't know what it is about Rocky. He's a nice guy, personable—he'll have dinner with you, shoot the bull. But there was always something mysterious about him, something I could never figure out.

He always drove a Cadillac on the old tour. I never had a Cadillac, and I was winning golf tournaments. I thought that was odd.

This Vintage ARCO Invitational tournament puts me in the pressure-cooker because it's played here at home. The Vintage Club is only a mile from our house in Palm Desert, and I think I've given out twenty-eight badges to friends.

A lot of players respond well to playing in their hometowns. I never have. Anytime I played in Louisville or near Louisville, I'd fall apart. With all those Frank Beard fans out there, I always felt like I was on stage and had to perform.

This tournament is the same. These are wonderful people. They know about me, they care about me, they pull for me—not just in golf, but in life. Still, I put that extra pressure on myself.

I went out early this morning and played my practice round alone. Drove the cart myself. No partners, no Susie.

It didn't help. I'm still nervous.

I'm also ticked off. I got some letters that were forwarded to me out at the course, and a few of them raked me over good for my latest column in *Golf World*. In the column I just basically set out my views on the "names" versus "no-names" debate. I pointed out that this is not necessarily a tour of great players; it's an exercise in nostalgia. And I gave some examples of golfers that people want to see and golfers they don't necessarily want to see.

I guess I made some people angry. It's apparent to me that the people who wrote me in rebuttal haven't read my article very closely. I haven't seen a copy of the column yet, but some of the words they attribute to me aren't even close. "You said this, Frank . . . you said that . . ."

Well, I *didn't*. It's not near what I said. I think there's a trigger in people's minds, and you say something close to what they don't want to hear, and that's what they hear.

I got some letters of praise, too, but that doesn't make up for the critical ones. I'm a perfectionist, I don't like to be told I'm wrong. I don't like to hear that I'm off the wall, that I'm sick, or that there's something wrong with me. They don't use those words, necessarily, but that's what I hear.

The lesson I should learn from this, which I never did learn when I wrote for *Golf Digest*—I was too young or too callous or too drunk—is that if you're ready to give your opinion in print, you'd best be ready to hear somebody else's in response.

MARCH 20, WEDNESDAY/INDIAN WELLS

J. C. Goosie tracked me down in the locker room this morning, and he was very irate. "Why'd you put my name in that article? What did you do that for?"

I tried to calm him down. "What did I say about you, J.C.?"

"Well, it just made me look bad."

"How did it make you look bad? Did I say you couldn't play?"

He frowned. "No."

"Did I say you were a bad guy?"

"No."

"Did I say you took one side or the other?"

"No."

"What did I say about you?"

"Well . . ." He didn't know what to say. "It's the whole article. It made me look like I was—"

I jumped in. "All I asked was who would sell more tickets— J. C. Goosie and Terry Dill or Julius Boros and Tommy Bolt. It was a very simple thing."

I explained that I had picked the names very carefully. The names I had used were those of players who had circulated petitions to get the older, better-known players kicked off the tour. These were people who felt very strongly about the issue. I told him I respected his opinion, I just didn't agree with it. And I said it wasn't personal. "You're a friend of mine. I didn't write that to hurt you or put you down."

I finally got J.C. soothed down a bit, but he's still not happy about the article. A little later, somebody stopped me and said, "Terry Dill's after your scalp." I just sighed and shook my head.

I'm sorry I wrote the damn thing. I expect some more of these fellows to corner me as we go along. It adds to the pressure of playing this week.

I had a great time last night, though. Mick Humphries is the guy that puts on the Vintage, and he has a pros-only dinner on Tuesday. It's a deal where we come in coats and ties, we pick up a little prize, and we honor somebody. This year it was Gene Littler, one of the truly neat guys. He's had terrible physical problems this year and last—a hip, something with the sciatic nerve. Rest seems to help, so he's missing a lot of golf. When he's healthy, he's still one of the best players out here, even at age sixty. But there are just some guys that are nicer and better liked than other guys, and Littler is one of those. I didn't count, but I'd almost bet you that every single pro was there last night.

Oh, it rained today. No pro-am. That's the desert for you.

MARCH 21, THURSDAY/INDIAN WELLS

I finally got around to reading my *Golf World* column. It's a very good article, I stand behind every word. But I'm not happy with how it was presented. The headline is "IN THIS CASE, BETTER ISN'T BEST—Senior Tour's Foundation Is Names of the Players, Not Their Games." In the middle of the page they ran side-by-side pictures of Gordon Jones and Julius Boros under the words, "Who sells more tickets?"

Somebody gave me a copy of the latest *Golf World* when I got to the course today, and I had something else to chew on. There was a letter to the editor titled, "Beard's Got It All Wrong." It was from a former tour player, Al Mengert, and it took me to task.

"If Beard and his pals had their way," Mengert wrote, "they would have a monopoly and split the pie each week and there would be no opportunity for rookies." And then he took a real shot: "An interesting trivia question might be: What has Frank Beard ever won? . . . Yes, the Frank Beards want a second chance, yet they are so selfish they don't want to give anyone a first chance."

I called Connecticut and talked to Geoff Russell, my editor. I told him I thought the headline was fairly inflammatory, and I thought the pictures tended to sensationalize what I had written.

"I'm not saying this is a yellow-journalism, tabloid-type thing, but instead of just letting me have my opinion, there was an attempt to draw attention to it. When you put somebody's picture, like Gordon Jones's, up against Julius Boros's and say, 'Who will sell more tickets?' that's pretty rough. You put a guy's picture there, you single him out. That was not my intent."

Geoff was very conciliatory. He said he'd pass my concerns on to *Golf World*'s editor, Terry Galvin.

When we signed the contracts, we never talked about editorial control. It just never occurred to me that an innocent little article like this would cause so much trouble.

MARCH 22, FRIDAY/INDIAN WELLS

I shot 75 in the first round of the Vintage. Three-putted here, three-putted there, couldn't make a birdie to save my soul. I'm nine shots behind the old workhorse, Jimmy Powell, who came in with a 66.

So I didn't play well. That doesn't bother me half as much as the other thing that happened today: Susie decided to stop caddying for me.

I still don't understand it. I don't agree with it. I've pumped her about it, and I don't think she was mad at me because I played badly. And it's nothing she did wrong. She's been around golf long enough to know she didn't contribute to my shooting 75. She just decided that was the end of the caddying.

"I think our relationship gets in the way of your focus on the golf course," is how she put it. "I think you need a professional caddy or somebody who is just a caddy and brings nothing more to the scene than caddying."

That wasn't good enough for me, so I kept after her for a better reason. She said, "I just don't feel like I can help you out there."

"You didn't feel that way at Ojai," I said. "You said you enjoyed caddying for me and wanted to do it again."

"This week feels totally different. If it had been like this, I never would have made that statement. Here I feel like I'm your wife at home, and I feel like I'm still your wife at the golf course. I can't feel that separation of home and work. I still want to caddy for you. But I don't at home."

I don't happen to agree with that. For her not to caddy for me after I enjoyed it so much at Ojai and was so looking forward to it here—it's a real loss to me. And I expressed that to her. To be able to share my golf with her is very special. It's almost like she's out there in my skin. Which may be her point. Maybe the caddy doesn't need to be that close.

I'm not going to cut my throat over this. It's just a real big disappointment. My best friend, Gary Colvin, who caddied for me at the Tournament of Champions, will finish out the weekend.

In short: hard day. It was tough out there, having all my friends behind the ropes and playing so badly. They didn't say a thing, they didn't put any pressure on me, but I put it on myself. It's just a tough venue for me, a very, very difficult tournament.

MARCH 23, SATURDAY/INDIAN WELLS

Gary caddied today, Susie and the kids walked behind the ropes, and Daddy shot 71. Susie said, "I think your attitude improved by 10 percent."

I was very tentative with my putter, and I'm not sure why. I feel very good with this long putter I'm using, I'm happy with it, but I just couldn't get anything going. I really think it's the pressure of the Vintage.

Also, I've always played my best golf when I play all day, every day, tournament after tournament. Somewhere around the third or fourth week, that's when I really hit my stride. Our early schedule has us playing a tournament here, taking a week off, playing a tournament there, taking a week off, and it's just too spotty. I don't use this as an excuse, but I can't seem to get into a golf mode.

It returns, though, to this business of playing in front of so many people who care about me. The pressure is self-induced, but it's no less real for that. I stand over too many shots with a lack of confidence, even fear. That shows up on a given shot as quickness. Most pros, not just me, miss shots when they get anxious.

My battle today on the golf course was to work on tempo. My swing is technically sound, but my tempo is thrown off by these dark images I have. I get over the ball and there's a pervading fear. I try to focus on the positive: "Where do I want the ball to go?" But I get a message back: "Oh, jeez, I don't want it to go over there." Once you start that, you're dead. Almost invariably you wind up hitting it right where your fears are leading you.

And right now, my fears are leading me all over the golf course.

MARCH 24, SUNDAY/INDIAN WELLS

Chi Chi Rodriguez won the Vintage today and jumped to the top of the money list. Lee Trevino finished in a twelfth-place tie, six shots back. It's unusual for Lee to finish that far down in one of our tournaments, but he's human like the rest of us. Just not as often as the rest of us.

I played better today and shot a 70, good for a twenty-seventh-place tie with Arnold Palmer, Simon Hobday, and J. C. Snead. I wound up winning about $4,600. Gary, my caddy, was crowing. I shot 71-70 for the weekend, and he held that over Susie's head. "You shot 3-over," he teased Susie, "and I shot 3-under." They had a big laugh over it.

My playing partners today, Harold Henning and Jim Colbert, also played well today and shot 69s. This was Jimmy's second tournament as a senior, and I was very impressed with the way he hit the ball. He's such a marvelous striker of the golf ball and he has such great confidence and presence on the golf course that I'm sure he'll do well here.

Jimmy and I go back a long time. We were bridge-playing

buddies on the regular tour and spent many wonderful hours gabbing and sharing things with our wives and kids. He's always been full of confidence. You might call it arrogance, but it's a neat kind of arrogance. He can produce.

When I started on the Senior Tour, Jimmy gave me a lot of support. He was doing tournament commentary for ESPN, and on more than one occasion he and I would sit in the locker room and talk about life and golf and what made each of us tick. Those talks helped me a great deal, and I've been waiting eagerly for him to drop the microphone and join us on the fairways. It doesn't bother me one iota that he finished two shots ahead of me this week and got a bigger check.

By way of a postscript, J. C. Goosie shot 73-75-73 and finished in a tie for forty-first. Terry Dill, however, shot 68-69-72 for 209—good for a share of fourth place and almost $22,000. If they were bothered by my *Golf World* column, they showed it in different ways.

I'm just glad to see the Senior Tour leave town. I'm not a work-at-home kind of guy.

MARCH 25, MONDAY/PALM DESERT, CALIFORNIA

I was too absorbed in my own goings-on to notice, but John Brodie had one of his better tournaments over the weekend. He shot a 68 in the first round and was only three shots off the lead Sunday before fading and finishing twentieth.

John, as you probably know, was a great quarterback for the San Francisco 49ers, but he's also played a lot of golf since his college days at Stanford. He gave up a great job as a football color commentator for NBC to play the Senior Tour, and he's done well . . . for a broadcaster. In six seasons out here, he's only been exempt off the money list one time—he was twenty-fifth in 1987—but he's exempt by way of the Q-School this year. As a former football star, he can play pretty much anywhere he wants anyway, just on sponsor exemptions.

Brodie is a great competitor, but he's never won a golf tournament and the odds are long that he ever will. People watch him hit balls and they see his confidence and his athletic ability, and they wonder, "Why is that? Why can't he win?"

Ralph Terry is another guy. Ralph was an all-star pitcher for the Yankees, a twenty-game winner, but he's a bench-warmer on the Senior Tour. He's a good swinger, he hits the ball very well, but he's having trouble playing championship golf.

Maybe it's a gross simplification, but I look at it this way. You're not going to beat me at golf when I've done it for forty years and you're just starting. It's just not going to happen. Brodie was knocking heads with linebackers and defensive linemen during his athletic prime. Terry was trying to strike out Ted Williams. They've played a lot of golf since they left those sports, but they can't catch up. Even Walt Zembriski and John Paul Cain have played competitive golf all their lives.

That's why I laugh when I read that Michael Jordan is going to play professional golf when he's through with basketball. He may *play*, but he won't win. His peers will be tournament-hardened guys like Paul Azinger and Mark Calcavecchia, guys that have spent their lives on the golf course and the range, guys that have hardened themselves with a couple of thousand rounds of tournament golf. I mean, I wouldn't give Jordan a chance against guys like Sam Snead or Jerry Barber, and those guys are in their seventies.

On the other hand, if you ask me if I'm impressed by athletes like Brodie and Terry, guys who can be all-stars in one sport and competent pros in another—yeah, I'm impressed. I can only play golf. And some days I can't even do that.

MARCH 27, WEDNESDAY/PALM DESERT

Ten or fifteen of our guys are over in Japan this week, trying to win a hundred and fifty grand in the Fuji Electric

Grandslam. I'm staying home. I've made up my mind I'm not going anywhere in Asia for less than a $15,000 or $20,000 guarantee. Appearance money, not prize money. And I'm not going to get too many of those offers.

It's just a killer trip. I played in Japan twice last year and once in '89, and it takes two weeks to get over it. There are no golf courses around Tokyo, and the last time I was there it was two hours to the tournament site every day. They treat you like gods, they pick you up in limousines and even helicopters, but it's too hard on the system.

Larry Mowry's another guy who's not going. "I went to Japan seven times one year," he said the other day. "The money's good and it seemed like the thing to do. But it's like our Monday things. I played an awful lot of 'em from '89 through the first half of '90, and I think that's why my putter started yippin' on me. I stressed myself out."

MARCH 28, THURSDAY/PALM DESERT

I see in *Golf World* that the Vantage Dominion sponsors down in San Antonio are unhappy because only one of the six former winners showed up for a banquet in their honor. One of the guys who canceled—it doesn't say who—called a club executive from the Dominion grill room and said he had the flu and couldn't attend. After making the call, this guy allegedly spent the next two hours at the bar, not knowing that the official he had called was sitting in the same area.

I wasn't there, but this doesn't make any sense to me. I'll buy that this one guy messed up, the guy who sat in the bar, but our guys are very good about attending tour parties. We go to the sponsorship parties and the pro-am parties, we have lunch with our pro-am partners, and we write thank-you letters after the tournament's over. I'm not saying it didn't happen, but I can't believe that six said they would attend and only one showed up. It's just out of character.

Here's what happens sometimes. The sponsors send out let-

ters months in advance inviting players to a social event—
"We're having a dinner and we'd sure like you to attend!"—
and if they don't hear anything back, they assume the players
have accepted. And sometimes we haven't even seen the
invitation.

I've already been contacted by the sponsors in Dallas, where
I'm the defending champion. They've asked me to attend three
parties and play in a little skins game, and I've agreed to
attend all four events. But they *called* me to confirm that I
would be there.

That's how you avoid these misunderstandings.

FIVE

APRIL 1, MONDAY/SCOTTSDALE, ARIZONA

Jack's back.

This week's tournament is the Tradition at Desert Mountain. Jack Nicklaus designed the course we'll be playing on—the Cochise Course, one of three Nicklaus layouts at the Desert Mountain development in the cactus canyons north of Scottsdale. That means we'll see Nicklaus, the player, for the first time this year. Jack hasn't shown much interest in the Senior PGA Tour, but he likes to promote his golf courses. He's the defending champion, too. He turned fifty a year ago January and won the Tradition in his first start as a senior. Jack being here brings all the press out and makes it a big to-do.

I could be wrong, but I think Lee Trevino gets his nose a bit out of joint when he sees the press flocking to Nicklaus. Nicklaus puts the great players like Lee and Gary Player back in the shadows somewhat, and I think they feel a little hurt. Lee has done a lot for the game the last couple of years, and Nicklaus really hasn't done that much.

Trevino finished twenty-fourth here last year, and I'm predicting he'll finish behind Nicklaus again. Lee's the king of the hill on this tour and he beat Jack in the Senior Open last year, but I think he gets flustered when he goes head to head

99

with the Golden Bear. Trevino is the better ball striker, but Nicklaus usually gets the job done better when they play. Which shouldn't surprise me—Jack's the best player who ever lived.

The tournament itself is wonderful. Lyle Anderson, the developer of Desert Mountain and Desert Highlands, would like to make this the Masters of the Senior Tour, and he's working very hard toward that. They've got a dinner on Tuesday night at which they honor all the guys over fifty who've won major championships. They bring back a lot of the older players, the fellows who don't play anymore, like Tommy Bolt and Ed Furgol. They have a great dinner for them and entertain them and make them feel that they're still part of the tour.

Susie and the kids will be driving over for the weekend, but I won't have to wait that long for family support. Jennifer, my twenty-two-year-old daughter from my first marriage, lives in Phoenix, and she'll be caddying for me. She caddied for me in Park City, Utah, last year—it's what she wanted for her birthday—and it went so well we're doing it again. Jenny knows very little about the game, but she brings a lot to the team. She's like Gary in that respect. She can't read putts, but I'll let her look at the putts anyway. Who the heck knows? She might see something I missed.

My oldest daughter, Randi, is going to caddy for me in Atlanta this year, and she knows even less about it, but it's something she wants to do. And I want her to. The important thing is that we can share something on a very deep level. That's something I've never been able to do with any of my children.

Anyway, I flew in early today so I could spend two or three hours on the practice tee with Jim Flick. Jim, of course, needs no introduction—he's one of the greatest teachers in the game. For the last couple of years he's done most of his teaching here at Desert Mountain, over at the Renegade Course. He's out there all day giving lessons, grabbing a quick sandwich, and then giving more lessons. He truly enjoys his teaching. Of course, he's got a pretty exclusive clientele, people like Jack Nicklaus.

Whenever I go to Jim, I start to play very well. If my brain was working right I'd go see him the Monday of every tournament, but like most golfers I get some help and then discard my teacher.

I don't know that Jim has a method. All he's ever talked to me about is trying to get the club on the proper swing plane. I've always tended to reroute the club a little bit, and that causes some problems.

Today, Jim explained the swing to me in a different way. He said, "Try holding the blade on the ball a little longer. When your blade hits the ball, it's moving too much, it's turning. You want to stabilize the left hand and arm through the shot."

That made sense to me. He also got me closer to the golf ball and had me aim to the left a little. "You seem to get aiming right and hitting over the top."

That made sense, too, because when I played my best golf I aimed a bit left.

We worked hard. It was a neat lesson, and I think it put me on the right track.

APRIL 2, TUESDAY/SCOTTSDALE

Jenny is a beauty, a real special gal. She was traumatized by the divorce and having to grow up with an alcoholic parent, but she's bubbly and full of life. She's never down, she's always full of ginger, and I'm real proud of her.

I mention this because Jennifer turned to me this afternoon and said, "Are you a loner, Dad?"

The way she said it, there was a kind of sadness. I tried to explain to her that I'm pretty busy these days, and while I used to mix more with people on the old tour, now I like to do my business, get back to the room, have dinner, get a shower, and go to bed. And the reason I played my practice round alone was simply that I didn't need a lot of conversation today and I hadn't run across anybody I wanted to play with.

And I'm thinking, Maybe I *am* a loner.

The truth is, I'm not interested anymore in going out with the guys and having a couple of Cokes while they're having a couple of drinks. I don't want to talk golf all the time. I'm more interested in my family and my reading and my personal growth.

So I guess I am kind of a loner. And that's fine. But I was shaken a bit by the sadness in Jenny's voice.

And then this afternoon, when we were getting ready to leave the golf course, I looked up and saw Seemore the caddy walking across the parking lot. He looked like a little old man. He looked old and tired, and I saw thirty years go by real quick.

He's been after me and after me about my bag. Maybe next time I'll say yes.

APRIL 3, WEDNESDAY/SCOTTSDALE

There's no pro-am at the Tradition. This is a seventy-two-hole, medal-play tournament. Jenny and I got up a little after dawn and were ready to play an early practice round. We wanted to finish quick and go shopping and spend some time together. I was planning on playing alone again, but Orville Moody and Jimmy Powell caught me on the tee and said they needed one more for an eightsome. There's this gang that plays on Tuesdays and Wednesdays, if there's no pro-am. They throw up balls to pick sides, and everybody plays everybody individually, and there's five-dollar medals and two-dollar skins. It's just a real fun thing. You'd have to play terrible, just terrible, to lose fifty or sixty dollars.

So I said, "Sure."

And immediately it struck me. Why did I say "Sure"? I mean, it happened quickly, it wasn't something I thought about or that somebody forced me to do. It comes on the heels of Jennifer asking me, "Dad, are you a loner?"

The bottom line is, I really don't want to be a loner. There are no such things as coincidences in life, and somehow I created this day for myself. I really wanted to play with those guys.

Jenny and I had a wonderful time. I played with Orville and his brother Lloyd, and my partner was Bert Yancey. Bert and I have been friends for twenty-five years, but we really haven't visited much in the last two years. Today, we talked about our families and friends and the good old days, and it was just a great, great day. And you know what else? I played good! I took the most skins and won part of a medal game and won about sixty dollars. That's not what made it a good day, but it all goes together.

The lesson for me in this was: "Get away from the loner. Get out of the shell. Join in, join the world."

God knows, it's not hard to have fun out here. Bobby Brue gave his trick-shot clinic this morning, and that's always a treat. He hits balls a hundred different ways—blindfolded, standing on one foot, facing the wrong way, with his club upside down, with a triple-jointed club, from under a newspaper—and every shot is a perfect draw down the middle. He's also a great comedian, and he had the spectators doubled-up with laughter. I've seen his routine a million times, but even when I'm hitting practice balls, like I was today, it's fun to stop and watch.

Some of the older fellows were out there, too. Tommy Bolt's always telling me what a great swing I have, and that always pumps me up. He told me again today. And it was fun listening to Lionel Hebert kid around. Lionel didn't do that well when the Senior Tour got started. I mean, he didn't do badly, but not as well as he would have liked. "I just wasn't ready the first time around," he told us, "but when they start the seventy-to-eighty division, I'll be ready for that!"

I tell you what, there's more people who would buy tickets to a dinner and listen to Tommy Bolt and Lionel Hebert tell golf stories than would pay to watch some of these other guys play. That's the gist of my *Golf World* article. I've been walking on pins and needles this week, waiting for Terry Dill or Ben Smith or whoever else was in the article to come up and say something. And I didn't write a thing about them, nothing. I just used them as examples of no-name-type people. It had nothing to do with the quality of their play or how they qualified for the tour.

I know I can't please everybody, but I'm very sensitive to the controversy this article has stirred up. When I was younger, I really didn't care what I wrote. I wanted to prove I was a great writer, a great politician. I was running for something, I wanted to kill people. I don't know what I wanted, but I didn't really care what I wrote. It was the truth—it was always the truth—but if the truth hurt people or aroused controversy, that didn't bother me.

At least, I don't remember it bothering me. Maybe I drank it away.

The point is, I don't need any controversy in my life now. These articles are just my opinions—things I can say, things I want to say, but not things that I'm *burning* to say. I don't need these critical letters, I don't need to be hiding from the players. I do have strong opinions, but if it's going to cause this kind of stuff, phooey! I'm not going to write it anymore.

APRIL 4, THURSDAY/SCOTTSDALE

Jennifer took me aside today, during the first round of the Tradition, and said, "Dad, you're a really tough person to caddy for."

I said, "Why?" I was about 4 over par at the time.

"Because you beat up on yourself. You're not having a good day, but you're still a good guy. You try as hard as you can. You just never give yourself any credit."

This was not a golfer saying this, it was one of my children. And she said it in the heat of battle. That was a risk for her and it made her vulnerable, but it kind of kicked me, and from there on I played a couple under par. Besides helping me on the golf course, it was a real growth point for us.

My partners today were Bobby Nichols and Harold Henning. Bobby hasn't let his financial troubles bother him, I'm glad to see. He's had a very good year so far, earning $60,000 or $70,000. He's playing well. Harold played terrible, shooting a 75, but he kind of held it together. He knows it's a four-round tournament, and the fourth round gives the better players a chance to come to the top.

We all think we're the better players or we wouldn't be out here. Harold and I are somewhere in the top fifteen, maybe the top twenty. If we're going to open with a 74 or 75, we'd rather do it in a four-round tournament than a three-round tournament. We've got plenty of time to catch up.

The first-round leader is Phil Rodgers, who shot a 65. Phil hasn't won a tour event since the 1966 Buick Open, but we all pull for Phil when he gets up there. He's a wonderful player, a great teacher, and a real humanitarian. Phil will do anything for you, give you anything, and he works harder on his game than anybody. He hits as many practice balls as Jimmy Powell.

Nicklaus is six back at 71, but he's got plenty of time to make up ground. Trevino, though, I don't know. He opened with a 75. He came here straight from that unofficial senior event in Japan, and he was really dragging himself around the course, he was really spent. "It's too tough on the body," he said. "Something's got to give."

The problem is, if he skips the event in Japan, he gives up an appearance fee of about $200,000. For that kind of money, most of us would ride back clinging to the wings of a 747.

As is so often the case, I was too swing-oriented today. I was thinking about my swing. It was a good thought, not a groping, searching kind of thought. I knew where I wanted to go and had confidence in what I was doing. I just had to think about it. And when you're thinking "golf swing," you pick the wrong club. You're thinking "golf swing," and you hit the wrong shot. You're thinking "golf swing," and you don't quite catch up and you're a little bit off the arc.

The other thing I did today was call *Golf World*. I told them I didn't want to do the columns anymore. I was pretty blunt: "I know I said I'd do it, we've got a contract, but I made a mistake." I told them if they make me finish up the year, the articles were going to be pap. "I'm not going to write any more controversial items. I'm a changed person."

The ball's in their court. I feel bad, because I did agree to write these columns. But I didn't realize how the controversy would affect me, and I'm learning the hard way. While I wrote the truth, and my opinion didn't hurt anybody, it's ruffled some feathers. I don't want to be running and hiding. I want to be able to hold my head up, to sit down and have lunch with the guys and not be worrying about who's mad at me and who's not.

I'm not going through that again.

APRIL 5, FRIDAY/SCOTTSDALE

Can I take back my prediction that Nicklaus and Trevino will finish one-two here? Jack shot a mediocre 73 today and he's twelve shots behind Phil Rodgers, who shot a 67 to go with his first-round 65. Trevino shot his second straight 75, and he's eighteen back!

Maybe Jack's poor play will blunt the criticism, heard whenever we play a Nicklaus course, that he only builds golf courses to suit his own game. This Cochise Course is supposedly the easiest of the three here, but it's a typical Nicklaus layout. It's generous off the tee and the fairways are receptive. It's not a back-breaking length, it's pleasing to the eye, and, like most Nicklaus courses, it's in good shape.

But I, personally, don't care for it. Nicklaus's greens just don't accept the ball. You have pin placements where the green is very narrow, not deep, not wide, and you feel you have to go straight up and down with your shot. There's no way to land somewhere close, and if you miss by the slightest amount you're off in a bunker. And once you miss the green, there's no recovery. You just feel you're dead.

There's been a lot of grousing about it this week, as there was last year. Trevino had a good line about the tendency of modern golf architects to pitch their greens from front to back. He said, "If you could play these new courses backward, they'd be perfect."

I played today with Lou Graham and Lee Elder, and I kept my record intact with Lee—we went eighteen holes and never said a word to each other. It's fine with me, and I guess it's fine with him. Louie's a different story. He's been a friend for almost thirty years, and we're always kidding each other about the University of Kentucky and Vanderbilt. (He's a dyed-in-the-wool, fight-to-the-death Vanderbilt fan.) We always have a five-dollar bet on the football game and the two basketball games they play against each other every year. We pretty much break even—because neither team can play, I guess.

Louie's got an enviable disposition. I'm sure he gets angry with himself, but you never see him get excited or flustered. He always looks calm and peaceful. I enjoy being around him because he settles me down, and I don't mean just on the golf course. He's had a lot of hand problems, wrist problems, and elbow problems, but he never complains. He just practices and keeps that smile on his face.

Lou shot 74 today and Elder shot 78, so my 70 was pure gold by comparison.

Jennifer continues to delight me. She took the caddying very seriously, drove the cart well, kept the clubs clean, had the towel there, hustled, did everything right on the greens, and was really in the game. I even let her read a few putts. I don't pay a lot of attention to what she says, but it keeps her in the game. She'll say, "Oh, it kind of goes off to the right edge," or something. But one putt, I looked at it and it broke right, broke left, went over here, up and down. And Jenny said, "It kind of looks like a drunken man going down through there." It described the putt beautifully.

I didn't see Phil Rodgers today or I would have told him how happy I was for him. He's got a six-shot lead over five players, so he must be playing some great golf. It looks like this will be his week, and there's nobody more deserving. He's helped everybody out here with their swings.

Meanwhile, Chi Chi Rodriguez is bragging about his win two weeks ago at the Vintage. "I was the tallest player to win a tournament on any tour," he says. It seems Danielle Ammaccapane, who won the LPGA tournament in Phoenix, is two inches shorter than he is, and Ian Woosnam, who won the PGA Tour event in New Orleans, is *three* inches shorter. Chi Chi says, "It was the only time in my life that I felt tall."

APRIL 6, SATURDAY/SCOTTSDALE

We've been warned to watch out for rattlesnakes on the course this week. So far, they've caught two big rattlers, five or six feet long. The first one was hiding under a rock near the clubhouse circle, and the other one turned up on the eighteenth fairway. Some of the guys were joking that Nicklaus probably put it there as a hazard.

They bagged the snakes and released them somewhere out on the desert, but I'm watching where I step. Trevino's caddy, Herman, says we have nothing to worry about. "I haven't seen any snakes," he told one of the golf writers, "and we've been in some places where you should."

I had a real neat pairing today—Bob Brue and Don January, two very good friends of mine. Both opened with 68s but shot 75s Friday, and none of us was outstanding today. Don had the best chance. He chipped in twice and got it to 6-under for the tournament, but then he had an unplayable lie and a three-putt and kind of lost his concentration.

The more I play with Don, the more I wonder why he doesn't win more. He's sixty-one or sixty-two now, but he's fourth or fifth in driving distance on our tour. He's a great iron player, a good putter, a good thinker, and he has unbelievable confidence. I mean, he goes right at it. But I think he falls into the trap we all do as we get older; we have our lapses, our mental vacuums, our trances, whatever it is. We play like old men sometimes. And that's not to take anything away from us, because hey, we *are* old men. We don't have the young golfer's ability to stay sharp and focused for four straight hours. All of a sudden you hit a shot and you think, "What?" You aren't thinking of something else—your mind just isn't there.

Don did that a couple of times today, and I did, too. I was 1-under on the eighteenth tee, a par-5. I had a good chance to shoot another 70, which would have put me in pretty good shape. I hit a good drive and had a little 4-iron to the green, and that's when I had one of those lapses I was just talking about. Without a thought in my head, I hit it into a bunker. Then I hit it from that bunker over the green into another bunker, and from there I made 6.

So I shot a 72, and that puts me right around twenty-fifth place. That's a hump spot on our tour. Below twenty-five, you really drop into no-man's land—a couple of thousand bucks, give or take a few dollars. If you make a move from there, you can get up to the big bucks, which I hope to do tomorrow. It's tough sitting on the hump. You can go in either direction.

At least I'm hitting the ball well. I've seen Jim Flick a few minutes each day for a little brush-up, and he's given me confidence.

Phil Rodgers slipped to 73 today, but he's still got a share of the lead. Jim Colbert, my old bridge-playing buddy, shot 67, and he and Phil are four shots ahead of Jim Dent and Ben Smith. Nicklaus proved he can play his own course—he shot 66 today—but he's still five back. Trevino got untracked with a 69, but he's on the wrong side of the hump.

Now that I check the prize list, I see that the hump here is lower than I thought—more like forty-fifth place. A twenty-fifth-place finish tomorrow would get me around $8,000, which isn't bad. I'll be disappointed, though, if I don't do better. This is our first four-round tournament of the year, and some people are just going to fall out of bed tomorrow. I've got a chance to make a move.

APRIL 7, SUNDAY/SCOTTSDALE

I don't know why anything Jack Nicklaus does should surprise me. He was twelve strokes behind Phil Rodgers after two rounds, and there's no way he could win this golf tournament. No way. But when he hopped in his limousine this afternoon, headed for the airport and his corporate jet, he was carrying the Tradition trophy and a check for $120,000.

Phil has to be terribly disappointed. I talked to his wife, Karen, this morning, and she said, "He's ready. He's really ready." Susan had written a little note for Phil. She didn't sign it, she just wrote, "You've worked hard for this, Phil. You deserve it, it's yours, go get it." I stuck it in his locker this morning, so I presume he got it. It's not often you pull for somebody in a golf tournament, but the Beards were in Phil's corner today.

It's not like Phil played terribly the last two days; he went 73-73. But Nicklaus finished 66-67, and if you're anywhere near the top that's going to pick up a lot of cookies. Jack's still the best. I don't know how I could relegate him to any spot but first. Maybe I just have a soft spot in my heart for Trevino, but even Lee defers to Nicklaus. "If Nicklaus says an ant can pull a bale of hay," Lee once said, "hitch it up."

I played well today. The swing started feeling better, and I made some two-putts for birdies and pars that I haven't been making lately. More than anything, I started playing golf. I decided, "Hey, let's get away from the swing, I've got a chance here to make some money." That's what my focus was today: money. I said, "What's the best thing I can do to make a 3 on this hole, a 4 on that hole." And the next thing I knew, I was 4 under par after twelve holes. I had some chances coming in to do even better.

I might not be so happy if I hadn't finished the way I did. On No. 18, the par-5, I had a 2-iron to the green, and I did the same thing I did yesterday—put it in the bunker. Then I played it over into the other bunker—again, the exact same thing I did yesterday. But this time I got up and down, making a tricky downhill trickler from four feet for my 5.

That's one of those putts you've just got to make. I mean, the last hole of a tournament, the last putt—if you miss that one and make bogey, it's just terrible. You're ruined for another week. But I made it, and you can't imagine how neat a putt like that looks going in. Sometimes they look really, really good.

So I finished with a 68, which tied me for twelfth. I won $16,000, which is a confidence booster. And I'm happy for Jim Colbert, who finished in a three-way tie for second with Phil and Jim Dent. Colbert has to feel great, cashing a check for $58,000 in just his third tournament.

The highlight of the week, though, has to be the time I got to spend with Jenny.

APRIL 8, MONDAY/PALM DESERT, CALIFORNIA

When I got out to La Quinta today, everybody was buzzing about Nicklaus coming from twelve strokes back to win the Tradition. One of the guys came up to me and said, "Is Nicklaus really that good?"

I said, "No, he's just been on a thirty-year lucky streak."

APRIL 10, WEDNESDAY/PALM DESERT

I've been brooding over that column I wrote for *Golf World*, the one about the players who circulate petitions because they can't make it under the Senior Tour's qualifying system. I've gotten a bunch of letters from people who agree with me, letters of congratulation and support. But I've also gotten some hate letters. Mean letters, calling me crazy and questioning my motives.

It bothers me that *Golf World* ran four letters on the controversy and three of the letters made me look pretty sick. I called Geoff Russell a few days ago and said, "How are the letters running? Pro or con?"

He said, "About fifty-fifty."

"So why didn't you print another letter from my side? You've got three letters slamming me and one saying I'm okay. Where's the support? After all, I'm working for you guys."

Geoff explained that they had weighted the letters the other way to give the dissenters a chance to have their say. I still didn't like it, and I told him it bothered me that they could put any headline they wanted on my story and write captions for the pictures without consulting me.

"I'll talk to Terry about it," Geoff said. "Anything we can do, we'll do. We love your column."

So I got a call this afternoon from Terry Galvin, *Golf World*'s editor. He was calling from the press center at Augusta National, where the golf world is gathered for Masters week.

"Jeez, Frank," he said, "at least finish the year with us, do the rest of the columns in the contract. We love what you're doing, the readers love it. I just had a conversation with Dave Anderson of *The New York Times*—I'm talking about a Pulitzer Prize–winning writer here—and he told me, 'Terry, Beard's the best columnist you've got in the book.'"

"Yeah?" That stroked my ego, pulled me up short.

"Yeah. And Dave meant it. You shouldn't take the letters so seriously, you're doing great. Whatever support you want, fine. You want us to call you with the headline, fine. I'll call and read you the headline. But stay with us. The column is too good to kill."

So we talked for eight or ten minutes, and the bottom line is, everything is fine. I'm going to keep doing the column.

Looking back on it, this whole brouhaha is just another example of my obsessive-compulsiveness. I blew the whole thing out of proportion. I tend to overreact to criticism or anything in my life I can't control. After fifty years of living and learning, you ought to know that you have to take what comes when you put your name to something. I'm fifty-two, and I still haven't figured that out.

APRIL 11, THURSDAY/PALM DESERT

I watched some of the first round of the Masters on TV today—some of it out at the club, the rest at home. I've already mentioned that I don't watch much televised golf, but the Masters, the Open, the PGA, and the British Open, I pretty much stay glued to the set. I become a golf fan for those tournaments. A special golf fan, because I've played in them. I know what it feels like to play under major tournament pressure, and I know the subtleties and nuances of the golf courses.

They had perfect weather today, and a bunch of guys broke par. A couple of fellows I know and like, Lanny Wadkins and Mark McCumber, shot 67 and are tied for the lead with Jim Gallagher, Jr., who's a stranger to me, a good young golfer. Tom Watson and Jack Nicklaus shot 68s, which tickled the hell out of me. And Tommy Aaron, one of us Senior Tour farts, had a 70. Aaron gets invited back to Augusta every year because he won the Masters in 1973. Tommy won only two official tour events in his career, but winning the Masters is like winning ten regular tournaments. Anybody who's ever played the game would love to have his name on that trophy.

APRIL 12, FRIDAY/PALM DESERT

More Masters observations from Frank Beard, the television golf fan:

- There's something about Phil Mickelson, the Arizona State University lefthander, that turns me off. He has this smirk and he turns his collar up—it makes him look a little smug. But then I reflect on what he's done at the age of twenty-one—two NCAA titles, winner of the U.S. Amateur, winner of a dozen or so college tournaments, Walker Cupper, winner of the PGA Tour's Phoenix Open—and I guess he can afford to be smug. The guy's obnoxious and shoots 80, you can hate him. The guy's obnoxious and shoots 60, you gotta love him.
- Seve Ballesteros is back on the scene. I can still see him as a young hotshot, the kid from Spain. He used to be all over the golf course. He'd make a bogey on a 5-par, the kind where I'd be hanging my head a little bit. It just seemed to tick him off to where he'd say, "I'm going to eagle this next hole." You could just see it on his face.
- Here's what I notice about the foreign players (I hate that term). They have a grittiness. Not that I think our guys give up, but they seem to be bothered more by a bad hole. (See above, under Beard.) Not to a man, but occasionally. The foreign players just seem more determined to come back. Maybe it's because the foreigners play in such crappy circumstances through their careers—rugged golf courses, bad weather, smaller purses. They learn, "This is golf, you're going to make a double once in a while. Let's get on with it."

I spent most of the afternoon rooting for Nicklaus and Tom Watson, who were playing together. Nicklaus, as far as I'm concerned, is not a senior golfer this week. He's Jack Nicklaus, the greatest player who ever lived, and I want him to beat the kids very bad. I got home too late to see his triple bogey on No. 12—it's a treacherous little par-3, and apparently he knocked two balls into the water—but I caught his string of birdies starting with No. 13. He got back to par for the round and finished four shots off the lead.

The thing that strikes me, as it has before, is that I couldn't tell from Nicklaus's expression that something terrible had happened on No. 12. That's pure Nicklaus. For years I've turned on the TV when Jack was on, and I've never known if he was five ahead or five behind, whether he was lying seven on a hole or two. The shot that he is hitting at the time is all that is ever on his mind. Jack doesn't hit the ball any better or worse than the other guys, I think, but he is a wonderful general. He has total command of his assets on the golf course.

The other guy I watched closely today was Watson, who shot his second straight 68 and took a two-stroke lead on Woosnam, Wadkins, McCumber, and Mark Calcavecchia. I'm pulling for Jack because he's meant so much to the game, but I'm pulling for Watson because the game means so much to him. I respect him enormously. I know how hard he's worked, and I know how much it would mean for him to win another Masters.

There was this wonderful moment on No. 18 when Nicklaus and Watson were walking up the hill to the green after hitting their approaches. Watson was ahead of Jack. The crowd started to cheer and clap, and Watson was sensitive enough to stop, turn, and wait for Jack to catch up. The two of them sort of put their arms on each other's shoulders and walked up together, and the gallery just loved it.

It was one of the best moments I've ever seen at a Masters.

APRIL 13, SATURDAY/PALM DESERT

Out on the range the other day, somebody stopped me and said, "What did you think about old Sam?"

I didn't know what he was talking about. "Sam who?"

"Sam Snead!"

It turned out that Slammin' Sammy played in the par-3 tournament they always hold on the Wednesday of Masters week, and he nearly won it. He's seventy-eight years old, half-blind, and can't walk, but he went out in front of a huge crowd on the most difficult par-3 course in the world and shot a 3-under-par 24, good enough to tie for first. The three regular tour guys he tied with—Rocco Mediate, Billy Ray Brown, and Kenny Knox—weren't even born when Sam won the last of his three Masters titles in 1954. God, I love it! Mediate won in a playoff, but Sam must have felt like a barefoot mountain boy again.

Another guy asked me if I missed being at the Masters, and I said, "You mean as a player?" Hardly anybody knows that I was going to be a TV commentator at the Masters until the crusty old chairman of Augusta National, Clifford Roberts, shot me down.

What year was it, 1977? I hadn't signed a contract with CBS, but I had done seven or eight tournaments as a color man. Frank Chirkinian was the CBS golf producer then, as he is now, and he told me at the beginning of the year that he wanted me on the team. He called me for this and called me for that, worked my appearances around whatever tournaments I was playing in. He paid me $2,500 a shot, I think. I was recognized as a CBS part-time guy, and I expected to be in the booth in Augusta, since I wasn't going to be invited as a player that year.

I was writing my *Golf Digest* column at the time. We were doing some articles for the annual Masters issue, and Robert Trent Jones, the architect, had just made some of the first changes to Augusta National. The bunker on No. 2, bunkers on No. 18, some changes on No. 14. Traditionalist that I am, I wrote a column, the sum and substance of which was that Bobby Jones, the golfer and codesigner of Augusta National, was probably turning over in his grave. I said, How *dare* they? I said, Bobby Jones and Alistair McKenzie are gods of golf! I said, I don't care if the players shoot 30-under for the week, you don't touch Augusta National! It's sacrilegious!

Cliff Roberts, who ran the Masters with an iron hand, didn't like that. He got on the phone to Chirkinian. He said, "We don't want Beard down here doing this tournament. In fact, we really don't want Beard on CBS at all."

I'm not making this up; Chirkinian told me himself. And of course, the Masters was the jewel in the CBS crown, the most prestigious event in their sports lineup. Roberts was always yanking their chain, threatening to take the tournament away if they didn't toe his line.

Chirkinian was apologetic. He said, "I can't take a chance, Frank."

I understood. I wasn't fired, because I never had a contract in the first place. I just never worked for CBS again.

APRIL 14, SUNDAY/PALM DESERT

Ian Woosnam won the Masters today, and Jose Maria Olazabal finished second. I had never seen either of them play, other than glimpses, and I was impressed with their golf swings. I mean, *really* impressed. What struck me most was Woosnam's boldness. Jesus Christ, whenever he could see the pin he just went for it. I'll never forget the shot he hit yesterday on No. 13, the par-5 down in Amen Corner. He was in the trees to the right, and I don't know who it was, Tom Weiskopf or somebody, said, "He's got to lay up." And Weiskopf was right, I've been there. It's not so much that you can't get across the creek, but a ball that gets across is going five thousand miles an hour when it lands. And you don't want to be going over that green to the left, because you can't get up and down.

Well, Woosnam took some kind of iron, and the minute he hit it I knew it was a great shot. And it was, right in the middle of the green. He has to have enormous strength to do what he did.

Tom Watson showed great resiliency. He double bogeyed No. 12 and seemed to be out of it, but he eagled both No. 13 and No. 15, which was sensational. He came to the final hole tied with Woosnam and Olazabal, but he fired a 3-wood into the trees on the right and ended up making double bogey. I was a little stunned at his last-hole collapse—Tom Watson didn't do that a few years back—but it's not fair to compare. He's human, and maybe the older we get the more human we get.

It was a great Masters, except there weren't any Louisvillians in there. Jodie Mudd wasn't doing well, or Fuzzy Zoeller. I'm like most sports fans, I'm partisan and parochial. I don't necessarily pull against the foreign players, but I'm American from top to bottom. I'd like to see the Masters won again by somebody who drinks in a bar instead of a pub.

APRIL 15, MONDAY/PALM BEACH GARDENS, FLORIDA

My friend Gary Colvin and I flew into Fort Myers last night because I had an outing today in Naples. He's caddying for me this week in the PGA Seniors Championship, and he's never been to Florida.

I'm always moaning and groaning about these Monday outings. Gary's heard my lament: fly in Sunday night, play all day Monday, fly to the tournament, get to bed late on Monday. "Damn, I've got to go to one of these crummy outings."

I make it sound worse than it really is. The truth is, we get from $2,000 to $6,000 to play in these things, the food is good, and the host company usually whisks us to and from the airport. Sometimes we even fly to our next stop on a corporate jet. It's not slave labor.

Anyway, I told Gary I had to do this outing for Mazda, and he said he'd like to go along.

As it turned out, somebody was a no-show at the outing and Gary got invited to play. So here I am, darting about from group to group, trying to play with all the executives, and I see Gary out on the golf course. He's playing a hole out by the Gulf, and it's a beautiful day. The sun's shining off the water, his hair is blowing in the wind, he's got the free Titleists and the free golf cart and the free visor and the free golf shirt. Somebody drives up every few holes with coolers of soft drinks and beer.

I pull up and say, "How ya doin'?"

Gary gives me this look. He says, "Don't you *ever* bitch to me again about doing an outing. You may fool Susan, but you're not fooling me anymore." He turned away, shaking his head. "And you're getting *paid*, on top of it. Unbelievable!"

After dinner, we drove Alligator Alley back to the Atlantic Coast, and Gary told me all his stories about Patty Sheehan and Beth Daniel, two LPGA stars who had played at the outing, and about the alligator that had crawled up on the tee box when he was getting ready to tee off on one hole. The thing that impressed him most, though, was one of the executives he had played with.

"Frank, he took off his golf glove on one hole, and you know what? His hand was totally white. The rest of him was tan, but his hand was white."

Gary shook his head. "Unbelievable!"

APRIL 16, TUESDAY/PALM BEACH GARDENS

This golf course, PGA National, is a typical Florida course. It doesn't always blow gales, but it blows enough to throw you off your game. I don't know who designed it originally, but Nicklaus came in and reworked it and there's some typical Nicklaus stuff here. He's made some of the holes unplayable. For the average guy, not for Nicklaus. It's almost as if he doesn't take into account that the wind is going to blow and humans are going to play.

The first three holes can take you out of the game before you're even warmed up. No. 1 has got out-of-bounds extremely tight on the right and a lake down the left, which is Jack's way of telling you you aren't good enough to play his course. No. 2 is a tough green to putt. No. 3 is a reachable par-5, but there's water again and some imposing bunkering.

Gary and I got in a good practice round with Ben Hogan's

old protégé, Gardner Dickinson. Gardner doesn't play much
these days. He's sixty-four and he's been through a whole
catalog of surgeries—his neck in '58, his back in '84, and last
year a triple-bypass heart operation. But he's hardly a fossil.
He's got a young wife, Judy, who's a good player on the LPGA
Tour, and he's got two-year-old twin boys.

"He doesn't have the distance," Gary told me, "but man,
he's got some great shots. I'd love to have seen him play in
his prime."

We played eighteen, we checked our yardages, and then we
left. Gary was stoked up to go to the Palm Beach Kennel
Club, but the track was dark tonight and we went to jai-alai
instead. We had a good time and lost the usual amount of
money, but I don't care much for that game. I don't like it
when I see the players down there on the bench, looking up
at the odds on the tote board. Gary's the same way. He said,
"I'd rather bet on animals than humans anytime."

We saw a caddy or two at the fronton, but no golfers. People ask me the difference between the Senior Tour and the
regular tour. I tell them the principal difference is how we
behave after dark. Daytime is the same on both tours. Everybody gets up in the morning, goes out and busts butt till 5:30,
grabs a shower, and goes out for dinner. On the big tour,
though, the night has just begun—women, cards, movies,
whatever the young guys want and never mind how late it
gets. It's different for the seniors. Most of us are in our rooms
by 7:30, reading or watching TV. Some of us may go for a
late dinner, a few guys might take in a movie, but that's a big
night out.

There's no mystery about it. Age and fatigue have forced us
to cut back on our after-hours activities. Carousing is out.
Dating is a distant memory. Even card playing, which was all
the rage when I played the big tour, is almost unheard of on
the Senior Tour. I've been out here thirty months now, and
I've been in exactly one card game—and that happened during a double rainout in New York, when nobody could think
of anything to do.

What we have now is a Bible study group that meets one night a week. I haven't partaken of that, but it shows how things have changed. Sure, there's still two or three seniors who chase women as much as they ever did, and there's two or three guys in the bar as drunk as they ever were, but they're the exception to the rule.

APRIL 17, WEDNESDAY/PALM BEACH GARDENS

I spent a few minutes with George Archer on the practice green this morning. "How's it look for Japan?" I asked.

"We don't know yet," he said. "Ted's still looking for a sponsor."

George has this friend who's got a tournament in Japan every November, and I'm planning on going again this year if the money's right and the date is okay. But the Japanese economy is as bad as ours right now. The guy lost his original sponsor because the company's gone under, and now he's out beating the bushes for a replacement. George is on pins and needles over it.

"I want to do it," I said, "but I need to know pretty soon."

"Me too. If we wait much longer, everybody will have other commitments."

Then I talked to Freddie Hawkins, who showed me some little putting tip that he'd just gotten from Dale Douglass. Freddie's in his sixties now, but give him a tip or a new piece of equipment and he's like a kid with a new toy.

Freddie's an interesting case. He's on the bubble this year. He's number seventy-six or something on the all-time money list, which puts him at risk for next year. I mean, he's the last guy. But he is the epitome of effort and he never quits. Here's a guy who's about finished as a player, but you'd never know it. He could be 215 over par and he'd be on his stomach, lining up that last putt.

Anytime I think I'm getting too old or I've had enough, I think of Freddie Hawkins.

The PGA Championship has never felt like a major championship to me. It's never had the mystique, the hype, or the
player acceptance. Of the three, player acceptance is the most
important, because players make the majors. The press can't
do it, sponsors can't do it, and governing bodies can't do it.
The players do it by answering a simple question: "Which
tournament do you want to win the most?"

You hear players say, "I want to win the Masters . . . I want
to win the U.S. Open . . . I want to win the British Open . . ."

Let's face it, you never hear anybody say, "I want to win
the PGA." Arnold Palmer might say it, because that's the only
major he's never won. But basically it's the Masters, the U.S.
Open, and lately, the British Open. The PGA—which, quite
honestly, has always had the strongest field of the four—has
just never had the acceptance.

That's carried over to the seniors. For me, this week's tournament, the PGA Seniors Championship, is just another tournament. Yes, there are differences—it's a four-rounder, the
committee people wear different-colored coats, and the PGA
of America, while it's not quite as arrogant as the USGA, has
its own way of letting you know that this is not a PGA Tour
event. That's fine, that's their privilege. But the PGA just
doesn't feel like a major championship, and this senior ver-
sion is no different. The only edge this tournament has on
our regular tour events is Jack Nicklaus. Jack's being here
adds something.

Maybe if I held the tournament in higher regard I might
play better this week. I caught myself again today: I was thinking of my swing during the practice round. There's no way to
play that way. You can't stand on the first tee or the fourteenth fairway thinking, "On this swing I'm going to keep the
head still and not let my right leg break down, and I'm going
to stay down through the shot longer and finish high." You
can't do that and play well. You can do it for six holes, maybe,
but on the seventh hole you lose a golf ball.

Listen to me preach! Since I worked with Jim Flick at
Phoenix, I've had nothing but swing thoughts on my mind.

My ball-striking problems come when I take the club back too much on the inside on the backswing and then swing straight out across the target line. It gives me this terrible underneath-inside-out golf swing that produces a toe hook. Flick got me to make a more inside-to-inside golf swing, one in which the club ends up more to the left on the follow-through. He's also got me aiming quite a bit left and almost hitting a cut shot, or what *feels* like a cut shot to me. It's hard for a hooker to aim left, and if you say the club is going to go left as well—that's scary. I know what he tells me is right—I don't ever hit a bad shot if I do what I'm trying to do, because a good swing is not going to hit a bad shot—but the rerouting, the inside-out stuff, all that is a consternation to me.

I'm not sure these swing changes look any different to the naked eye. Phil Armbruster from Power-Bilt followed me some today. He said, "Frank, your swing looks pretty good."

I'm sure it does. I played well at Phoenix and I'm still hitting some good shots. But I'm hitting some godawful shots, too, and to post a good score you've got to hit it consistently.

I'm just not able to shake my old mental images and go with something new. As I told Phil, "The old way has me by the scruff of the neck and won't let me go."

APRIL 18, THURSDAY/PALM BEACH GARDENS

I stand on the tee sometimes, and I feel the old fear floating up. It's like a ghostly specter standing there. I feel all this old stuff from 1977, when my game was in shambles. Dread pervades my whole being.

Is that a good enough excuse for shooting a 75 in the first round of the PGA Seniors Championship?

Aw, hell, I just flat-out played poorly. I think it bothered Gary more than it bothered me. He's my friend to a fault, and he doesn't know what to do for me when I'm not going well. He wants to *do* something. He's like me, he wants to fix everything. So I'll hit bad shots and have bad holes, and he'll stand there with this helpless look on his face, a look that says, "What can I do?"

He doesn't know how much he does for me just by being here. Off the golf course, I'm having a wonderful time. We're talking a lot, we're going to the dog races every night. He even likes to eat like I do, so we've been going to greasy places where we can pig out without our wives bugging us.

Gary teaches me new things about the word "wonder." He has wonder and awe about everything he's ever seen. "What a beautiful, beautiful place," he'll say. "I just love the plants, the different flora and fauna. You see plants here you've never seen before."

Last year, Gary went with me to the tournament in Richmond, and we made a special trip up to Washington, D.C. We toured the Smithsonian, which is about a four-day excursion, in four hours. I'd never been to the Smithsonian and never wanted to go, but with Gary it was fun. I wound up on a bench under the Wright Brothers airplane, too tired to move. We also went into the Capitol Building, scammed some guards, and went some places we weren't supposed to go. We wound up in the bleachers watching the House of Representatives shoot the bull. Kind of turned my stomach, but it was interesting.

This afternoon, Gary asked if we couldn't drive down the coast highway, A1A. So I drove him for an hour or so, up and down the highway, past the big houses in Palm Beach, past the Kennedy estate. We drove by John Lennon's mansion and Donald Trump's place. I would never have done that on my own, but I wound up having a wonderful time.

He's teaching me lessons at age fifty-two.

My playing partners today were Doug Sanders and Jimmy Powell. Doug showed up on the first tee in one of his more conservative outfits: yellow-green pants, chartreuse shoes, and a bright yellow shirt with green trim. His entourage followed him all over the course. Volunteers, marshals, scorekeepers, fans—women from thirty to eighty, all following Dougie. Big smiles on their faces. "Hi, Mr. Sanders, how are you today? . . . Oh, Mr. Sanders, I love your outfit! . . . Make a birdie for us, Doug!"

Doug is suave personified. It's, "Ladies, how are you today?" and "What a pleasure to have such beautiful and lovely ladies with us today." He's got his lines, and they eat it up, they love it. If he could still shoot golf scores like he did in the sixties, I bet Doug would give Trevino and Chi Chi a run for their money.

APRIL 19, FRIDAY/PALM BEACH GARDENS

Jerry Barber came over to me on the putting green this morning. Just out of the blue, he said, "Frank, I want your opinion on something."

Jerry and I are friends, I guess. We're speaking, at least.

He said, "Down in San Antonio a while back, Mike Fetchick came to the locker room, picked me up by the collar, and said he was gonna thrash me. He said I had driven into him on the golf course. He was very threatening."

I waited for Jerry to go on.

"Now you know I can't drive into anybody. I can't hit it far enough."

I didn't say a word.

"Here's where I want your opinion, Frank. We had a pro-am earlier in the year, and I was kind of the honoree. It was right after Las Vegas. And before we went there, the guy that was putting it on showed me the list of invitations and said, 'Do you like who we invited?' And I said, 'Well, you didn't invite Doug Ford.' He said, 'Well, we invited Mike Fetchick.' And I said, 'Well, why don't you drop Mike Fetchik and invite Doug Ford?' "

I still hadn't said a word. I was listening to this whole thing.

Jerry said, "Do you think Mike Fetchick came into the locker room in San Antonio and picked me up and was gonna thrash me because I drove into him? Or do you think he did it because I dropped him from that pro-am?"

I said, "I don't know, Jerry."

I went back to putting, and he walked off.

That's the total conversation. I don't know any of the facts of the case, other than what Jerry told me. I don't even know that he wanted me to ask for details. I think he wanted me to say, "He attacked you because you dropped him from the pro-am." And then he would have gone off satisfied.

This is only funny to someone who knows Jerry.

We have our pettiness out here. We have fellows like Jerry and Mike, some of the older guys, who played back when there wasn't any money and every nickel counted. I've heard stories about the gamesmanship that went on. Not cheating, but what you might call "unethical conduct"—little stuff that might intimidate a fellow or play with his mind. For instance, a guy would wear white shoes on the golf course and make a point of standing in your field of vision. Just as you were getting ready to drive, he'd take a step with the white shoes. You'd see the flash of white and miss the shot. And he'd say, "Oh, sorry—didn't mean to do that."

I've heard the older guys talk about Dutch Harrison. Old Dutch had a marvelous golf swing, and he'd fool you with his golf clubs. He'd tee up on a par-3 that he knew called for a 4-iron, and he'd take out a 3-iron and put this big, easy swing on it. And when the ball was in the air, he'd yell, "Get up! Get up!" He'd get you thinking, "Hey, it really must be a 3-iron." You'd pull your 3-iron out and bust it completely over the green.

Today, it wouldn't cross our minds to pull such stunts, but some of the older guys used to work one another over. You might have trouble beating a guy with your clubs, but you could still beat him with a little gamesmanship.

From that has come these long-standing rivalries, even feuds. Sometimes you can see the old guys circling out there. They talk to each other, but they stay at arm's length.

I suspect Jerry's monologue on the putting green was part of that. I don't think this Fetchick and Barber thing started in San Antonio.

Don't get me wrong, our tour isn't a bunch of old guys shooting daggers at each other all day. If you pressed me, I'd say it's a kinder, gentler tour than the one I played on in the sixties.

Arnold Palmer had a tough day today. He made a 7 on the last hole, shot 78, and missed the cut by a stroke. That had to kill him. But I saw him signing autographs outside the clubhouse afterward, and he was the same old Arnie. To this day, he won't leave the golf course until he's signed every autograph there is to be signed. Arnold is a great guy, and it hurts me to see him play badly.

Readers of *Pro* may remember that I didn't always see Palmer in this light. When I joined the PGA Tour thirty years ago, I was a young guy, and like all young guys I wanted to be number one. And Palmer was number one. I gave him credit for popularizing the tour and making it possible for us to make so much money, but I wanted to knock him off his perch. He was the King, and I was the Man Who Would Be King.

So when I wrote *Pro*, I made the point that guys like Palmer, guys who were number one, didn't get to the top by looking out for anybody but themselves. They went after what they wanted and didn't let anything stand in the way.

I could have expressed myself more tactfully, but I was trying to be honest. Was there some jealousy mixed in? Sure. I shared that with a lot of the lesser tour players. We spent so much time in Arnie's shade that we had trouble growing.

So when the book came out in 1970, a lot of people took the things I'd written about Arnold's fame and his fans as a personal attack on him. A bunch of golf writers surrounded him after the book came out, and one of them asked, "Will this change your relationship with Beard?"

Arnie looked baffled and said, *"What* relationship?"

I always thought that was a great line. And it was totally factual. We had no relationship. Not then, not now, not ever.

But times change and people change. What I see today with Palmer, that I don't think was present before, is a higher regard for his peers, the other tournament players. He is softer now, he's kinder. I remember when I joined this tour in Houston in 1989. He came right over and asked about Susan, asked about my kids. He told me he was glad that I had licked a few personal problems and that I was back in the game. I can't tell you how much that meant to me.

He seems to be more one of the guys now. He eats lunch with us, he tells jokes in the locker room. Things he never did before. His intensity on the golf course and the practice tee hasn't been affected. He still tees it up and thinks he can win. He just seems softer.

I realize now that Arnold Palmer has been a wonderful part of my life, even if we've never really been close. He has more guts and determination and more youthful belief in himself than anybody I've ever seen.

A few quick notes about the tournament. Nicklaus shot his second straight 66 and leads Jim Dent by five strokes. More important, he leads Trevino by twelve, Chi Chi by thirteen, and Player by fourteen. Those are the only guys who can hope to beat Jack, and they don't seem to be on the same planet with him this week.

On the fashion front, Doug Sanders went out today in a snappy fuchsia number. He looked like a tropical sunset and shot a 72 to go with yesterday's 73.

As for Beardsy, I got off to a glorious start, hitting one into the lake off the first tee. I played good golf after that, though, and shot a 70. I'd still be in the hunt if Jack weren't playing.

Jim Dent will be paired with Nicklaus tomorrow. He ought to try wearing white shoes.

APRIL 20, SATURDAY/PALM BEACH GARDENS

I was on the fifteenth green with George Archer today when the wind came up and angry clouds started gathering to the west. I was 1-under at the time and I really wanted to get over to the sixteenth tee and drive before the sirens went off. The wind was behind us and I had a funny feeling, the way the front was coming in, that it was going to change.

The rumbling of thunder told us we weren't going to make it, but we hustled over our putts anyway. The way the rules read, if just one of us had teed off on No. 16, all three of us could have finished the hole before heading in. I was thinking, "If I finish this round well and have a good round tomorrow, I can make some money—ten grand, maybe."

But there was another peal of thunder as we finished putting, and then the sirens went off. We barely made it back to the clubhouse before the skies opened up and all hell broke loose. The rain came down in sheets, and you couldn't see fifty yards out the clubhouse windows. Gary thought the world was ending. "I've never seen rain like this or lightning like this," he said. "It's frightening."

When we came back out after the storm, the wind had shifted. It was blowing forty miles an hour, right in our faces. No. 16 is a difficult par-4, and I managed a 6 there, real quick. That killed any comeback chance I had. I was just on the fence anyway—I had to make a couple of pars and a birdie to finish 2-under for the day, which would have been a good score. I wound up making double bogey there and bogey on the last hole, and instead of finishing 2-under, I wound up 2-over. A big difference. A swing like that changes your whole attitude.

The tournament is something of a joke, anyway. Nicklaus shot 69 and has an eight-stroke lead on Bruce Crampton. That's the biggest lead in Senior Tour history. Jack won't have any trouble mopping up tomorrow, unless he sprains his back opening his wallet or something. It's galling, when you think about it. You complain about how hard his golf courses are, and Nicklaus refutes your argument by shooting three super scores and making a shambles of the tournament. How do you argue with somebody like that?

I guess you don't. Gary and I are going to get something to eat and go back to the dog track. I've had as much luck there as I've had on the golf course, which is zero. But Gary's done well. "You know," he said, "I've made more on the dogs this week than I have caddying for Frank Beard."

I said, "I'm sure you're not the first caddy to make that statement."

APRIL 21, SUNDAY/PALM BEACH GARDENS

Looking back on the week, I just never got out of the chute. Those first three holes intimidated me. I put one in the lake on No. 1 on Friday, trying to keep it away from the out-of-bounds, and I did the same thing today. So I started two of my rounds with bogeys. I three-putted the second hole a couple of times. The third hole is a par-5 that I can reach in two, but I managed to knock it in the lake one time and make a 6, and I hit into a bunker on two days, stuck it right under the lip, and made 5s when I should have made 4s. Today's round was the worst, a 78.

Nicklaus was never pressed. Bruce Crampton played very well today, considering how windy it was, and he got to within four or five shots of the lead at one point. But Jack just kind of left-handed it in. I can see why Lee Trevino gets his nose a little out of joint when Nicklaus is around. Trevino is the king of the Senior Tour, and here comes Jack, like he's on holiday, shaking the rust off his clubs and winning three out of every four tournaments he plays.

Not a bad week, though. I've become two people. I'm still Frank Beard, the golfer, but I'm beginning to recognize Frank Beard, the person. Frank Beard, the person, is someone who likes to drive down A1A to look at the houses with Gary Colvin.

The old Frank Beard would never have taken that drive.

The golf totally absorbed me. But now I'm beginning to separate the two, and the more I get them apart, the more I'm going to enjoy life. This week in Florida, I had some fun. I enjoyed Gary and I played some pretty bad golf, but I kept it separated. I had some legitimate anger and frustration over my golf game, but I didn't let it infect the rest of my life.

That's the theme for the week of the PGA. I'm not going to hang my head because I can't beat Jack Nicklaus. Who can?

SIX

APRIL 23, TUESDAY/PALM DESERT, CALIFORNIA

The terrible paradox in the world of golf is that when you're
playing well, you get late tee times. That means you can get
drunk the night before. You've got all morning to sleep it off.

I told that to *Sports Illustrated* a couple of years ago, and
they used it to lead off a story about me. Put it in italics with
my name under it, as if it were a quotation from Shakespeare
or George Bernard Shaw.

Since my own alcoholism makes me something of an expert
on the subject, I've got a few general comments to make on
booze and golf. First of all, there are two or three fellows on
our Senior Tour who I think have a drinking problem. I will
not name names, but I see them drinking at the club the way
I did. Grabbing a few beers to relax after a round, drinking
martinis with dinner, having a nightcap at the hotel bar. The
kids on the big tour, I don't know. They're a different
generation.

Overall, though—especially on the Senior Tour—we tend to
take better care of ourselves. We know our bodies don't function the way they used to, and we're anxious to hold on to
what we have. So while there's a lot of good food and a lot
of laughter, I don't see much drinking as such. And I see no
drug use at all. I never saw it on the big tour, and I don't see

132

it now. There were rumors about a couple of guys, and there was probably some marijuana use, but I never saw any, and I haven't heard of a touring pro, to this day, who had a drug problem.

Maybe I'm oblivious to it. A very prominent trait of alcoholics is their loneliness, and my own experience tells me that a lot of drinking gets done in private. Sometimes I'd grab a couple of beers at the club—Westchester sticks in my mind because there was a lovely porch off the clubhouse there— but I did most of my serious drinking at home.

I'm often asked: "Didn't anyone try to get you to stop?"

My answer: not really.

From 1965 on, my drinking got progressively worse, but no one confronted me. Not my family, not my first wife, and not my friends. Not that it was their responsibility.

Oh, I had people come up to me and say, "Hey, Frank, do you think you're drinking a little too much?"

Well, no, I didn't think so.

I truly couldn't see it. After all, I didn't behave like a drunk. I didn't beat up on my wife and kids, I didn't fall down stairs, I didn't do ugly things. And I could quit! I'd say to myself, "Well, I'll just drink beer this week." Or wine. "I won't have anything but wine this week." Which is bull, because you get just as drunk on beer and wine. I'd say, "I'll drink only 3.2 beer for a while," and I'd drink two cases of it.

I did all those things. I'd quit cold for two weeks to prove I wasn't an alcoholic . . . and that gave me permission to drink for the next ten years.

Denial is part of the disease. To this day, I think I can go without my AA meetings. I'll go a few weeks without a meeting and the dry drunk comes back. The anger. The resentment. It was easier to deny back then, because I was doing pretty good. If I had been missing cuts in 1969, maybe I'd have seen the red flags, but I was the leading money winner. "What do you mean I'm drinking too much? I just won the Westchester Classic!"

I planned my drinking as I planned my practice time; I

knew all the tricks and ruses. I would never go to a restaurant unless I knew it had a bar, and I wouldn't visit friends without bringing my own bottle as a "gift." Toward the end, I even learned to drink so that Patty, my first wife, wouldn't know.

I'd make an announcement: "Hey, Pat, I'm only going to drink beer for a while. Only beer. Just a couple."

We'd sit down at four o'clock, we'd talk about the kids, and I'd drink a beer. I'd have beer on my breath, but that was okay. She knew I was going to have a beer.

"Oops, I'm out of razor blades. I'd better go down to Ralph's."

I'd drive down to Ralph's supermarket and buy two quarts of beer, and I'd drink one of the quarts before I got to the checkout counter. I'd pay for the two quarts, get in the car, and drink the other quart on the way home. I'd get home with beer on my breath, but so what? Patty would think I'd had just the one beer. And what I'd really had was a six-pack.

When I look back, I recognize how much stress it put on me and my golf. It takes a lot of effort to hide the elephant in your clothes. It's a real job making sure you have enough to drink while remaining "respectable."

The hardest part is dealing with your own conscience.

APRIL 25, THURSDAY/PALM DESERT

This week's tournament is the Doug Sanders Kingwood Celebrity Classic down in Houston. I'm passing it up for three reasons. One: I'm sticking to my commitment to my family and not playing three straight weeks on the road. Two: It's a celebrity pro-am, and I steer away from those, my affection for the old Crosby notwithstanding. It's terrible to play with celebrities; they're always on stage. Three: The money is not that good.

If the last reason sounds cold, so be it. You've got to skip somewhere. I look at the schedule and see that this tournament in Houston has a purse of just $300,000. And the tournament in Newport, Rhode Island, is just $300,000. The schedule is full of tournaments with $500,000, $600,000, and $700,000 purses, right on up to a million dollars. It's not hard to choose.

On the other side of the ledger, you've got Dougie himself. His lifestyle and the image he presents—the nightlife, the colorful clothing—have been good business for him and for our tour. It's just sad that his golf has suffered so drastically. In the sixties, he was one of the best golfers alive—his twenty tour wins attest to that. But he pursued his high living, and I think it's taken its toll. I haven't witnessed any of his late-night escapades, but if just one-tenth of what he says he does is true, it's a miracle he can play golf at all.

He's done a lot for the game, but he hasn't done much for Dougie.

APRIL 29, MONDAY/PALM DESERT

Mike Hill won the Doug Sanders tournament down in Houston yesterday. Lee Trevino stumbled on the back nine, George Archer three-putted the eighteenth green, and Mike got his sixth win as a senior.

There's a story there. Mike won only three tournaments on the big tour, and I think he didn't win more because he was full of anger like his brother Dave. Dave voiced it and Mike didn't, but both of them walked around with chips on their shoulders. Mike's line is, "I'm just right of Attila the Hun," and the title of Dave's autobiography was *Teed Off*. Does that tell you anything?

Nice guys, mind you—I've always been good friends with both of them—but tough guys, too.

Davey's still angry, but Mike has lost his belligerence. He's still tough, but I suspect he's solved a few riddles and made peace with himself. He can't be full of anger, not the way he's playing.

I'm only guessing, but the Hills' anger must go back to

childhood, to their upbringing. I look at Jack Nicklaus and I see something completely different. Jack had a good family background and grew up with extremely high self-esteem. Golf is important in his life, but it's not the whole world. Tom Watson is another. I've always felt that if Watson or Nicklaus lost an arm in a car wreck, they'd end up on top in some other endeavor. They'd go on and be the world's best insurance executives or the world's best golf commentators.

I don't want to say it's a blue-collar thing, the anger. But you see it most often in players who feel they weren't always welcome inside the country-club gates. Mike and Dave grew up on a dairy farm outside Detroit, and they learned the game as caddies. Mike spent four years in the Air Force and drove a beer truck when he got out.

Maybe that's why Mike bought his own golf course when he got the chance. He owns a municipal course, Hill's Heart of the Lakes, up in Brooklyn, Michigan. I'm sure all the guys up there were watching TV and whooping it up for Mike yesterday. And nobody's prouder of Mike than his big brother, Dave.

APRIL 30, TUESDAY/LAS VEGAS, NEVADA

I checked in at the Desert Inn around noon today and then went out and played a practice round with Bruce Devlin. I love Bruce. We became friends way back in 1963 when we played a tournament in Ardmore, Oklahoma.

Bruce had been in a desperate way that week. "I had a wife, two kids, and $400," he said today, "and I was over here from Australia. Can you believe that? My back was really against the wall."

We weren't playing for much money then, but Bruce finished third at Ardmore and third a week later at Oklahoma City, winning $3,000 between the two. That kept him alive, and now he's a millionaire. He's built golf courses, he's done television—he's just made a wonderful life for himself here.

"But I'll never know what would have happened if I'd finished out of the money at Ardmore," he said.

Bruce has got a son, Kel Devlin, who plays the Hogan Tour, and I follow his name in *Golf World*. I counted up, the other day, and there's eleven senior players that I know of from our top fifty who have boys playing professional golf and trying to get on the tour. There's Bruce, DeWitt Weaver, Dick Rhyan, Bobby Nichols, Charlie Coody, Jack Nicklaus, Al Geiberger, Gary Player, Miller Barber, Don Massengale, and Gibby Gilbert.

This blows my mind. I told Bruce today, "Almost all of these kids I patted on the head when they were one year old. It just happens too quick. It's unbelievable."

He said, "Just wait till your boy Mike is out there. Then you'll really feel old."

MAY 1, WEDNESDAY/LAS VEGAS

I enjoy Vegas. I like the glitz and the glitter, and if I didn't watch myself I could probably turn into an out-of-control gambler. I won my first Tournament of Champions here in 1967, and you always have a warm spot in your heart for cities that have been good to you.

Seemore is here—Melvin Johnson, the caddy I used in Miami. He wants my bag. I ran into him by the caddy tent, and I just said, "We'll see, Seemore." I'm not ready to commit.

I may use him, though. These three weeks here, from Vegas through the Legends, I've got a young fellow named Steve carrying the bag. He does a good job, but I'm not completely comfortable with him. My problem, not his. Sometimes I feel too much energy coming from the young guys. They've got money on their minds, and they expect me to perform.

Some of these caddies are businessmen. Bruce Edwards, who caddied for Tom Watson for years and now carries for Greg Norman, sells real estate when he isn't caddying, if you can believe that. We've had guys who were lawyers, accountants, teachers. They get into caddying for the adventure, sure, but if they get a good bag like Watson, that's a business.

There was a time when I thought the middle-class caddies were pretty irresponsible. They'd caddy for a year, and they'd act like they were a little bit bigger than the job. "I'm not really a caddy," they'd imply, "I'm just out here on a lark." But they'd stay forever. And they didn't all have Tom Watson to caddy for.

I've learned not to judge. If a guy wants to caddy, and he's happy—why not? A lot of them are happier than I am.

I think, though, that I do better when I have a caddy who knows he's a caddy. It's not that the older guys are more menial, but they've settled into the caddy position. They say, "That's my lot in life, that's the best I can do, and I'm comfortable with it."

This new breed, I can feel them grinding. They're bustin' their balls. "We're gonna win this tournament, Frank, we're gonna win." A certain energy is okay, but sometimes it goes beyond that. And if you don't do well, the energy reverses. They can't find the rake. They don't get the pin. They don't give a damn because they're not going to make any money.

So maybe I'll use Seemore. I'm leaning that way.

The pro-am today was a little different. About three or four times a year we play a modified scramble. The pro plays his ball out on every hole, and he always putts first so he doesn't get help with his line. Otherwise, it's a scramble. Everybody hits, you pick the best shot, and everybody hits again from that point. It's great fun for the amateurs, and it has the added advantage of speeding up play.

One thing never changes, though: They're scared to death.

I've got this little speech I give my pro-am partners on the first tee. "The best way to play is like you don't care," I tell them. "Too many guys come in with unbelievable expectations. You think the pro expects you to play five shots better than your handicap. Well, I not only don't expect you to play five shots better, I bet you'll shoot five shots worse. Minimum!

What usually happens is, you play nine holes as badly as you've ever played in your life. Then you grab a sandwich and a couple of beers at the turn, and you do ten strokes better on the back side. Because you're relaxed. So I say, let's do it now. Pretend you've had the couple of beers. Walk along the rope, talk with your wives, and have some fun."

That, more or less, is what I say to calm them down on the first tee.

Does it work? No. Nothing you say can relax them. They've got five thousand people on the fairway and they're playing with a golf pro. They haven't got a prayer.

MAY 2, THURSDAY/LAS VEGAS

Beard's Army is at full strength again. I met Susie and the kids at the airport this evening, and we went straight to Caesars Palace for dinner. After that, we moved over to the Excalibur to check things out.

Vegas is not a new haunt for Susan. She and I have been here a bunch of times, and she played here on the women's tour. But the children have never been here, so we thought we'd take them around. We thought they'd be dazzled by the bright lights and glitter. They aren't. They've been to Disneyland a few times, traveled on 747 jets, and grown up on Nickelodeon and music videos. Nothing astounds them.

But Vegas has a certain attraction for me. I walk through the casinos and see the gamblers pouring their money into the games, and it's almost like going to an AA meeting. The compulsive gamblers are just like me.

As I noted here the other day, I don't go very many days without reflecting on my drinking. Every week, when I'm playing a tournament, I see some pro-am guy heading out after the round, and I know he's drunk. One of my pro-am teammates the other day was worried about his buddy. He said, "I don't think Charlie can get past the sobriety checkpoint on his way home."

I got this flash, a picture of myself twenty years ago: getting into my car with a buzz on and driving away. That's the thing that still shocks me, the number of times I drove drunk, the times I left the club legally drunk after a drink or two. Although it was never a drink or two, it was six or seven. Whatever it took to get really blotto.

This is hard to believe: I was never stopped by the police for drunk driving. I never got caught.

One time, though, I nearly killed myself and a friend. I did a 360 one night on an exit on the Hutchinson Parkway from New York to Connecticut. I was staying in Greenwich with Dick Schaap, my coauthor on *Pro*, and I was headed for some party with Jerry Kramer, the Green Bay Packer star. Jerry was about as drunk as I was. It was wet, I was going to miss the exit, and I whipped it onto the exit going fifty miles an hour. I spun the car around. I did everything but flip it.

I remember apologizing sheepishly to Jerry. Neither of us laughed. And we took our sweet time getting to the party from there. Whenever I pass that exit, I realize how fortunate I am not to have died in my car or killed somebody.

Because most alcoholics hit bottom. They wind up in a ditch, they kill somebody, they land in jail, they lose all their money. I was lucky. I just stopped winning golf tournaments.

No, that's not true. I lost my first family.

MAY 3, FRIDAY/LAS VEGAS

Bridget came to the ropes a couple of times today and asked me what club I was going to use. I told her, and she said, "Oh, Daddy, let me kiss it. It'll be good luck!" So I let her give my clubheads a few good-luck smooches.

Even with Bridget's help, I shot 76 today—a not-too-auspicious start. Play was suspended for about an hour this afternoon when thunderstorms came through, but that didn't have anything to do with it. I just didn't play well. The golf swing is distracting me.

Bruce Crampton and Kenny Still shot 67s for the tournament lead, but they must have been playing a different golf course than I played. This Desert Inn course is very tight. It's not a hard golf course if you're playing well, but if you're not playing well you're going to hit it out of bounds and in the water.

Kenny, I think I've mentioned, is a real piece of work, the ultimate sports fan. No one will get him mixed up with Trevino, but he's got some pieces of business, some shtick. He's got a line he uses when somebody moves when he's about to hit. He backs off and says to the offender, "You know my brother Stan? Stan Still?" If they don't get it, it's probably because he says it with a smile.

Tonight, Susie and I took the kids to Circus Circus. They love animals, but all they wanted to do when we got there was play the carnival games upstairs. We could have been at the Pomona State Fair. Fun, though. Daddy spent about forty dollars and won his daughter a big teddy bear.

These are things I didn't do with my first family. Or if I did them, I wasn't there the way I am with Michael and Bridget. Before, everything revolved around golf. I played golf, and everybody else had to fit in the slot where I put them. My ex-wife's job, for example, was to take care of the kids. I said, in effect, "Bring them out when you can, and I'll come home when I can." I was a pretty sorry excuse for a husband and father.

I have a totally different feeling now. There's a real effort to make this foursome work. We're a real unit. And that's 180 degrees from where I was before.

I must be doing something right. Bridget went to sleep clutching her teddy bear.

MAY 4, SATURDAY/LAS VEGAS

Good news on George Lanning, I guess you would say. He underwent triple-bypass heart surgery today at a hospital here. His wife, Eloise, is with him and everything seems to be okay. Just another in the string of medical problems and crises that seem to dog us seniors. I don't know how long George will be out, but I know he'll be impatient to get back. He's one of those guys who's made a whole new life on the Senior Tour. He was in the Air Force for about twenty years, and then he was a club pro for a while up in Tacoma. He's pretty far down the money list this year, but he's exempt based on his career earnings as a senior.

Bad news on Frank Beard, though. The Senior Tour's Daddy of the Week shot 75 and came in fourteen strokes behind Gary Player. I played with Bob Goalby, and when we got off No. 18 I asked him for some help. "I don't want a golf lesson," I said, "but you're one of the guys who played with me in '69 and '70. What looks different? That's all I want. Not what looks wrong, just what looks different."

Bob was very helpful. "I don't think you're turning, Frank. You're setting up on your right side and kind of sliding in front of the ball. You really need to turn and stay behind the ball at impact."

He seemed somewhat touched that I had asked him for help.

As I mentioned earlier in the week, I've pretty much decided to go back to some of the caddies I used earlier in my career, the older black caddies. I enjoy them. They're comfortable with what they're doing and I don't feel I have to perform for them.

The guy I had in mind was Seemore. Ever since I saw him walking across the parking lot at the Tradition, looking so small and old, I guess I've wanted him to caddy for me. And he's been all over me this week, hoping to get my bag.

Anyway, he caught me again after today's round. I said, "I tell you what, Seemore. You've been after me and after me, and I'm kind of filled up here and the next few weeks. But I don't have anybody at the Tournament Players Championship and I don't have a caddy at Syracuse. What do you say we try those two tournaments?"

His eyes rolled back in his head when he heard

'Tournament Players Championship.' That's a big-money tournament.

He gave me that toothless grin. "You can count on it, Frank."

And I said, "Well, I'm *gonna* count on it, pal." I don't know if I felt sorry for him or what, but I wanted to reach out to Seemore. There's a lot of years there, and that ought to mean something to somebody. I must be the guy.

Tonight, I was going to take the family to the Mirage to see the lion tamers, Siegfried and Roy. I've got a good friend who's in charge of public relations there, Bob Halloran, and he was going to get us some tickets. I'll be damned if one of the stars—Siegfried or Roy—didn't pull a muscle. Bob called and said they'd had to cancel the second show, so we didn't get to do that. But we went to the Mirage anyway, and Bridget got to see the white tigers, which they keep in a big cage between shows.

It was a great evening, but my mind kept going back to the tip Bob Goalby gave me. I'm going to work on my body turn a little more tomorrow and see if that helps any. I'd really like to uncage my swing and shoot a round of golf I can be proud of.

MAY 5, SUNDAY/LAS VEGAS

We got a scare this morning. Susan and the kids were standing behind the gallery ropes on the right side of the first fairway when one of my playing partners, Howie Johnson, let his second shot get away from him. Howie hit one off the toe, and the ball went screaming, head high, right at Bridget, who wasn't even looking. Susan, who *was* looking, couldn't open her mouth or get her arm up, it happened so fast. The ball shot right by Bridget's head, missing her by inches.

My heart fluttered, but it was all over in a fraction of a second. I ran over to Bridget because I thought she was scared, but she didn't know anything had happened. It was *Susan* who was scared; she had seen it coming. Susan said she actually heard the ball buzz past.

"My God, Frank, it was headed for her like a magnet. If she'd moved the wrong way, she'd be dead."

Susan told me later that Bridget's life had flashed in front of her and that she had felt this powerful awareness of Bridget's importance in her life. For the next three holes, Susan hugged her so tight I thought Bridget would pass out.

I was shaken for only a few seconds. I have a way of taking something like that and pretending that it didn't happen. Number one, it's too terrifying to contemplate, and number two, *it didn't happen*. I mean, Bridget didn't get hit.

I've hit people or come close to hitting people so often that I've almost learned not to react. I hit a guy in Akron once, and when I walked up he was lying on the ground, surrounded by people. He had blood everywhere. His glasses were shattered, his eye was bleeding profusely, and I thought, "My God, I've put his eye out." It turned out I'd only cut his eyebrow, and he was just fine. No glass in his eye, nothing.

But you learn on the tour that people are going to get hit. We don't take it lightly, but there are so many near misses that you find yourself saying, "Oh, I missed another one," and you get on with it. That's what Howie did today. He just marched on down and hit his next shot. Of course, he had no idea it was my wife and kid he'd almost killed. Howie's kind of unflappable, anyway. He's kind of in a fog when he plays.

My other playing partner today was Bert Yancey, and Bert and I spent some time visiting between holes. I've known Bert since '64 or '65, and I consider him a good friend. I think he feels comfortable with me, too. Maybe that's because I understand him a little bit. Not a lot, just a little bit.

If you don't know the story, Bert is a West Point graduate whose career on the regular tour collapsed when he began to exhibit bizarre and disruptive behavior. Somewhere in the

late seventies he started showing up for tournaments un-
shaven and disheveled. Tom Weiskopf, who was a friend of
Bert's, actually walked off the course one day looking for a
tour official because he thought Bert needed medical attention. Tom got fined $3,500 for that, which is pretty incredible
when you consider what happened later. Bert had what was
then called a "nervous breakdown" and wound up being taken
to a hospital in a straitjacket.

It turned out Bert is manic depressive—he has an illness
caused by a chemical imbalance in the brain. Medication
keeps him normal these days, and Bert's doing very well. I'd
heard, though, that he'd been in the hospital a couple of
weeks recently, and I asked him about it.

"Yeah, I went in," he told me. "My body metabolism gets
out of whack and I just don't medicate myself properly. Last
year was a bad year, three episodes that I recognized, so I
took my doctors' advice and went to the hospital and got
straightened out."

It's interesting that people put a label on Bert: "mentally
ill." I say interesting, because I have much more of a psycho-
logical problem than he does. There's a craziness, a ber-
serkness in Bert when his bubble bursts, but it's truly a
chemical imbalance. It's not something you go after with
therapy.

Actually, the Bert I know has always been a very calm, very
sane person. I do remember once in New York, back in the
sixties, when he was on the threshold of a manic attack. I
didn't recognize it. I thought, "Wow, is he talking a lot. Is *he*
wound up today!" I wasn't educated.

When I joined the Senior Tour, Bert was playing some and
piddling with his medications. We had dinner one night, and
I said, "Bert, you seem a little hyper."

"I like to know that," he said. "It helps me with my medication. But most people don't have the nerve to tell me."

Bert wasn't close to the edge. He was just "up," not quite
himself.

I suspect the medication slows his metabolism down a little—not drugging him, just slowing him down. He got off it a couple of times in the eighties and kind of went off the edge again. He thought the medicine slowed him down just enough that he couldn't function as a keen athlete.

To me, he's the same old Bert—kind of a thinker, obsessed with the science of the golf swing. He talks about his kids, he talks about mutual friends, he's fine. But he's not playing golf very well, and that's what Bert really wants out of life, to play this tour and win golf tournaments. He's exempt, but you've got to make some money or you can't afford to play.

"I've got two strikes on me," Bert says, "and the pitcher looms big and tough."

Bert actually had one of his better rounds, a 3-under-par 69. He won about $3,000, and that has to be his best check in a while. Howie didn't do as well, shooting 76. I finished fairly well with a 71 and made a little better than $2,000.

It was just a tough week of golf. The family being here helped, but I hit too many bad golf shots. Maybe Vegas is not a good place for me to play, with all the distractions. I feel like I'm close—*real* close—to playing well, but it's one of those "so close, but so far away" feelings.

MAY 6, MONDAY/DALLAS, TEXAS

I played an outing in Tyler, Texas, today, and it was a huge success. They must have had twenty-five thousand people there and scads of volunteers. We didn't do a clinic, but we had a pro-am scramble with the proceeds going to charity. The way the townspeople turned out, I bet they raised a lot of money.

When we do these things, people always come up and say, "Gee, we sure appreciate you taking so much time for our charity."

I never know what to say, because we're *paid* to be there. I don't mean this as a shot at me or any of the other pros, but there's very few of us who would do a lot of these events for nothing. Most of us would do a *few* of them for nothing, but not a lot of them.

The net result is, we're doing it for the money. And we don't know what the hell is going on. What's the charity? Who's going to benefit?

Sometimes it's pretty clear. They'll have the little girl out there with the leg braces on, God bless her, and you know it's for polio or the children's hospital. Other times, you're in and out so fast that you don't quite catch the drift. This one in Tyler had something to do with sister cities and education—training students, something like that. I left without ever learning where the sister city is.

This afternoon, I caught a plane into Dallas. I'm staying at a hotel in North Dallas, not far from the golf course.

It always feels strange to me to stay in a Dallas hotel, because I was born and raised here. My dad was the golf pro at Cedar Crest Golf Club, a semipublic course that was run by a family whose name I've forgotten. That's where I started to play golf, when I was twelve years old.

Cedar Crest was my dad's big chance to make a bunch of money. The family that owned it had a couple of deaths and had to settle the estate, so they came to my dad and offered him the golf course. This was during the war, about 1942. They offered him the whole golf course—clubhouse, machinery, and everything—for $150,000. And it was a good golf course.

Dad didn't have any money. The only guy that would go in with him was a member of the club, a gambler named Benny Bennion. Dad, while he liked Bennion, didn't feel comfortable going into business with him, so he backed away from the deal. Bennion wound up in Las Vegas some years later, a big success.

So Dad missed his big chance. The owners sold the golf course to the city, the city put in their own pro, and Dad was out on the street.

Dad was kind of a dreamer. He cared about inventions,

things like that. He and Mom had made some money at Cedar Crest, so they decided to get into the cellophane bag business. They bought a couple of these machines that made cellophane bags, and Dad's job was to sell the bags to candy companies and whoever else used cellophane bags. He used to take me with him when he drove to Fort Worth to visit this one candy company. I still remember the smell, down where we made the bags and boxed them up.

The cellophane bag business didn't work, and Dad lost most of his money.

After that, Dad got into a business that restored worn-out auto batteries. That didn't work, either. He bought a liquor store, and that didn't work. He was a great guy, but nothing worked.

All this was going on during my childhood years in Texas. I started playing golf when I was twelve because I couldn't play anything else. I've always said I might have been a basket-ball immortal if I'd been about eight steps faster. My half-brother Ralph *was* practically a basketball immortal—two years an all-American at the University of Kentucky.

So I backed into golf. I couldn't do basketball, but I could do that.

I was a sophomore in high school when my dad's father died and left him this hand-quilting company in Louisville, Kentucky. Dad went back there for a year to see if he could make a go of it. Finally, he sent for us, saying, "Yeah, we can make it go." We moved to Louisville between my junior and senior years in high school.

But the quilting company didn't work either.

What the hell. The point of all this is that Dallas engages the side of me that wants to look back, nostalgically or other-wise. A guy at the hotel tonight, a guy who recognized me, said, "You grew up here, you must've played a lot of golf with Lee Trevino, right?" Because this is where Lee made his reputation as a hustler at some pitch-and-putt course, playing guys with a Dr Pepper bottle and only a few bucks in his pocket.

I could have made up something, but I told the guy the truth. "I never heard of Lee Trevino until he showed up that year at Baltusrol and finished fourth or whatever it was in the Open."

We never called my dad "Dad," by the way. He was always "Pro."

SEVEN

MAY 7, TUESDAY/DALLAS

There was a big sign in the parking lot when I drove into the Stonebriar Country Club this morning: "Reserved for Frank Beard, Defending Champion."

When was the last time I was defending champion of a golf tournament? They had wooden shafts, I remember that. We played on sand greens.

Seriously, it has to be 1972, because the last tournament I won on the regular tour was the 1971 New Orleans Open.

The sign makes me a little uncomfortable, as do the posters and programs with my picture on them. I'm flattered when people recognize me, but I don't like the pomp and circumstance that goes along with it. If you put two balls in the air, I'd pick the one that says, "Beard, you'll never be recognized again." That would relieve me of the pressure of having to be the Frank Beard of 1969.

I know, the guy driving the cab says, "God, Beard, you're moaning and groaning. I'd like to have that just *once* in my life."

I look at the cabdriver, and then I look at myself, and I think, "What's wrong with me? Why don't I feel that way?" I suppose my happiness and peace is going to come when I finally put all these pieces out on the table and begin to believe in myself.

150

*   *   *

The full name of this tournament is the Murata Reunion Pro-Am, and the format is like that of the regular tour's pro-am at Pebble Beach. We each have an amateur partner for the week. He and I are a team. There's a cut Saturday night to twenty-four and twenty-eight low teams, and if we get by that, the amateur gets to play on Sunday. That puts enormous pressure on the amateur.

Last year, I had a partner assigned to me. It costs thirty-five hundred bucks to play, and I don't know anybody who wants to spend that kind of money to play golf with Frank Beard in Dallas. Add the travel expenses, and it costs five grand. So I went to Joe Denton, the tournament chairman, and said, "I can probably get a partner, but you must have some local people who'd love to play. Just put me with somebody."

So Joe paired me with a Stonebriar member named John van Brunt. John's got a business here, he makes decals and bumper stickers. A real nice guy, probably in his forties. But hyper! Holy Jesus, his feet never hit the ground for fifty-four holes last year. He was an 8- or 9-handicapper, and he either eagled two holes in a row or I couldn't find him. But he won the thing. Sunday, last year, John was not only playing in the final group with the leader of the tournament, he was also playing with the runner-up, Dale Douglass, and he was leading the pro-am himself as my partner. All the club members were out there cheering him on, and we won the tournament.

John and I are partners again. We had lunch today in the clubhouse, and it was a nice reunion for both of us. He remembers every shot he hit in the final round last year. Great guy. But he's still hyper. I mean, he's not one of those guys you walk up behind and tap on the shoulder. He might jump out of his clothes.

After lunch, they took me into the interview room for the defending champion's press conference. It's a weekly ritual on all the golf tours. You go in and sit behind a microphone for a half-hour or so, and the local media throw questions at you. It's a very relaxed thing, a way for the golf reporters to gather material for their pretournament stories. Mine wasn't grandly attended by the whole Texas press corps, but there were five or six writers. They asked what I thought about the course and how much it had meant for me to win here last year. No hardball stuff.

The drinking story has kind of run its course. I decided last year at Richmond that I wasn't going to tell it anymore. *Sports Illustrated* and *Golf World* had done good pieces on my comeback, and my attitude was, "I've spoken my piece, let's get on with life."

I got a little flack from Alcoholics Anonymous for being so public in the first place. *Sports Illustrated* did its story on me in 1989, right after the U.S. Senior Open. I heard the magazine was out, so I went out and picked up some copies and came back to the house. I read the story, liked it. I'm sitting there, the magazine's still warm. The phone rings. It's some guy from Connecticut taking me immediately to task. He says, "I'm shocked. I'm stunned that you would stoop so low. Don't you know we have a tradition that we remain anonymous at the level of the press, radio, and television?"

It hit me right between the eyes. The reason for the tradition is obvious: If Frank Beard goes public that he's in AA, and then two weeks later he gets drunk, it hurts the program.

I was not totally naive. I was sort of aware of the "rule," but I thought I could help more people than I could ever hurt. And all I got, in the end, were a couple of negative phone calls and letters—against about 150 letters from people who decided to take action after reading my story. Many AA people called to let me know that they had made great strides in their own lives. I even had two close friends who joined the program because of the *SI* article. I know in my heart I did the right thing.

But I'm tired of talking about it. And it's not something you can tell in ten or fifteen minutes. I don't want to sit down in the press room with some guy and try to compress a three-hour story into a sound bite. If I'm going to do it, I want to do it right. The point of my speaking out is not to attract attention to myself; it's to help others.

After the press conference, John and I went out and played in a $10,000 skins game. It was a nice departure from the usual Tuesday Shoot-Out—more exciting, to be honest. It was a nine-hole, pro-and-partner deal. The other pros were Charlie Coody, Homero Blancas, and Harold Henning. Charlie represents Murata; Homero's partner, if I got it right, was the guy who put up the money for the skins; and Harold's partner was a successful Dallas jeweler. I'm not a good estimator, but I think we had a couple of thousand people following us.

Sad to say, John and I got blanked. Came up zip. I had a shot at a $5,000 skin on one hole. I made about a fifteen-footer for a birdie, and Henning's jeweler partner was left with a fifteen-footer—downhill, sidehill, fast, and breaking to the right. No way he could make that putt. But the guy hearted it! And there was never any doubt, from the second it left his putter, that he had hearted the thing. We're talking about a 12-handicapper here. I didn't think he'd come within two feet of the hole.

We had one other good shot at a skin. There was an extra-hole playoff for a couple of thousand dollars, and on the first playoff hole John hit a putt dead at the hole that would have won us the skin. But it lipped out. Harold and his partner ended up with most of the money, but it was a lot of laughs and a nice thing for Dallas.

MAY 8, WEDNESDAY/DALLAS

Today was a rare day off. There was no pro-am, and I was glad to get away from the golf course. I just stayed in my room and read and tried to relieve the pressure I'm beginning to feel.

The pressure, as always, is self-induced. When I step onto

the first tee on Friday I'll be introduced as the defending champion, and after all these years that still frightens me. I've got a lot of friends here, family, old schoolmates. I don't want to disappoint them, and I don't want to play bad golf in front of the local media. Yesterday I kept hearing, "Hey, there's the defending champ," and "Go get 'em, champ!" Instead of getting pumped up, I just got tighter and tighter.

I apparently choose to live in this world of pressure. Last night at the pairings party, some well-wisher told me, "You played great last year, Frank—let's do two!" I went nuts inside: Oh, my God, Jesus, I'm trying to find a way out and this lady wants me to do two in a *row!*

It's just a tough situation.

I find myself, lately, spending more and more time in my room. I very rarely have dinner with anybody. And I'm a little concerned about it. I enjoy my reading and my thinking and I enjoy sports on TV, but it's sort of a replay of the old days, when I was drinking. Between my marriages, I couldn't wait to get home and close the apartment door.

When I do go out with friends and have dinner, it's not bad. I don't hate it. But I've never been good around people, whether it's a cocktail party or a small gathering of friends. I don't know what to talk about, or I talk too much and wish the hell I'd kept my mouth shut.

Anyway, I spent the whole day talking to Frank Beard.

This evening, I had dinner with my sister, Marianne. She's a year younger than me and the closest thing to a genius I have ever met. Marianne entered a convent right out of high school, joining the order that had taught us here in Dallas when we were kids. Her order sent her to Belgium, and she got a doctorate in nuclear physics when she was only twenty-two or twenty-three. Something to do with Einstein's theory, something a little over my head. She came back with her doctorate, and the order—and this will sound like an indictment of the order—put her to work as a high school math teacher. After that, she served two or three hitches in the Belgian Congo, living in mud huts and teaching the children

English and religion. When she came home again, she had a stint at the University of Dallas as a professor of math and physics. The order, as I understand it, was practically out of money and had no leadership, so she had to generate income on the outside.

Somewhere around the age of thirty-eight or forty, Marianne decided she wanted to be a doctor. She completed medical school in three years, and again she was magna-magna-summa cum laude. Never has she made less than an A-plus in anything scholastic—a test, a paper, a thesis, oral exams, a degree, anything.

So now she's a D.O., a Doctor of Osteopathy, specializing in holistic medicine. She has a clinic near here in Arlington and she works sixteen to eighteen hours a day, six or seven days a week.

Sad to say, Marianne and I have never been real close. Politically, she's about as far left as anybody I know, and we're both very stubborn. I think, down deep, we both want to reach out, but we don't know how to do it. Maybe it's not the time to do it. But we try, and we feel the love coming from each other.

She's proud of me, I know that. She was one of the first to recognize my drinking problem, and she's proud that I dealt with it.

MAY 9, THURSDAY/DALLAS

It's not a bad golf course, Stonebriar. It has some funky holes. It's a development course and it's in Texas, where they don't have trees or anything, so it's wide-open, sort of bleak and stark looking. But twenty years from now it'll be a good golf course. It'll have trees and homes around it, and it'll all be blended. Right now, it's kind of rough. Hit it off the fairway and it's kind of muddy where machinery's gone through. The tees and fairways and greens, though, are in perfect condition.

It's Texas. Texas is like Florida, the wind blows like crazy. You live with it, that's all.

People who "knew me when" keep coming up to me. Some of the guys I played junior golf with showed up with old pictures from the *Dallas Times-Herald*, pictures of us as kid golfers. Guys that I went to grade school with were there, the wife of my Little League baseball coach, friends from Jesuit High. I saw my first basketball coach, Bill Durick. I even had a couple of guys come up today who said they were *sons* of guys I went to school with. I mean, these boys were twenty-five years old. It was a real shock.

When I meet these people—and some of them I haven't seen in forty years—it amazes me how old they look. I go look in the mirror, and for some reason, I don't think I look that old. It's really weird. My mortality must be playing more and more on my mind.

I had a chat with Babe Hiskey on the practice tee. Not about golf. Babe is the guy that organizes the Bible study on our tour. He has a brother who's a minister, and Babe is very staunch in his spirituality and his belief in Jesus. I remember hitting balls with him once on the practice range at Park City, Utah, minutes before a tournament round. I'd kind of stopped practicing and he was standing there with a club in his hand, looking at the Wasatch Mountains. He turned to me and said, "You know, every time I see these beautiful mountains it irritates me that the scientists are still trying to prove their Big Bang theory. How can they argue that something other than God created us?"

I said, "I'm with you, pal."

MAY 10, FRIDAY/DALLAS

I was very nervous on the first tee this morning. They introduced me as "our defending champion," and I felt all the eyes swing my way. And I happened to be paired with Chi Chi

Rodriguez, for Christ's sake, so there were ten times as many people staring at "our defending champion."

Have I mentioned that the first tee has always been the most difficult place on the golf course for me? Not the eighteenth hole, not the holes where the TV cameras are on you, but the first tee. The first tee is where you sort of step up and announce to the world, "I'm a professional golfer. Watch me do it." Everything is magnified on the first tee.

Professional golfers don't worry about whiffing, but we all have our fears and doubts. I was fortunate today in that the first hole, a par-4, doesn't call for a driver off the tee. I usually hit a 2- or 3-iron for my first shot on this hole and then go for the green with a wedge or 9-iron. Today I hit a 2-iron pretty good—a nice round of applause for "our defending champion"—and then hit a nice wedge to about eight feet. I missed the putt, but I thought I held up pretty well under the first-hole microscope. Chi Chi, who can't have been nervous at all, hit his tee ball way right, knocked his second into a bunker, and wound up bogeying the hole. Which only shows that you can't necessarily judge a player's emotional state by the shots he hits.

I hadn't played with Chi Chi for a while, and today's round just drove home for me again what a wonderful, wonderful player he is. I was talking about Chi Chi with Larry Mowry yesterday, and Larry said that Chi Chi has vowed that he is going to be number one this year. "Hell," Larry said, "he bought a jet plane! Here's a guy that said, 'To hell with it, I'm going right after that Trevino. I can beat him.' And he's doing it. I think it lends some credence to those positive thinking things."

Chi Chi didn't have a great round by his standards—a 71— but I wouldn't bet against him winning again this week. And he's not bad to play with, either. Everybody thinks he's tough to play with because he talks to the crowd and does his sword dance, but he's actually very considerate of his partners. His dances and routines are never disturbing.

I played pretty well today and shot a 69, but my partner,

John, really struggled. He couldn't make a shot, he was wound up like a clock on a homemade bomb. If I didn't know better, I'd say he was scared to death. I made my usual efforts at small talk. "The shot wasn't that bad, pal. . . . Isn't it a pretty day? . . ." I just couldn't penetrate. If we exchanged a thousand words today, nine hundred of them were mine. I need to talk to him tomorrow and let him know that winning this golf tournament is not quite up there with ending world hunger and finding a cure for cancer.

MAY 11, SATURDAY/DALLAS

Well, it didn't work so well for John van Brunt and me this year. I'm 3-under after two rounds and I've made seven or eight birdies, but John just couldn't get it together. God bless him, he must have missed three one-footers the last two days. We missed the pro-am cut by two shots, and he could have cut his throat.

At times like this, I kind of wonder if we should put the poor amateurs through the wringer of tournament competition. They choose to take part—I know that—but Lord, John was miserable. Winning last year, he put a lot of pressure on himself, and his hyperness just seemed to work against him. He disappeared afterward. He went looking for a rock to crawl under.

What a good guy, though. I'm sure we'll play again next year.

I shouldn't say this, but it's kind of a relief not to be leading the tournament. Last year, I shot a 66 in the wind on Friday and had a two-shot lead. On Saturday I went out early and shot a 67 before the wind kicked up, and I left the golf course with a six-shot lead. I'd never had that kind of lead before, so I turned on the radio as I drove away and listened to reports from the golf course. It was about an hour's drive to my sister's house, and nobody was making a move on me. Dale Douglass finished at 5-under, and that was it. I had a six-stroke lead.

My first thought was, "I've won the tournament!" Then I slapped myself. "Whoa! What did you say, boy? Don't *say* that!" But it kept coming back to me, and I thought, "Well, if I can't say that to myself, at least privately, then I'm not worth my salt. It's not over . . . but it *is* over."

It was scary. I'd never had a six-stroke lead, and it put a pressure on me I'd never felt before. If I didn't win on Sunday, I'd have pie on my face. Big-time embarrassment, big-time shame.

Sunday morning, I got up with a lump in my stomach like I hadn't had in a long time. It was worse than U.S. Open pressure. I couldn't eat. I felt giddy because I thought I was going to win the tournament, but I felt terror that I might not. When I got to the golf course, I told somebody—I don't remember who—that I didn't know what to do with a six-shot lead. And he said, "You know what? There ain't too many people you can ask."

My good friend Steve McGee was my caddy that week, and I told him, "Keep taking the right club out of the bag, the ones we've been using." I had played very aggressively the first two days, taking drivers where I usually wouldn't and hitting my irons close to the pin. But once we got out on the course, I wasn't as convinced about what I wanted to do. I'd aim for a flag, and on the way down it was, "Don't shoot at it!" I'd bail out and put the ball thirty or forty feet on the wrong side of the hole. I wound up three-putting three of the first six greens because I was not committed to the plan, and by the seventh hole my lead on Douglass had shrunk to two.

It was real clear to me that I'd gotten caught between two philosophies, but it never occurred to me that I wouldn't win the tournament. I drove across the corner on No. 7, a par-5 with water, and wound up with a 6-iron to the green. I didn't make an eagle, but I made a birdie, and that stopped the bleeding. (There's something therapeutic about a birdie, even if everybody else is birdieing the same hole.) I birdied No. 9 to go three strokes up on Douglass, bogeyed

No. 11, missing a three-foot putt, and then made a fifteen-footer for birdie on twelve. Dale made a hell of a par there out of a bunker, but my lead was back to three with six holes to play. I wasn't popping any corks, but I felt like I was in charge again. I was thinking, "I'm going to win my tournament!"

I had the feeling, too, that the gallery was pulling for me. Not against Dale, but for me. And that was a wonderful feeling, too.

I was 9-under when Dale three-putted No. 14 to fall four shots back. But Steve suddenly said, "Look what Zembriski's doing, the little turd!"

I looked up on the board, and I couldn't believe my eyes. Zembriski was at minus-8! Our leader boards don't give the hole, and I didn't know if he had finished or if he still had holes he could birdie.

So we got to the fifteenth hole, a little downhill par-3—128 yards to the pin with water on three sides. The wind was kind of gusting—left to right, I thought—but apparently it was more left to right and behind, because the damndest thing happened. I hit it right over the pin and into the water. All I could think of was double bogey, but I got to drop my ball almost on the green and I made a 4. When I looked up at the board, I saw that Zembriski had gone right past me. Steve said he had birdied No. 17 to go 9-under.

I remember how I felt; I was hanging my chin a little bit. But there was no despair. I didn't agonize or ask myself where all the strokes had gone. I told myself, "I can win." Steve has to take some credit for that, because he kept me in a winning frame of mind. He kept saying, "You are not going to lose this tournament. You are not going to lose."

So it never left me, the conviction that I was going to win. Zembriski had made a triple bogey on No. 18 the day before, and somehow I knew he was going to have trouble on eighteen again. I had three holes to play, all straight downwind, and I was sure I could birdie one of them.

Sixteen was a funny little hole. I hit a 3-iron and a little sand wedge to eight feet. But I missed the birdie putt.

Seventeen was the key. It's a par-5, and I hit a driver and a 3-iron to the middle of the green and two-putted for birdie to get back to minus-9.

Steve said, "I don't know if you want to know or not—"

"Sure I want to know. I want to know everything." Because I knew what he was going to say.

Steve said, "Zembriski knocked it in the water on eighteen."

I'm a little ashamed, because I've never pulled against anyone and it's not the way I wanted to win. But we found out Walt had made double bogey on the hole, giving me a two-shot lead.

Now, I hadn't played eighteen like a rocket scientist myself. It's a tough little hole with water right and left. But they had set the course up for a south wind, and the wind had turned until it was right behind us. The tee markers were up a bit. It stunned me that Walter had made a double bogey on the hole. With the wind in my face it would have been a driver and a 7-iron, but I turned to Steve and said, "I think we should hit a 2- or a 3-iron." I could have played the hole with a 5-iron and an 8-iron, but I wanted to get further down. Anyway, I knocked the 2-iron down the left side of the fairway and then hit a pitching wedge to the middle of the green. It was all over.

I've been asked what it felt like, that walk up the eighteenth fairway to the green. Surprisingly, I was not overwhelmed. I had dreamed of winning as a senior, and I had gotten close a few times. When I played the scenario in my mind, I got teary-eyed. But now that it was happening, it was as if I had won ten tournaments in the last two years. I was happy, I was ecstatic—I don't want to sound blasé—but it was almost like I was watching a movie that should have been playing the last eight years.

"This is where I'm supposed to be," I thought, walking on the green to the traditional ovation. "This is what I'm supposed to be doing."

The first thing I did after I tapped in my par putt for the victory was give Steve a big hug. Neither of us said anything.

We both knew that winning that golf tournament meant more than anything that had ever happened to me in golf.

That's because the tournament was about me. It wasn't about golf at all. I don't mean that the other players and the galleries were hanging on that, but to me it was about *me*, the man.

Ten years before, to the week, I had met Susan. Ten years before, I had weighed over two hundred pounds. Ten years before, I had not one meaningful relationship in my life. Zero. Kids, spouses, nothing. I was drinking. I couldn't break 75. I owned a little Chevrolet and part of a small condominium, and my net worth was probably $10,000.

Ten years later, all that had turned around. My health was good, I had wonderful relationships with my wife and kids and other people, I had a beautiful house and money in the bank, and I could break 75. I could only thank God that I had been given the chance to come back.

But, as I told the press afterward, there wasn't the excitement and euphoria I remember from winning my first PGA tournament at age twenty-three. It was more a feeling of satisfaction and relief. And later, as Steve and I drove away from the club, I thought, "I should be more excited about this." It was just a little glow inside.

I liken it to a farmer who has just built his own farmhouse. He kind of stands back and looks at it. He doesn't whoop and holler and he doesn't care if anybody else knows about it. It's just something he did, and he worked hard to do it.

MAY 12, SUNDAY/DALLAS

In the sports pages this morning, Lee Trevino took some pretty hard shots at his caddy, Herman Mitchell. Trevino was 7-under yesterday and about to run off with the tournament when Herman gave him the wrong distance on the thirteenth hole. Herman said it was 141 yards to the pin. It was really 130, and Lee hit it over the green and into a bunker. From there he made double bogey, and I guess he was pretty hot about it afterward. The *Dallas Morning News* and the *Dallas Times-Herald* both had headlines that said, in effect, "Herman Screws Up."

Herman was sitting in a golf cart near the locker room this morning, and I stopped to commiserate with him. I said, "Herman, in my opinion, that was not called for. Lee didn't say much in the paper about all the good things you've done for him. I don't know what happened yesterday, but he didn't need to say those things."

Herman said, "You know, I really appreciate that."

It was pretty presumptuous of me to stick my nose in Trevino's business, but I thought somebody needed to say something to Herman. He's been Lee's caddy for fifteen years, and he was obviously hurt by Lee's remarks.

After that, I went out and shot a 73. Finished thirteenth and won about $7,500. I hate to say it, but the way I've been going that's a pretty good check. A 66 would have put me close to the playoff between Chi Chi and Jim Colbert, but there are no 66s in my bag right now. I was never really in the hunt.

I'm leaving Dallas, and I'm no longer anybody's defending champion.

MAY 13, MONDAY/AUSTIN, TEXAS

Trevino let another one get away yesterday, and I guess people are beginning to wonder if the success he had last year was a fluke. Lee shot a final-round 75 and fell all the way down to eleventh, just a stroke ahead of me and six shots behind Chi Chi, who beat Jim Colbert in a four-hole playoff.

Larry Mowry and I were talking about it today, and Larry thinks it's burnout. "Lee played all last year, and I don't think he played more than two corporate outings," he said. "And those were Toyota deals. This season, he's tied up with Motorola, with Spalding, with Cadillac. . . . They're paying him enormous amounts of money and they want a chunk of him, not just a piece. He leaves one tournament, goes to New York for a commercial, goes to a party the next day, goes to an outing, and maybe somewhere along the way he plays in the golf tournament."

Larry said, "I played with him the other day, and he was just burned to a crisp. He was absolutely gone."

I agree with Larry, but I think there's more to it. I suspect Lee reached his goals too quickly. If you meet your goals, your intensity has to go down to some degree. And like me, he's got a second family to think of. I suspect Claudia is not happy with him playing thirty or thirty-three tournaments a year. I mean, she can't carry their new baby along every week, and if she does, she's not gonna like it. Nobody can like that traveling life *all* the time.

In short, I think Trevino has truly burned his candle—a big, big candle—very quickly. He had a whole career in one year.

I know, I got into big trouble saying the same thing about Nicklaus in my first book. I said, "Jack's done it, he's never going to be what he was again," and Jack went out and had some great years after that. But people misunderstood. I never said he wouldn't win again. I was saying, "Holy Jesus, what can he do for an encore? He's already proved he's the greatest player in history."

That's how I look at Trevino today. He's going to win again. He's going to win a lot, simply because he's head-and-shoulders better than the rest of us, even Chi Chi. But I don't think he'll ever get back the intensity he had last year, when he had so much to prove.

Frank Beard—now there's a guy with something to prove. The seven thousand and change I won at Dallas gives me $93,677, good for seventeenth on the money list. Chi Chi Rodriguez, who's on top of the list, has about $400,000. Does that mean he's four times better than me? Yeah, I'd say so.

One way to change my situation is to work harder, so I busted butt today. I hit a lot of balls on the range at Barton Creek Country Club, the tournament site. Caesar Cenudo gave me a few tips that helped. Caesar played some on the regular tour, and now he's a rep for one of the golf companies. He shows up from time to time, and I feel like I can use his eyes. Our egos are such that we try to fix things on our own, but when the pain gets bad enough we go to somebody we can trust. Usually it's somebody we've played with for a long time. I can always turn to Charlie Coody or Dave Eichelberger and say, "What do you see? What's different today from when I played a month ago and won the tournament?" Everybody has somebody they turn to, even if they sneak up on that somebody on the range and make it look like an informal gab session.

When I got done I was hitting it pretty good.

I've never been afraid of hard work. I know I could play better golf if I spent most of my waking hours hitting balls and playing practice rounds. But I want to be with my wife, I want to be with my kids. And that's why I'm at a real cross-roads right now. I've half a mind to ditch the seniors and go home to my family. But the energy, the impetus, the *push* in my life—my personal joy—comes from playing competitive golf. I don't have another business, I'm not a social animal, I don't have hobbies. Nothing else interests me.

So how do I find the proper balance? This drives me crazy. I mean, it's preyed on my mind the last two or three weeks and may have something to do with my poor play.

Then again, it may be my swing.

MAY 14, TUESDAY/AUSTIN

Chi Chi Rodriguez says he's sorry it took a playoff for him to win in Dallas. He says, "I don't like playoffs. If two players are tied at the end of the round, they should both win. If you go to a playoff it's like match play, and I don't like match play."

I understand where Chi Chi's coming from, but I don't agree with him. You have to have playoffs, you *have* to have a winner. You can't leave it with the Lakers and the Bulls tied, 110–110, and just send everybody home. You've got to have a little blood on the floor.

And let's face it, we're one of the few sports that doesn't leave some blood on the floor every day. We take four days to declare a winner. We're boring. Give *four* guys a trophy on Sunday afternoon and we'll have people running for the exits.

My own record in playoffs is undistinguished. Here's a trivia question: Do you remember what made Lee Elder famous? The answer is: the five-hole playoff he lost on national TV to Jack Nicklaus in the 1968 American Golf Classic at Firestone Country Club in Akron, Ohio. Well, there was a third person in that playoff: old Frankie boy. I lost on the first extra hole.

Another time, I lost a four-man playoff in the old World Tournament at Pinehurst. Johnny Miller, Jack Nicklaus, and Bob Murphy were in that one. I had a six-foot birdie putt on the first hole and couldn't make it. I also lost to Larry Hinson in a playoff in New Orleans.

Two years ago I lost my first one on this tour, a four-way playoff at the Northville Long Island Classic. My playoff opponents were Orville Moody, Don Bies, and Butch Baird. Butch and I were talking about it just the other day. The playoff started on the tenth hole, which is a par-5. Both Butch and I wedged up to about four feet, while Orville and Don weren't quite so close. After both those guys missed their birdie putts, the tour officials had to measure to see who was closer to the hole, me or Butch. According to the tape, we were both *exactly* 43½ inches away. So we flipped a coin. I called heads and won the toss. I went to putt first . . . and missed. And then Butch made his putt to win the tournament.

I didn't realize I had won the *choice* of putting first or letting Butch go ahead. In retrospect, I should have let him go first. I like to know what's going on, I like to know the whole picture when I stand over a putt like that. For some reason, I won the toss and just walked right over and lost the tournament.

Or maybe I didn't. When it came up the other day, Butch said, "No, I asked an official if the coin toss was for who would putt first or who would get to choose. And he said it was for who would putt first. But you know"—and Butch began to laugh—"I don't think he knew. He just didn't want to look like he wasn't sure."

So that's how you compile an 0-4 record in playoffs. Pressure? Yeah, there's pressure. But the excitement far outweighs the pressure. I remember a real elation, being in those playoffs. It was like jumping on a merry-go-round. That's probably why I never won one. I'd sign my scorecard, take some practice swings, they'd flip coins to see who went first, and all of a sudden I'd be out. I remember hitting some reasonably good golf shots in playoffs, but I never thought clearly.

I ran into Jim Colbert today, and he was pretty much over his disappointment. Jim hasn't won yet, but in just six times out he's earned almost $150,000. I told him, "You're going to win, no doubt."

He smiled and said, "Yeah, I expect to do well. I can drive my golf ball and I can play golf."

That's Jimmy. He has an absolute belief in himself that's beyond anybody I've ever known—almost including Nicklaus.

Where he gets that confidence, I don't know. When Colbert came out on the regular tour he couldn't hit a bull in the ass with a bass fiddle. I mean, he was a terrible golfer. But he was the most intense competitor I've ever seen. In time, he learned how to play golf, and then he started winning tournaments. He might have won some more on the regular tour if he hadn't left to run his golf course business in Las Vegas.

So Jimmy didn't need my encouragement. He's going to be a force out here, a top-five force, for as long as he can tee it up.

Larry and I joined up for a practice round, and I wouldn't bet the house on us this week. Larry is about fiftieth on the money list, and I haven't played worth squat. I've had 1½ good tournaments. The Tournament of Champions was a good one, and I played pretty well at the Tradition. Otherwise, my play has been mediocre to poor. And Larry's been in a tailspin all year. First it was the smoking—trying to quit—and then it was some health problems his wife has been having. He's tried to lose some weight without much success. And now he tells me that he broke his toe in Las Vegas. He ran into a table in his hotel room and fell down.

You'd be surprised how important it is to play well here. The Legends of Golf is a very special tournament. It's not a PGA Tour event, but it's a big-money tournament with a special niche in the history of senior golf. The first Legends was played back in 1978, when guys like Sam Snead, Gene Sarazen, Julius Boros, and Doug Ford were dropping out of sight because they couldn't compete with the kids any longer. Someone got the idea of playing a televised tournament, a best-ball exhibition, featuring the great players of yesteryear—the "Legends." The tournament was so successful that it spun off other senior tournaments around the country, until finally the PGA Tour stepped in and established a formal tour. That was in 1980.

From what I hear, the early Legends tournaments were a lark for the old-timers—the reunion aspect was paramount and the competition secondary. That has changed. Until I played in my first Legends last summer, I had forgotten how tough partnership competition can be. It's not like your typical tournament where you, the individual, take all the credit and all of the blame and nobody's looking over your shoulder. There's a totally different kind of pressure when you're standing over a four-foot putt and your partner's counting on you. The only thing I can compare it to is the Ryder Cup, which is also a team event.

Fortunately, there's a wonderful camaraderie that develops if you have the right partner, and Larry is the right partner for me. He and I are totally alike—philosophically, politically, religiously, and every other way. It's like two brothers doing something together, or two close friends who go hunting.

When we finished third last year, Larry and I felt we had really accomplished something.

And there's just a beautiful ambience, the week of the Legends. Sam Snead comes back, Roberto de Vicenzo and Tommy Bolt come back. The Legends truly brings together the greatest names in golf. Anytime our tour looks like it's going to get in trouble—and I've discussed the rumblings over the horizon, the arguments that we should make it tougher for the old stars to get into our tournaments—all we have to do is look at the Legends of Golf.

MAY 15, WEDNESDAY/AUSTIN

I saw Sam Snead in the grill room today. He's seventy-nine years old and he can't get around as well as he could just a few years ago, but he still plays golf and he still commands respect wherever he goes.

I went over to pay homage. I hadn't laid eyes on Sam for at least ten years, so I wasn't sure he'd recognize me, or even remember me. Not that he should, we were never fast friends. But I played a fair amount of golf with him. I played with him when he broke his age in a tournament round at Quad Cities.

He remembered me. I didn't say much, something along the lines of, "Sam, I've missed seeing you. I hope we get to play again sometime."

Sam said, "Well, I can't see out of one eye, you know."

I said, "I heard that."

And that was about all. I said, "Well, I'm glad to see you here," and I moved on.

Not a very exciting exchange. I just wanted to say something to Sam. For me to say he's done a lot for the game would be trite, but he *has*. In my lifetime, the Sneads, the Demarets, the Burkes, and the Souchaks built the game to where it is today. Somebody else invented golf, but these guys built it, and I respect them for it. Saying something to Sam was just my way of saying thanks.

After that I went out and played in the pro-am. This Barton Creek is a good golf course, a Tom Fazio course that runs up and down the side of a wooded canyon outside Austin. Fazio has become my favorite architect; he makes playable golf courses. He has a real awareness of who's going to play his golf courses—middle and high handicappers, mostly—so his greens are receptive and puttable. His courses aren't easy by any means, but they're fair and they're fun. I think those of us who play golf professionally, as well as the architects who build our courses, tend to lose sight of that: Golf is supposed to be fun. Too often these days my fun on the golf course is directly proportional to how well I play and how much I earn. And that's pretty far off-base.

Larry and I didn't play together in the pro-am, but I hit the ball pretty well today and he told me at dinner that he played better also. We can do well here.

The best-ball format works like this: Each of us plays his own ball, and the lower score for the hole is our team score. If I make 4 and Larry makes a 6, our score is 4. If both of us make a 2, our score is 2. It tends to be a putting contest and kind of a lottery, too. If you both make twenty-footers on the same hole, it's no good. It's a waste.

The only rule I have in team play is this: no apologies. Larry and I have an agreement never to say "I'm sorry" after a bad shot or a missed putt. We all do the best we can. I don't need to hear my partner say, "I let you down," and I *sure* don't need to beat up on myself any more than I already do.

Compliments are fine. I'm always happy to hear "Nice shot" or "Way to go, partner!"

MAY 16, THURSDAY/AUSTIN

It's not often you blow a best-ball tournament on Day One, but Larry and I may have done that today. Our best-ball was a disaster, a 69. We couldn't make putts. We couldn't hit shots together. And the harder we tried, the more we got in each other's way. We were both very frustrated at the end of the day. Our 69 puts us eight shots behind the leaders, George Archer and Don Bies.

The only bright spot was playing with Mike Souchak and Jack Burke. They're both over sixty and they're both truly legends on our golf tour. They've lost a lot of their skills, as have the rest of us, but you could still see flashes. There were chip-ins and putts made and lots of stories and laughter. Burke's an independent sort of person, and he had some acrid comments about course architecture and golf club design. And Souchak—what a warm personality. He makes you want to love the day.

Feisty guys, though. This tournament has a Super Seniors division, same as on our tour, only here they call it the "Legendary Players." Mike and Jack refused to compete in that class, preferring to go head to head with the likes of Trevino and Archer and Bob Charles. It's like, "We're going to play with the kids or we're not going to play at all." I admire them for that. They don't have a chance to win, but they still have that keen competitive sense. As I told Larry within their earshot, "You've got to admire these old fossils."

Souchak looked at me and growled.

Just before noon, we got some thunderstorms over the course and had to come in for a while, and then there was a three-hour delay this afternoon. We didn't mind. All the guys gathered in the grill room, and Snead and Burke and Bolt talked about how the tour started back in the thirties and forties—the poor purses, the hard travel, the weird rules. Not many people realize that most of the players back then had regular jobs, and there was a winter tour, a spring tour, and a summer tour, all sort of spaced. Jack Burke said, "I was the leading money winner on the winter tour one year with $13,000. I'd won four straight tournaments and they asked me if I was gonna play the summer tour. And I said no, I had a job in

New York that I could make $35,000 at. I said, 'Do you think I'm gonna give up that job to make another $13,000?' It didn't make sense."

Now Snead, I don't guess he had to starve. But he didn't make a *lot* of money, and you could tell from listening to him that he always played for the love of the game. I can't talk about the Calcavecchias and the Baker-Finches, because those guys are twenty-eight years old and these guys today were sixty, but I think the old-time players got more out of one another. They were always intense competitors, but they loved and liked one another for who they were and they played golf basically for the fun, the competition. The kids today are dazzled by the money and the fame and can't take their eyes off the top of the mountain. I was guilty of that myself, and I think that's why my game collapsed.

"That was really neat, hearing the old guys rehash it," I told Larry when we came out after the delay. It reminded me how lucky I am to have played with Hogan and Snead and Middlecoff and the Hebert brothers and Boros and Mangrum. It made me proud and grateful to be a pro golfer.

MAY 17, FRIDAY/AUSTIN

I can't believe it. I just can't believe it. I got to the golf course this morning and learned that George Lanning died yesterday.

What can you say? Jesus, he was a good friend. A good friend died. Kenny Still saw him last week and said he was pink and happy, practicing his putting on the rug and getting ready to play again. *Boom.* He's dead.

Don Bies lives up in Washington, and he was one of George's good friends. Don said they had talked by phone on Tuesday and George was feeling great. "George probably took better care of himself than anybody I know," Don said. "He's been on a low-fat diet for years. He didn't even eat much chicken because he was worried about his heart."

All these things are happening in my life now, and I'm sure

they're happening for a reason. After today's round, Larry Mowry's caddy, Winston, complained of chest pains, and they thought he was having a heart attack. He'd felt like hell all day and he could hardly walk this morning because his ankles were so swollen. This afternoon, they came and took him away in a helicopter. He was scared to death.

I just talked to Larry and it wasn't a heart attack, but Winston does have high blood pressure and they say he's suffering from gout. They sent him back to his motel with some medication and orders to elevate his feet and get some rest.

George Lanning's death and Winston's collapse really bring it home to me: We don't have yesterday, we don't have tomorrow, we only have right now. It's an important thought because I think over the last several months my success on the tour has begun to outshine my family and my spirituality. There's a side of me that says, "I want to be a star golfer again and make all the money and win all the tournaments."

That can't happen. I did that once. I had those things, and I thought they were what I wanted, but when my life turned sad, it all vanished. My pseudofriends left me, the fame left, the money left, the fancy cars left. And basically I was left with just myself.

A lot of it comes down to my feelings about myself as a man. I have a friend, Brian Berkstrom, who's very much into the Men's Movement, and he's made me more aware of Robert Bly and some other writers. I respect Brian and that movement, but it's a teeny bit away from me right now. Playing the drum, initiation rites—they're not quite where I want to be. There's still a part of me that says, "I'm a man, I've got to talk about sex and baseball games." And that's fine, I don't want to change that completely. But I've started to read John Bradshaw on the Inner Child, and I'm reading *Fire in the Belly* by Sam Keen. He's not in the Men's Movement, but he writes about men who disregard their feelings. I'm beginning to understand more about the pressures that are put on us by society, by our parents, by the church—all the people and institutions that inform us how men should act.

This, more than golf, is what is on my mind as I get ready for bed tonight. George Lanning is dead, and I wonder what meaning this great sadness has for my life.

MAY 18, SATURDAY/AUSTIN

Larry and I shot 64 yesterday. We didn't play much better than we did Thursday, but we sank a few putts and made fewer mistakes. It looked like we might get back in the tournament and make some money. But today we shot another 69, a really bad score.

Both of us played poorly, but a bad best-ball score is mostly a matter of bad timing. You can shoot six birdies each, and if you make them on the same six holes you're only 6-under. Shoot them on different holes, you're 12-under. You can make three bogeys each, as long as you spread them out. But Larry and I birdied the same holes and bogeyed the same holes. We got nothing out of the round.

I don't know. Last year we had a chemistry, and this year we don't. It's a good thing we get along so well.

After the round, I drove over to Winston's motel to pay him a visit. I knocked on the door, and he opened it. He looked kind of shocked. On the tour, there's this way of looking at things: "We're stars and you're caddies." We hand these men and women this somewhat demeaning, menial task, and we end up with human beings who feel somewhat less than human.

Winston's full name is Winston Prince III, and he's the son of an attorney down south somewhere. He lives in Seattle. He's around forty, a little chubby. He likes to tell dumb old jokes and laugh a lot. Last summer we went to a few ballgames together with Big Steve, my caddy. We saw the Yanks play, ate hot dogs, and had a great time.

There was a time when I wouldn't have done that with a caddy. The lines were drawn very sharply; the pros went here and the caddies went there. We stayed with our own. So

Winston answered the door and was embarrassed. He said, "Gee, Frank, you didn't have to come by."

I said, "Well, I wanted to."

I wanted Winston to know that I cared about him and that I didn't think he was a "less-than" because he was a caddy, that he was a "less-than" because he had some physical problems, or that he was a "less-than" because he had some fears. We just talked for a while, man to man. And it was a wonderful thing. We cried a little. I gained immensely from it, and I think Winston did, too.

That's very much where I am right now. I want to be with people, I want to be involved with people. My lasting memories, when I'm honest with myself, are not of golf shots and money. My lasting memories are of the times I give of myself.

MAY 19, SUNDAY/AUSTIN

Sam Snead was in my peripheral vision and in my thoughts today. As I've mentioned, he can hardly see out of one eye and he can't walk much anymore. I watched him hit some balls on the range, and he doesn't hit them like he used to. And I don't mean the way he hit them forty years ago. He doesn't hit as good as he did *ten* years ago. But he's still got that swing.

We talked for a minute. Sam said, "You know, those fellows at the Masters were going to let me win that par-3 playoff. They kinda whispered among themselves, and I knew what was goin' on. But I got up first on the playoff hole and I bladed it over the green. They couldn't do a thing about it."

I spotted him later on the course. Sam was short of some green by fifty yards or so, and I was amazed to see him get out of his cart, walk all the way up to the green, look around, and walk back. The energy, the intensity, the *will* to play good golf—Sam Snead still has those qualities.

I found out afterward that Sam made six birdies on his own ball today, and he and Bob Goalby shot a 64. That really tickled me. We live in a world of lower scores and high-tech equipment and television, but I still love Babe Ruth and Joe Louis and Sam Snead. I'm a traditionalist. "Sam Snead rips one down the left side of the fairway . . ." I just love that stuff. Seventy-nine years old, and he's playing in a big-time golf tournament.

Larry and I played the final round with Walt Zembriski and Peter Thompson. Nobody played well in our group. Larry started hitting the ball a little better than he had been, but the handwriting was always on the wall. We shot 69-69 the last two days, and it was just miserable. We made too many bogeys and three-putts, and we couldn't bury the par-5s. I was angry at the end, and Larry was, too. Not at each other— we were just angry that we didn't play better as individuals. We finished way down the line and got $5,000 apiece, our guarantee.

I did what I could to pump Larry up for Philadelphia next week. I'm going to take a couple of weeks off, but he's going on to play in the Bell Atlantic Classic, and he really needs a kick in the butt to get going. His putting is very poor, and he has a stroke that's kind of a Band-Aid. I said, "Larry, your stroke is just flat-out no good. You're going to have to make a change. And get rid of that goofy putter, it doesn't work anymore."

He didn't want to hear that. He told me, "This putter worked real good for three and a half years." He just gave me this blank look.

Larry's kind of living in the past right now, and that won't cut it. I've learned that we seniors are at the stage where we can't go back. We can't go back to the way we played when we were youngsters, and sometimes we can't even go back as much as a year or six months.

This, for some of us, is hard to grasp. Our approach to golf used to be pretty consistent because our bodies and minds were strong and dependable. But now our bodies have begun to change, we're in physical decline. I don't mean that in a dark way, but we have to find ways to keep our energy and vitality. Old strokes and old clubs are not going to cut it. I truly believe that the seniors who succeed are those who are willing to try new equipment, new putting strokes, and new swing concepts.

Larry doesn't see that yet, but I think our talk is going to help. He's going to start putting better.

EIGHT

MAY 20, MONDAY/PALM DESERT, CALIFORNIA

Life is tough.

Scott Peck says that in *The Road Less Traveled*. Life is tough. But that's the way we grow, and there's a plan for it, there's a reason. I have a saying now that I try to fall back on: "Life doesn't make sense . . . but it's not supposed to." I think, for me, that's the test of faith. If life made sense, we wouldn't need a God, we wouldn't need spirituality, we wouldn't need anything. It wouldn't be any fun.

These last three weeks are tied together in my mind. George Lanning's death, Winston's gout attack, going back to Dallas and seeing those people from my past . . . even the golf. A year ago, Larry and I were going to finish third, we were laughing and kissing and hugging. This year, we're two alcoholics walking up different sides of the fairway beating up on ourselves, afraid to look each other in the eyes.

I would love to be more intent on my golf, more focused on playing well—just for the joy that comes with it. But there's an upheaval going on, and it has to do with my spirituality. I remind myself, "God will give you everything you need. He always has and he always will." But I think I have to do more, I have to create more. And that's when I get in my own way and mess the whole thing up.

178

I'm not trying to go on a preaching jag, but this is what's going on in my life. This is what's standing in the way of my playing good golf.

It's a different and very difficult time.

MAY 22, WEDNESDAY/PALM DESERT

A few leftover observations from my last trip:

- Gene Littler got $5,000 in room credits from the Hilton Hotel people for breaking my course record at the Murata. He shot a 7-under-par 65 in the second round, proving that timing is everything. I didn't get an extra penny for my 66 last year; Hilton wasn't one of our sponsors last year.
- "Can a Super Senior win one of these tournaments?" Someone asked me that at the Legends. I said, "They can and they *have.*" Sam Snead won a lot of tournaments after he turned sixty. This year, Littler almost won in Dallas, Don January's come close a couple of times lately, and so have Jim Ferree and Miller Barber. Mike Fetchick shot a final-round 64 and took Lee Trevino to five holes of sudden-death at last year's NYNEX Commemorative. Joe Jiminez finished in the top ten a bunch of times. That's our drawing card. Baseball and basketball players can show up for their old-timers' games, but they can't play. We can show up *and* perform.
- Ferree had a double eagle on the eleventh hole at Dallas. Rare among rare. I've made twelve holes in one, and I'd give eleven of them for one double eagle. Not to take anything away from Jim, but we all had a shot at it that day. It was downwind and the pin was right in front of this funky little green, the only place where you could possibly get close. I hit a 4-iron for my second. Didn't make it, though.

MAY 29, WEDNESDAY/PALM DESERT

Larry Mowry called today. "You know, Frank, I was kind of mad at you for what you said about my putter. But I've been fooling around with a long putter like yours, that Slotline. I've worked with it now, and I think I'm probably as good or better now as I was in my heyday, when it seemed like I was making everything."

I said, "I told you so, dummy."

MAY 30, THURSDAY/PALM DESERT

Some guys at La Quinta were talking the other day. "I don't get it," one of them said. "That Jenkins kid—" (not his real name) "—I'd a sworn he'd be a star on the tour. He can bust it a mile and he's got the course record on half the courses in the Valley, but he can't make a penny on the tour."

They turned to me and asked what I thought the kid's problem was. I said, "He can't play golf."

I wasn't being flip or mean. I meant that he had never been taught to play golf. Hit a golf ball, sure, but not play golf.

I've brought this up before, and I should maybe explain it better. You see, I learned to play golf before I ever learned to hit a golf ball. My dad was a golf pro, but he didn't have a pro job at the time. He and Mom both had to work, so they turned me loose on the golf course. I started teaching myself. I had some clubs, I was reading about the game . . . I was getting ready to be a golfer.

The trouble was, there were some little caddies down there in Dallas who started taking my nickels and dimes away from me on the golf course. This was at twilight, when everybody was gone. They had these old, beat-up clubs. I thought, "I've got better clubs, I've got a better swing . . . but they're beating my brains out!" It occurred to me that I had better start making some threes or fours or I was going to lose all my money. So early on, I learned the value of getting it in the hole no matter how it looked.

The kids today learn to hit the golf ball first. They become marvelous athletes, marvelous strikers of the ball, but they almost never learn to play the game. The winners do, but your local favorite who shoots 69 every day on his home course and looks great doing it—he ain't got a clue.

That's why I tell my son Michael, "Learn to play golf."

He says, "Well, what does that mean?"

So I teach him. Today we were playing the Citrus Course and I got him up on the tee at one hole. I said, "The book says on this hole you hit driver. What does your stomach say."

He looked at the tight landing area and said, "Oooooh. My stomach says to hit a 3-iron."

"If you do, what will your friends say?"

"They'll say I'm chicken. I should hit a driver."

"Can you beat them with a 3-iron?"

"Yeah."

"Well then, what do you care what they say?"

That's the simplest explanation of it. On another hole, Mikey grabbed his 3-wood to hit over a creek that was 190 yards away. I stopped him, and he said, "Yesterday I hit a 3-wood here and it carried the creek."

"How do you feel today?"

"I feel great."

"Okay, if you know you can make it. But before you try, go way down deep inside. And if you hear a voice that says, 'I don't know if I can make it'—don't try! Ask yourself, 'Who am I today? What's going on *today?*'"

It's a point I make again and again with my pro-am partners. If on a certain day all you've got is a toe hook, then play a toe hook!

The book says don't do that. The book says you should make some adjustments. But by the time you're through making adjustments, you're 6 over par on the twelfth hole. And it's too late.

MAY 31, FRIDAY/PALM DESERT

Seemore the caddy called me at home this morning.

"Frank," he said, "I'm down in Fort Worth visiting a sick

relative, and to tell the truth, I ain't got no money and I don't know how I'm gonna get up to Detroit."

It's happened to me a couple of times in my career, a caddy calling for money. I learned that you don't send them money. Caddies are a little less than responsible when it comes to drinking and gambling, and you sure don't want to give them a handful of cash when they're two thousand miles away.

But I did want to help him. So I said, "I'll call you back, Seemore."

I called the Greyhound people, the 800 number, thinking I would send Seemore a prepaid ticket to Detroit. No luck. The bus line said I couldn't charge the ticket to my credit card. So I called Seemore back at his sister-in-law's in Texas.

"Seemore," I said, "the bus station is in Indio. I'm not driving all the way to Indio to stand in line for you."

"Well, I guess I can't get there." He really sounded down.

Okay, I like Seemore. The feeling is over me. I see him again walking in the parking lot in Phoenix, this little old man.

"Look, Seemore, I tell you what I'm gonna do. I'm gonna wire you some money."

Susan looked up. She couldn't believe it.

But I decided to take a shot at it. I called Western Union, and they gave me three different numbers to call to send money by credit card. The bus ticket from Fort Worth to Detroit was $118, so I decided to send Seemore $200. That way, he'll have money to travel on and I can take it out of his check next week. Western Union wanted its cut, of course, so the whole thing came to $250.

I called Seemore and told him the money would be in Fort Worth in thirty minutes. Forty minutes later, he called me back.

"Frank, they won't give me the money."

"Why not, Seemore?"

"I can't identify myself."

"Don't you have a driver's license?"

"Well, it ran out, and I had to get a temporary, and they

don't put your picture on a temporary." His voice brightened. "Let's give them a code word. The code word's 'Seemore.' " He picked that because I had sent the money to Melvin Johnson, his real name.

Okay, I called Western Union. They said we couldn't use a code word. "He's got to identify himself."

I called Seemore back. (This is four or five phone calls now.) "Seemore, is there anybody there who can pick up the money for you? If somebody can pick up the money, Western Union says the rest is between you and whoever picked up the money."

"Oh, yeah," Seemore said. He perked right up. "My sister-in-law's got a driver's license. Call that Western Union back and change the name to her. We'll go pick it up."

Before I left him, I said, "Seemore, I've got a lot of calls and time invested in this caper. I've got my money in this. The minute you get the money, I want you to call me here at the house, collect. I want to know you got the money."

"Yes sir, Mr. Beard, I'll do that."

It's bedtime now, and I haven't heard from Seemore. He probably got the money, but I wish he had called.

JUNE 4, TUESDAY/DEARBORN, MICHIGAN

I'm in Detroit, and no Seemore. I called Western Union, and somebody in Fort Worth got the money, either Seemore or his sister-in-law. I went by the caddy tent this afternoon, and none of the caddies here knew where he was. When I told them that I'd sent some money to him down in Texas, where he was visiting a sick relative, all the black caddies began to laugh. Herman Mitchell said, "Hey, he doesn't have any relatives in Texas. They're all in Georgia!"

I guess the joke is on me. I've got a one o'clock tee time in tomorrow's pro-am, and I'm giving Seemore till then to show up. But it looks like I'm out $250.

The golf course this week is the TPC at Michigan, a new

Jack Nicklaus course. The players I met on the practice range said it was a typical TPC. In other words, they were rolling their eyes over it. Phil Rodgers said, "You'd better be shooting to the middle of the greens this week, because if you're just a little bit off, you're dead."

It's getting so that all you have to do is say "TPC" or "Jack Nicklaus" and half the guys would rather stay home and watch on TV.

I hate to hear everybody talking about the golf course because the Players Championship is one of our big events, a million-dollar tournament. Eligibility is limited to the top seventy-eight money winners since last year's TPC, which was held at Dearborn Country Club.

It's a four-rounder, too, and I always like my chances when we go seventy-two holes.

JUNE 5, WEDNESDAY/DEARBORN

It occurs to me that we're starting the sixth month of the year, and I not only haven't played a round with Jack Nicklaus, I haven't even talked to him. Not that this is unusual. I was coming out of the Dearborn Hyatt last year, and I spotted Nicklaus in the lobby. I turned to whoever I was with and said, "You know, I can't remember *ever* staying at the same hotel as Jack Nicklaus. Not in thirty years."

Maybe Jack was there and I didn't see him, I have no idea. We were just never thrown together on the old tour. Palmer was the same way, and Gary Player. They lived in another world. On the Senior Tour I see them occasionally, but they're still on a higher level. There's a kind of arrogance about them—a good kind of arrogance, a deserved kind. They don't go out of their way to demand respect, but they know who they are.

Seemore didn't show, so I went to the caddy tent thirty minutes before my tee time. I got the last caddy, a young kid. I was hoping for a high school or college kid, someone local, but there were none left. And this boy, this Dirk, was standing there. So I took him. And Dirk did a good job today. I didn't ask much of him, but he hustled, kept the clubs clean, and did his job.

As for the golf course, I'm not going out on a limb to say that the players, to a man, do not like it. It's pleasing to the eye and it's not overpenalizing for bad drives. But you find yourself having to play to the middle of the greens, almost never daring to shoot at the pins. I feel like I've got to hit the green or I'm looking at a bogey. And I'm pretty good at getting up and down.

Of course, Jack would say, "Well, you'd better work on your iron game." And to a certain degree, he's right.

But everybody's complaining about the course. I mean, I haven't heard *anything* nice about it, except that it's pleasant to look at and easy to walk.

I don't admire the golf course, but I have to admire Nicklaus. He's not letting the criticism get him down. I mean, he's getting *killed* with his golf course, but he has so much self-esteem, it doesn't faze him. I don't know what he's like inside, but my guess is that, while he would prefer some kind of consensus that it's a great course, the criticism doesn't bother him that much. It's like, "If you don't like the course, that's fine. I do."

If I got half the criticism Jack gets, I'd crawl under my bed and hide.

As for the pro-am—now, this is funny. This is where I am now in my life, this little story I'm about to tell. I played in the pro-am today with a couple of Ford executives and some guys from a truck company. Good guys, just a nice day at the pro-am. But I wasn't scoring well and they weren't scoring well, and I'll be honest, I wasn't into it. I was faking it. The course was hard, we weren't in the hunt, and I just lost interest on the back side. We all did.

Coming in, my teammates made three or four putts from across the green, but it didn't matter. Fifteen-under figured to be the winner, and we were gonna shoot minus-11 or -12. Finally, on the last green, this guy made one from thirty-five feet and we finished 12 under par. We shook hands. Just another pro-am, and nobody makes anything.

I'm hanging around later, and I pick up a copy of the pro-am summary, just to see who won. And it turns out the scores are very high—which figures, because the course is twice as hard for the amateurs as it is for us. My team tied for fourth, and I won $250.

Was I surprised? Listen, if somebody on the eighteenth green had offered me five cents for what I'd won in the pro-am, I would have taken it.

But the amazing thing was the *amount* of the prize money: $250, the exact amount I had sent Seemore.

I don't know, do they connect? I did what I thought I had to do with Seemore. I came from an honest place in my heart and I tried to help another guy. And now I get this money, and I have absolutely no idea where it came from.

Susie has this belief that everything gets taken care of. I'm beginning to think she's right.

JUNE 6, THURSDAY/DEARBORN

Everybody is talking about yesterday's pro-am and all the golf balls that were lost. Jimmy Colbert said his group lost twenty-two balls, but John Brodie wasn't impressed. John said, "We had a guy who started with two dozen balls, and by the time we got to the eighteenth hole he only had one left. Then he lost that one, and he had to borrow a ball from me to finish."

I played the first round with Mike Fetchick and Charlie Owens, and I like both of those guys. They're Super Seniors now, they're in the sixty-and-over group. Mike had an 80 today, but Charlie shot a 70, a really fine round. Charlie, if you don't recognize the name, is the guy who introduced the long putter to professional golf. He's got a stiff leg from an old war wound, and the long putter allows him to stay in the game. It really amazes me how well he plays, because that leg forces him to hit the ball on a strange angle. That's why sometimes his shots are not real pretty. But he's got a good short game and he can putt. And Charlie is another one of those guys with a great attitude. If he hits a bad shot or has some bad luck, it doesn't seem to faze him. I could play golf with Charlie Owens every day.

My round today was a 70. I played really good golf, and I was very happy. The best round of the day, though, was a 66 by Jim Albus, a club pro from the metropolitan New York area. Jim's not exactly your behind-the-register club pro. He's played in a bunch of Opens and PGA Championships, and he tied for thirtieth at the 1984 Open at Winged Foot. He tied for eighth last week at the NYNEX Commemorative, and I guess that's why our tour commissioner, Deane Beman, expanded the field to eighty-one—to let Jim and a couple of other guys play here.

The guys continue to criticize the golf course. I talked to George McCabe, who's the vice-president of public relations and marketing for Mazda. He's always very upbeat, but he was very concerned about the pounding the course is taking. Mazda has put up the million-bucks prize money and several million more to sponsor and promote this tournament. They've done everything we've asked, including moving the tournament to the Tournament Players Course. And Mazda is sort of getting a black eye because the players are complaining about Nicklaus's course. It's not fair. It's just not right.

But what can you do? Nicklaus's approach to green design is almost sadistic. You stand there in the fairway with a 6-iron in your hand and you look at the pin, and you realize you've got about twenty feet of green and a yawning bunker on either side. Twenty feet—that's not much for a 6-iron. And these bunkers are straight down.

Here's how tough it is: Nicklaus shot 77 today on his own course.

JUNE 7, FRIDAY/DEARBORN

Bobby Nichols has been playing very well lately despite his legal and financial problems. He hasn't won a tournament, but he's won about $115,000 to this point. I stopped him in the locker room today and said, "I know what's been going on, I know about the trauma you and your family have been going through. And I just want to congratulate you on the way you've played."

He thanked me. "It's been tough, all right, but I'm really glad that I've been able to keep pushing and playing well. And it's a good thing, too, 'cause these legal things can drag on for years."

Out on the practice range, Dave Hill was working on his swing. "My driver is giving me fits," he said. "But like I always say, it's not the arrow, it's the Indian."

I continue to fiddle with my golf swing. I keep going back and forth with some of the things Jim Flick has told me. My golf shots the first two days have been pretty good, and to the naked eye I look like I'm walking along a pretty wide line. In truth, it's a really thin line, one that I seem to have to walk more and more often these days.

But it's working now, and I'm very pleased. I shot a solid 71 today. That puts me at 3-under for the tournament and four strokes behind Trevino, who's got the lead at 137. I'm in good shape.

Charlie Owens didn't have the luck he had yesterday, but he shot a 74. I think he finished third or tied for second in the Super Seniors, so he'll get $6,000 or $7,000 on top of what he gets for the four rounds. Jim Albus, the club pro from New York, shot a 74 and slid back in the pack.

All in all, the scores have been pretty low. Trevino shot himself into the lead today with a 67, two shots ahead of Dave Hill and Bobby Nichols. There were ten other rounds in the 60s, so the course wasn't exactly unplayable. But you have to consider the weather: sunny, comfortable, hardly any wind. If the wind comes up, you're going to see some outlandish scores.

Nicklaus shot a 70 and got back in contention. Actually, he's ten shots behind Trevino, but after what happened at the Tradition nobody wants to count him out.

I should be happier than I am, but I'm still caught up in this family muddle, the old home-one-day, gone-the-next dilemma. I lie in my room with a book, and other thoughts keep intruding. My boy's home playing a golf tournament, my girl's giving a piano recital, and Susie's back there with them. And I'm thinking, "Is this where I want to be?"

I'm not a cat with nine lives. I don't get to have three or four more families. This is it. It's so bad this week that I'm thinking of canceling out of Syracuse and going home early.

The other side of the coin is, I want to play. As narrow as it may sound, that's what I do, play the tour. I'm not a fisherman, I'm not an artist, and I don't do music. I play golf.

It's become a real battle. I just wonder if I'm in the proper frame of mind to play well at Syracuse. Or anywhere, for that matter.

I mentioned this to Susie when I called her from the locker room after my round. She listened, but she's at the point now where she says, "Frank, you've got to figure it out for yourself." I think I've begun to wear on the relationship in terms of being a needy person. She's a codependent person herself, so she has to be very careful with someone like me. She has to back out and let me make my own decisions. It's not that she lets me, she has to *force* me.

My head says my family is going to be fine without me. But my heart says I need to be at home.

And soon.

JUNE 8, SATURDAY/DEARBORN

That thin line I was walking? I fell off it today. I just kind of lost it, to be honest. My score wasn't embarrassing—a 73— but the golf course was just a little too difficult for me. The winds, thank God, were still gentle, but they've begun to dry the course out and make it play harder. You land your ball on the green and it just jumps right off again like a rabbit. I got in a couple of those deep bunkers today, and I just didn't feel I had any chance at all. I'm not Gary Player out of the bunkers, but I'm pretty good with my little brown club. Out of one bunker today, I hit the ball exactly where I had to hit it, and it went twelve feet by the hole. I'd let Player and Chi Chi shoot at it, and I don't think they could do any better.

Maybe I need to explain myself. I don't want a golf course where I shoot 61. That's no fun. But I don't want to walk around with my heart in my throat, either. Who needs that? What do we prove by playing golf courses where Jack Nicklaus shoots 77 and Frank Beard shoots 80? I know the public thinks we're crybabies, but we're seniors now. We've already proven we can play. Now we're out to have a little fun and give some vicarious thrills to the fans. We don't need to play four rounds on the hardest golf course in the world, embarrass ourselves, beat ourselves up, and then complain about it.

And for what? Will somebody tell me for what?

Now, the kids—the guys on the regular tour—they can do it. They're out to see who is the best golfer in the world. As much as I hate the USGA for what they do with U.S. Open courses, I can't refute what Sandy Tatum, the former USGA president, said on the subject. He said, "We're not trying to embarrass the best players in the world. We're trying to identify them."

So maybe they still have to do that with the kids—play the hardest courses, put the pins in the toughest places, and let them prove who's best.

The seniors, no.

Hey, the young guys don't like it either. They used to hold part of the Bob Hope Desert Classic on Pete Dye's course at PGA West, but they left because the rounds took forever and it was no fun. We're all human. No one likes to be embarrassed.

If I sound unhappy tonight, I am. I've pretty much decided to skip Syracuse and go home after Monday's outing. I'm just not in the frame of mind to play good golf, and I have too many things to work out at home. I messed up badly with my first family, and I'm not going to allow that to happen again.

JUNE 9, SUNDAY/DEARBORN

Today was one of the best days I've had in a long, long time. I didn't play particularly well—I shot a 74, good enough for nineteenth place—but I was really happy with my decision to withdraw from Syracuse. It was the kind of feeling that told me I'd made the right decision. Which is important, because I'm not the kind of guy who can make a decision and stand by it. I need validation.

When I called Susan and told her I was coming home after the outing tomorrow, she said, "Wonderful. It's just what you should have done." She keeps her hands off and lets me make decisions, but it was nice to hear that.

So I was happy. I played with Gay "I'll Trade for Your Club" Brewer and Don Massengale, and I held it together enough to win $13,000 and change. I haven't done that well in a while, so that was nice. It was another one of those deals where I played okay, but if you'd known what was going on inside me you wouldn't have thought I could get out of the 500 Club.

This evening, I shared a seat with John Paul Cain on a bus out to the airport, where we were catching a charter to Jacksonville. John's a stockbroker down in Texas, and he didn't turn pro till he was fifty-two years old. He was what we used to call a "career amateur." He'd played in the U.S. and British Amateurs, a few U.S. Opens, and he'd won all the Texas amateur events. Then he came out on our tour and won a tournament in Grand Rapids, which was a pretty big story. He and Rives McBee shared last year's "Ironman" award by playing 115 official rounds on our tour. Everyone jokes that John is trying to make up for the thirty years of pro golf he missed.

But it hasn't been a good year for John until today, and he said he'd been putting too much pressure on himself. "I need to be in the top thirty-one to stay exempt," he said, "but I've played really badly and I've kinda been scared that I'll lose my spot. This was a big boost for me."

He wasn't kidding. The $41,000 John made today was more than he'd made all year.

The tournament had a wild finish. Dave Hill had a four-shot lead going to the eleventh hole, but he hit his drive into some long grass and wound up making a triple. It's that kind of course; you can make a double or triple bogey on a good as well as a bad shot.

Hill's crack-up opened the door for Trevino and for Jim Albus, who was still hanging around near the top after three rounds. Trevino bogeyed the sixteenth, which meant he was a stroke behind Albus when he went to the seventeenth, a 521-yard par-5 with water all along the left side to the green.

Sometimes Lee just doesn't think. He was one stroke behind a club pro who was playing a hole or two behind him. Instead of thinking clearly—"Whoa, now, I've got two holes to go, a lot can happen"—Lee takes a driver off the tee, which he shouldn't have. (Remember the seventeenth at Tampa, when he hit his driver into the swamp?) He got away with it, he hit a good one, but it's just not a driver hole. And then he takes a run at clearing the water with his second shot. He goes right at the flag, which he just can't do. Even if he carries it to the green with a 3- or 4-wood, it'll bounce into the water behind.

It turns out he used a 7-wood. I heard Herman, his caddy, say he tried to go *around* the water, that he wanted to hook it and run it down through that little narrow opening. Believe me, that's a one-in-a-million shot.

The point is, Lee didn't need a one-in-a-million shot. Albus, as good as he's doing, is probably not going to do much more than play it safe and make pars coming in. Lee could have played a prudent 5-iron down to where he could almost throw it on the green for a birdie.

You have to know Lee. He's a great front-runner, but I think he gets flustered when he's behind. This was, after all, a club pro he was trailing. So he tried not only to erase the lead, but to do it with a *flourish*, the way the greatest player in the world should do.

Okay, he's done it before. I described the 5-wood he hit to win the Dominion tournament at San Antonio. But it didn't work this time. Lee hit his 7-wood into the water, had to take a drop, and then pitched his next shot into a bunker behind the green. Why he made an 8 after that, I don't know. He had a bad lie and exploded over the green and back into the water. But I suspect that it was over for Lee when the first ball went into the water. He was done.

So Jim Albus, the club pro, wound up winning one of our biggest tournaments by three strokes.

People are going to ask, "How can this happen? How can a so-called nobody beat up on Lee Trevino, Jack Nicklaus, and Dave Hill—not to mention Frank Beard."

There are some underlying circumstances.

First of all, the obvious: Jim Albus is a good player. He's a guy who could have played the tour, but I understand his family didn't want him to. But he's played in all the Met tournaments, won all those things, and he's won a bunch of Florida tournaments with good players. I've already mentioned his appearances in major tournaments. So he's been around.

Second, he finished eighth the week before in one of our tournaments. Nobody even knew he was in the tournament, but here's a guy who was still on a high from that experience.

Third, Albus is the bulldog type, a guy who's got a lot of confidence in himself. If he was scared down the stretch, he didn't show it.

Finally, the tournament was played on a golf course that was difficult, even for Lee Trevino. If he gets just a little bit off his game, which he did, he can blow up in a hurry. We're not talking about a course where a good player can have a bad day and still shoot a good score. Can't do it.

So all those circumstances come together and you get an

unexpected result: Jim Albus wins a championship. But it didn't shock me that he was playing well, and it doesn't shock me that he won. Given the golf course, the Players Championship was a crap shoot anyway.

JUNE 10, MONDAY/JACKSONVILLE, FLORIDA

A bunch of us flew down last night on a Delta charter to play a one-day tournament with a bunch of players from the National Football League. Cadillac sponsors it. Each pro golfer plays with two NFL players and a businessman. It's your typical Monday outing except you're playing with football stars and the whole thing is being taped by ESPN.

My football teammates this year were two guys from the Phoenix Cardinals: Al Del Greco, who's a punter, and Rick Proehl, a second-year wide receiver. Everyone dresses in plus fours and color-coordinated shirts, so we looked like a hundred Payne Stewarts out there. My group was decked out in Phoenix maroon and white with white caps, and I confess, I felt a little conspicuous.

I've been teased about my wardrobe through the years. I run and hide from bright colors, and you'll see me wearing a barrel before you see me in plaid pants. Sometimes I lose my mind and wear a green shirt in a pro-am, and Susan will say, "Why not in the tournament?" But I'm just not one to make a fashion statement. Blacks and grays, navies and whites, that's me.

Doug Sanders was one of the guys who used to tease me, but I don't think of Doug as a great dresser. He's a flamboyant dresser. The wild colors and Liberace-type accessories suit his personality. In my opinion, the guy who could really dress was Tommy Bolt. Bolt used to say, "I've got one outfit that cost more than Dougie's whole wardrobe," and he was probably telling the truth. Another time, he said, "Dougie must dress in the dark."

The way I see it, shirts are shirts. If you don't like mine, my only comeback is to say, "Yeah, but I'm getting twenty-five grand to wear it."

Anyway, it was a nice day and we did our thing with the NFL. Joe Theismann, the former Notre Dame and Washington Redskins quarterback, ran around with a microphone and did the interviews. I gave my guys some lessons and did a "Tip from the Top" segment, which was taped. Then we went out and played.

It's an outing for us, but they run it as a tournament. Last prize is $4,000 and first prize is $18,000, so there's enough money in it to keep you from falling asleep. How you do, of course, depends on who you have for teammates. John Brodie won it last year with a couple of 49ers, including Bill Romanowski, who shot a 76 with a 22-handicap or something ridiculous like that. Brodie had Romanowski back again, and I'm sure everyone asked him if his handicap had improved any.

My guys, Al and Rick, represented the two extremes. Rick is sort of a beginner and Al is a scratch player, neither of which are very good in handicap events. Al and I sort of duplicated ourselves, and Rick, as hard as he tried, was still a 22-handicapper. Still, it was fun to play a pressure-free round of golf and watch guys like Dan Marino and Phil Simms running around.

I don't know who won. I just know I'll be home in a few hours, and I can't wait.

JUNE 15, SATURDAY/PALM DESERT, CALIFORNIA

Mikey had a junior golf tournament Friday, and he's got another one Monday and yet another the Monday before I leave for Kansas City. So we've spent a lot of the week practicing together. We go down to the range and hit balls every day, and Thursday I took him out for a practice round. He's got it by the short hairs, having a dad who can get him on golf courses.

Bridget was with us when she wanted to be. She doesn't like the golf part, but she wants more of my attention, too. I was determined, when I got home after the TPC, to give her more of my time, and today she said, "Dad, you're paying more attention to me than you ever have."

These things tug at me. My four older kids probably said the same things, but I didn't hear them. I didn't *want* to hear them.

What do I do? Quit the tour and stay home with the kids? Play twenty tournaments a year and be satisfied with half the income and half the fun of competition? Commit to a full-time playing schedule for a few years and hope that the kids will have time for their dad when he finally comes home?

Susan and I have gone round and round it this week. We've talked a lot and we've cried a lot. As I've told her, when I'm home I want to be on tour, and when I'm on tour I want to be home. So I'm no good either place. I'm useless. Useless as a golfer out there, and useless as a parent and spouse at home.

"The kids are like little sponges," she told me the other day. "They feel Daddy's aloneness. Especially Bridget, she feels whatever you feel. The first three days, when you're gone, she'll get teary-eyed out of the clear blue, because she misses Daddy. Michael gets sad at night. But they feel it most strongly when they talk to you on the phone. When you're emotional, they pick it up and act it out for me. It's almost like they're my little barometers to your feelings."

She isn't telling me to quit the tour. She's telling me to *decide*. It's either come home and get a job or get on with life—play the tour, do the family thing when I can, and get through the next four or five years.

She's right. She's dead-on right.

My trouble is, I'm a great mind person. I'd be a great arbiter, because I love compromise. I see where 2 plus 2 equals 4, but I could make it 3 plus 1 equals 4. But I don't see any compromise here. I've compromised as much as I can with the logistics.

Susie had more to say. "This is about *our* relationship, too," she said. "You have a tendency to look at things negatively, so I have to play a game with myself to stay up. I don't mean to ignore your problems or deny your feelings, but I need to look at things more positively. If I get too absorbed in your stuff, it's bad for both of us. The last three or four months, you come home and want all this attention. Here I am, juggling everything while you're gone, trying to keep everybody else up and moving, and there's no one there for me. I want attention, too."

She said, "Frank, we've got two needy people here."

I take what she said very seriously. I mean, she laid it right out. It has to do with two people knowing each other's needs and wants and being able to satisfy them.

While I don't like confrontation and arguing—or being told what I need to do—I've learned to listen to Susan. My MO for years has been to let people cater to me and give me everything I need. But I've always been told that when you give, you receive. And I'm sure that's right.

The tour seems awfully far away right now.

JUNE 16, SUNDAY/PALM DESERT

Watching Jack Whitaker do his U.S. Open commentaries from Hazeltine reminds me of what an old pro he is. Guys like Whitaker and Vin Scully, they're smooth. They open that show up and never miss a beat.

I remember on the big tour, when I was playing in the CBS Golf Classic, they'd bring us out early in the morning to tape some interviews. Everybody would be gulping coffee and gnawing on Danish, and I'd be there with three other players. One of Frank Chirkinian's guys would be frantic. "Where's Jack? Where's Jack?" And I'd know that Whitaker had had a few drinks the night before. Don't ask me *how* I'd know, I'd just know.

Suddenly, Whitaker would be there, looking perfect. Chirkinian would say, "Want to run through it?"

Whitaker would shake him off, and we'd start to tape. No

notes. He'd introduce all four of us, lay out our records, the tournaments we'd won, the state of our games, and highlights of our rounds that week, and never miss a word. There wouldn't be a retake unless the sound was off or the lighting was bad, or maybe he just didn't say what Chirkinian wanted him to say. But he never stumbled, he never misspoke.

I couldn't get six words out like that. That's why I always say anchoring takes a pro. Whitaker, Vin Scully—those guys are pros.

JUNE 17, MONDAY/PALM DESERT

Rocky Thompson is 1-for-612. He won the tournament in Syracuse yesterday, and I bet they're organizing a ticker-tape parade in Toco, Texas. Actually, as mayor, I bet *he's* organizing it. He can get up on a platform and present himself the key to the city.

Even the bad-luck fairy couldn't stop Rocky this time. He was tied with Jim Dent coming to the last hole, and just like he did in San Antonio he hit a drive down the fairway, only to see it kick left under a tree. This time he had a shot, and he hooked an iron onto the green and made par, while Dent went long and three-putted.

It's a pretty incredible story, if you think about it. Rocky's busted his butt for twenty-seven years trying to win a golf tournament, and now he's done it.

Doesn't make him any less mysterious, though.

JUNE 18, TUESDAY/PALM DESERT

Larry Mowry is sick. I mean, really ill. It turns out he was already having problems the week we teamed up at the Legends—vertigo, difficulty focusing his eyes, that sort of thing. He's been walking wobbly ever since, and he can't play golf. The doctors have put him through the wringer: CAT scans, EKGs, blood tests, the whole ball of wax.

I heard about it through the grapevine, not from him. I phoned him today, and he says they've made a diagnosis. "It's something called Meniere's disease. It causes vertigo, nausea, and all kinds of crap between your ears." He says they've got some drugs to take care of it, but he sounded worried. And it struck me, as we were talking, that I was worried, too. I hadn't realized how much I cared about Larry.

He said, "I'm going to be fine, Frank."

And I said, "I know you are, pal."

JUNE 22, SATURDAY/PALM DESERT

I just read this thing in *Golf World*, something by a guy who covers golf in Denver. It's a review of ABC's U.S. Open coverage, and the writer gets on Bob Rosburg something terrible. He writes, "Would somebody please explain why they've left this guy around for so many years?" And he goes on to blast Rosburg for being out of position on a couple of shots.

This is classic. I mean, Bob Rosburg knows more about golf than all the newspaper writers put together. I'd like to see the guy who wrote the review go out there with a microphone and walk two hundred acres.

What happened was, Payne Stewart had to delay his drive on the twelfth tee for something, and Roger Twibell said, "What have you got going there, Rossie?"

Rosburg told the truth. "I'm down the fairway, Roger. I don't know what's going on."

You know why Rosburg was out of position? Because he was standing where somebody had told him to stand. He doesn't go where he wants to go, he goes where he's told to go. Believe me, Bob Rosburg can describe what's going on, given the opportunity.

There's so much wrong with golf on television, I can't

believe that someone would go after one of the few guys that knows the game. It reminds me of Ben Hogan's old comment: "If someone dropped an atom bomb on the sixth hole, the press would wait for a golfer to come in and tell them about it."

JUNE 24, MONDAY/PALM DESERT

I looked at the money list today, and I'm slowly but surely digging myself into a deep hole. I've played ten tournaments and averaged over $10,000 a tournament. That's not a bad percentage, but it's still not going to quite get it. Because these guys grind it out. Everybody's played fifteen tournaments except me. Me and Nicklaus.

To be honest, how you rank on the money list doesn't mean a whole lot unless you're in the top five or six. Those are the spots that get you bonuses and entry into the Tuesday shootouts, that sort of thing. We do have a tournament in Puerto Rico at the end of the year, the New York Life Champions. Only the top thirty-one money winners are eligible. It's a million-dollar tournament, so I'd like to play in that.

I'm twenty-eighth now. There's no reason I shouldn't play well the rest of the year and stay right up there, but . . .

Worried? Yeah, I suppose I am. I know I'd be higher on the money list if I was playing more. But I don't blame my family. I don't even blame *me*. But it gnaws on me, the knowledge that I'd play a lot better if I played more.

I'm still hung up on money, too. My mind works very quickly, very mathematically. I'm in better shape financially than I've ever been, but I know I'm not going to be able to play tournament golf for twenty more years. We start going downhill when we reach fifty-six or fifty-seven. I'll work as long as this body works, but that may be only four or five more years.

And as much as I love golf, I'd like to spend more time with Susie, travel some for pleasure, be with the kids, go fishing.

You have to have money for that. Especially for the kids, because it'll cost a bundle to put them through college.

So for me, the difference between eleventh and twenty-eighth on the money list is substantial. Carry that difference out for three or four straight years and it's very substantial. It's the difference between retiring nicely and maybe still having to make some money.

I leave tomorrow for Kansas City and then Cincinnati, a week later. It's about time I cashed a big check again. That $50,000 from the Tournament of Champions wasn't meant to last all year.

NINE

JUNE 25, TUESDAY/KANSAS CITY, MISSOURI

Bobby Brue shared one of his swing thoughts with his clinic audience this afternoon. "Here's one," he said, addressing the ball with an exaggerated waggle. "Why does sour cream have an expiration date?"

He hit the ball while the people were laughing.

I ought to try some of Bobby's swing thoughts. They might work better than my own.

I'm not sure the two weeks I was home I got a lot worked out. My feelings are not as intense, and that's a step. And I'm more determined and more clear about playing the tour. I've decided that when I'm on tour, 90 percent of my energy has got to be here, and when I'm home 90 percent has got to be there. Up until this point, it's been equally split. It sounds cold, but I've got to take my family out of my life when I'm playing. I'll still call home, but maybe I'll call when I *have* to instead of calling every time I'm near a phone.

I've also been doing some thinking about Michael. He and I have built up a very special relationship, but it's almost unhealthy. He's such a neat little guy that I've sort of made him my best friend. We play golf together, we watch TV together, we talk about sports. I enjoy having someone idolize me. It validates me, boosts my self-esteem.

But just this last week it dawned on me that I had totally dominated his time. I showered him with attention, I arranged for us to play at golf clubs, I took him out for hamburgers, the whole bit. I made his life with me so appealing that he didn't want to be with his friends. At the end of the week, I had to practically *force* him to go play with his cousins. It was, "Just go play, Mikey. Play golf with your buddies. Go swing in a tree."

I'm going to have to watch that more closely. Michael needs a father more than he needs a fifty-two-year-old playmate.

On the way to my car, I came across Al Geiberger in the club parking lot. He was standing in this sea of white Cadillacs, looking lost. "They didn't have a spot marked for me," he said, "and now I can't remember where I put my car. You seen a white Cadillac anywhere?"

Another guy would've been steaming, but Al just took it as a good joke on him. You have to wonder how he can keep such a sweet disposition in the face of the setbacks he's had. He had colon surgery a few years back, and then a few years ago his two-year-old son, Matthew, drowned in a swimming pool. I don't know how you come back from something like that, but Al has whatever it takes. He's been off his game, though. He fell out of the top ten last year, and the best he's finished this year is fifth.

As I drove away, he was getting into one of the Cadillacs. I hope it was his.

JUNE 26, WEDNESDAY, KANSAS CITY

I caught up with Orville Moody this morning, just off the practice tee. He won last week at Charlotte, and I could see the difference in him. He looked pink and fit again.

"I feel better than I've felt in a long time," he said, "and I feel like my golf swing has come back, too. Winning again really meant a lot to me."

I was very happy for Orville. I think the two of us have felt a special bond since our one-two finish in the Senior Open at Laurel Valley two years ago. We had a mutual respect there for two solid days, and it continues unabated.

My pro-am guys were hot today. They were making putts from all over and knocking in wedge shots, and we wound up shooting 49 and winning the pro-am. I made $500, and that's not bad when you consider I shot 72 on my own ball.

This Loch Lloyd golf course is a pleasant surprise. It's miles south of town in farmland. The back nine crawls through some beautiful wooded ridges, and there's plenty of creeks and ponds to contend with. It's hard to believe the course is just a year old.

Would Nicklaus say it's too easy? Probably. The other ninety-nine players, no. There'll be no complaints this week because we'll all enjoy the golf course.

After the pro-am, I found Larry Mowry and the two of us drove down the road to Snead's Barbecue, a little hickory-smoke place with a gravel parking lot. Over beef and pork sandwiches, Larry and I had some discussions that were semi-intimate. They revolved around where he'd been in his life, and I shared some things about the relationship problems I'm having with Susan. Not marriage-threatening things, but changes I have to make if I'm going to be a healthy partner. He recommended that I read a book called *Illusions* by Richard Bach. "I think it might fit really well into the lifestyle change you're trying to make. It might help you clear your mind of all this stuff."

I asked him about his health, and he said it was an off-again, on-again thing. "With any head movement, my eyes don't catch up with my head. When my head moves a little, my eyes aren't still looking at the ball. They might be looking off somewhere else."

"How the hell do you hit the ball?"

"It's very difficult." He began to laugh. "Actually, it's just about impossible."

Larry seems happy, and at least now he knows what he's got to battle. It's not going to kill him. But he's not quite ready to play, I don't think. In fact, he'd told me over the phone that he wasn't coming to Kansas City, and that's why I've got his caddy, Winston, this week. It's not just the focusing problem and the vertigo—Larry simply hasn't played in a month. I'll be surprised if he holds up in the hundred-degree heat that's expected tomorrow.

After lunch, I went back to the club, found Winston, and beat on it pretty good. I had hit some terrible 3-irons during the round, so I hit 3-iron after 3-iron. That's the way I am. It could have been a 7-iron or a 4-iron, but today it was a 3-iron.

What was I working on? The same thing I've been working on for fifteen or more years: on finding a golf swing that I have confidence in. I've been working on it intently the last four years, and I mean *intently*—minute by minute, hour by hour. I think about it as I go to sleep at night. And nothing has worked.

Mostly the problem is with my longer clubs: driver, 3-wood, 2-iron. I get pretty comfortable when I get down around the short irons: 6, 7, 8, 9. Which means, parenthetically, that there is a swing there that should work. If I could swing my driver like I do my 7-iron, I'd be fine. That's what I tell people when I give clinics—"Swing the driver like you do your 7-iron"—but it's not good enough for me. I'm a star. There has to be something very complicated and obscure wrong with my game.

So I hit 3-irons while Winston watched. I think I'm laying back on my right side too much, kind of lagging behind and hitting some high hooks. I'd hit a few and then turn to Winston. "See anything funny?"

Winston would shrug. "Not really."

What a bunch of rocket scientists we are.

JUNE 27, THURSDAY/KANSAS CITY

Lee Trevino was in the locker room this afternoon, kidding around with some of the guys. He said he'd been in Kansas City the week before to play in an outing that Tom Watson puts on every year for a local children's hospital. The other two pros in the outing was Paul Azinger and Fred Couples, and Trevino had some funny lines. Particularly about Couples, a long-hitter who gets criticized for being too easygoing, too laid back.

"Freddie is so loose," Trevino said, "he just stays between the gallery and figures that way he'll get back to the clubhouse."

Another Trevino crack about Couples: "Here's a guy whose wife has to turn the shower on for him."

Chi Chi will have to put his writers on overtime to keep up.

I went out and had another good pro-am day. Today's team didn't do as well as yesterday's, but I shot 66 on my own ball and finished third. Five hundred dollars yesterday, $325 more today . . . hey, it adds up. I only wish it had been an honest 66 instead of one of those all-over-the-yard, chip-it-in-twice 66s.

As usual, I did what I could to help my partners—swing tips, reading putts, that sort of thing. My philosophy is to give them what they need. Sometimes it's swing stuff, sometimes it's course management. Yesterday I took a guy who was down off the edge of the fairway on No. 12, and I said, "What are we going to do here?"

He had a sidehill, baseball-type lie with the ball well above his feet, but he was an 8-handicapper, a good-enough player to make the stroke. He said, "I'm kind of stuck between a 7-iron and an 8-iron."

We went through the whole thing. I said, "Your ball is going to come out flying. You're downhill and downwind. The best you can hope for, if you try to go over the trees, is to land on the front of the green, and if you hit it long you're in the lake. Would you be happy if you could land it on the front fringe and maybe have it bounce up there a few feet?"

"Oh, I'd love it."

"Okay, how far is it?"

He frowned. "Well, the pin . . ."

"No, how far is the front of the green."

"Gee, I hadn't thought . . ."

I said, "It's only about 115 yards. A 9-iron would probably do it, and an easy 8 would be very good."

He ended up hitting the easy 8, and his ball wound up well onto the front of the green, a fine shot. I said, "That's course management." He was getting ready to hit a submarine simply because that's what the yardage to the pin called for.

After the round, he said, "I bet I could cut two or three strokes off my handicap if I had you by my side every time I played."

I had to agree with him.

JUNE 28, FRIDAY/KANSAS CITY

Two under today! A 68. Not bad, considering my confidence level when I started.

I was floundering on the front side. I was hanging on this mechanical thought, the one about bracing the right hip and leg. But I didn't feel very good. I was at even-par and I'd made some putts, but I didn't feel good over the ball. Everything felt forced.

On No. 11, I kind of sculled one off the tee with a 2-iron. It's just a little hole and I was in perfect position, but it was a pretty hokey swing. And as I walked down the fairway it occurred to me, as it has before, that I was in pretty good shape in spite of how I was hitting the ball. I suspect when I look at the paper tomorrow, par will be a pretty good score. So I began to think of it as another enormous piece of evidence that said, "Frank, have some faith. Move your feet a little bit, but let life take care of you."

I know, I'm sounding spacey. But all of a sudden, a swing came to me. Not a brand-new one, not some kind of miracle swing, but something that I used a little at the TPC and have been in and out of ever since. The swing came to me in a very smooth, relaxed way. I used it on the twelfth tee, and I used it the rest of the way. And the last seven holes, I played as good golf, from tee to green, as I have played in fifteen years.

Understand, I've played seven holes *better*. I've shot lower scores. I've put the ball closer to the hole for seven holes. But not with this flowing feeling. The swing just came to me, and I think it's because I made a genuine effort to let things unfold.

What this tells me is that tomorrow, if I just trust it from the first swing on, I can play well enough to win this golf tournament. Fear is going to creep in, but if I can accept the fear and say, "Okay, fear, thanks for rearing your ugly head, but I think I'll just put you aside and trust what's going on here," I can play well enough to win.

While I was finding my swing, Larry Mowry was making a brave effort to play, but he just couldn't do it. He made a 7 on No. 13, came back with a deuce on the par-3 fourteenth, and then made an 8 on No. 15. He withdrew after the round. "Trying to play was a big mistake," he said. "The heat alone was enough to make me wobbly."

He didn't seem broken up about it. I'm sure he churns inside like the rest of us, but Larry doesn't hate himself when he plays poorly. He took off right after his round, but he had some parting advice for me: "Let it go when you're out there, Frank, and don't worry about the results. You'll turn the corner with your golf game when you learn that you can be a nice guy and still be a tough competitor."

JUNE 29, SATURDAY/KANSAS CITY

There's a story we tell in AA about this guy and a rock. The guy's walking along with this big rock under his arm, and he falls in a pond. His friend says, "Turn loose of your rock!

You're going to drown!" And the guy says, "I can't! It's my rock!"

It's a story that bears repeating, and not just for alcoholics. Al Geiberger and I were paired today, and the subject of his little boy's drowning came up. "I thought I was getting over it, but you really don't," he said. "I hear a kid cry in the hotel lobby, and I don't think of the two at home. I think of the one who's gone."

I look at the rock that Al carries—the loss of his son—and I look at mine, and I feel ashamed.

All this is prelude to a couple of golf scores. Al Geiberger shot 65 today, the best round of the tournament. He's tied with Jim Colbert for the tournament lead. I shot 74 and fell to 142, nine shots back. The swing that I thought I had found yesterday was gone. I couldn't find it on the range, on the first tee, or anywhere on the golf course.

I have to face facts: I am powerless. I can't control this. I shoot a 68, and I'm on top of it for a day, I have a little confidence in my swing. "I've solved it!" And every time I do that, every time I feel like I have a little control, I just fall right on my face.

It was another hot, sunny day. I got up early and drove around until I found a bookstore that had a copy of *Illusions*. I took it with me to Loch Lloyd and read for about an hour in the locker room. Larry was right, it's fascinating. But I didn't get to the chapter that tells about curing a toe hook.

Good crowds again today, maybe twenty-five thousand. Kansas City hasn't had a tour event in thirty years, and you can tell that the city is golf-starved. Most of the spectators found shady spots on the ridges bordering the final holes and behind the waterfall on the eighteenth green, which is set into a natural amphitheater.

Al gave them plenty to cheer about. On the back side he made one putt that was literally a hundred feet long, and he nearly came out of his shoes he was so surprised. On the next tee, he said, "That's got to be the longest putt I've made in my whole life." I was happy for him, and I hope he goes on and wins the tournament tomorrow.

JUNE 30, SUNDAY/KANSAS CITY

When I got to the course today, I went straight to the transportation desk and made arrangements for my departure this afternoon. I told them, "I want the car out front and the motor running when I get off the course. My feet aren't going to touch the ground between the scorer's tent and the curb."

They're used to that sort of thing—players jumping into cars in their socks, their shirttails out. If you aren't in contention when you finish, the only thing on your mind is flying to someplace where you *can* be in contention. Or home.

I was particularly anxious to get away today because I was flying into Louisville to spend a day and two nights with my mom. The 6:05 flight out of Kansas City would get me into Louisville at 8:30, but the later flight, the 8:15, wouldn't get me there till 11:00—pretty late for Mom, and I knew she wouldn't let me go to bed without some peach cobbler.

I suppose the travel-agent side of pro golf can be a distraction, but I've always been able to put it out of my mind once I start to play. Today, I don't know. Yesterday's round took me out of the tournament, and I couldn't get anything going today either. I had a chance to birdie the thirteenth, a par-5, but I didn't. Then I bogeyed fourteen and fifteen, and that buried me.

So I got up on the seventeenth tee, and I'm not sure what happened. I just sailed one straight into the woods on the right, way up on the hill overlooking the fairway. I don't think the people lining the fairway even knew a ball went over their heads, it was that far off-line. I reloaded and hit my next drive into the creek running down the left side.

After that, I was on automatic pilot. I wound up making quadruple bogey—sort of a complimentary ticket into the 500 Club. Hero that I am, though, I birdied eighteen and escaped the 500 Club by a stroke.

I didn't hang around to brag about it. I signed my card, paid Winston, hopped in the cart, and burned rubber to the clubhouse entrance. I almost panicked—the car was waiting, but my driver was missing—but he turned up immediately and we were out the gate and headed for the airport by the time the next group was putting out. The guy driving me knew exactly where he was going, and we got to the airport with thirty minutes to spare.

I had some time to reflect on the tournament during my flight. Obviously, I'm disappointed. And angry. For a few holes on Friday I thought I had found a swing that would work, but it proved to be just another cul-de-sac. There seems to be no road out of the place I'm in.

Why do I play tournament golf? Part of me says I do it because I can't do anything else. When I quit the big tour, I got my broker's license and tried to sell limited partnerships for a New York firm. Tax shelter stuff, but good products. I couldn't do it. I had bigger knots in my stomach than I had playing in the U.S. Open. So I envy people who can just drop what they're doing and try something else.

I can always go back and be a club pro again. Those years I spent at the Canyon Club in Palm Springs, 1982 to 1987, were pretty easy. It was a real peaceful time in my life, a good time for Susie and me. But there was no fulfillment. There was no pain involved, but there was no bliss, either.

There's where I'm hung up. My ultimate bliss is playing tournament golf and hitting good golf shots. Along with that comes pain. Real pain. And if you're into something where the pain and the gain are equal, you've got a mathematical equation that comes up zero.

I got to Louisville around eight o'clock. My brother-in-law picked me up and drove me home. Mom, God bless her, had meat loaf and peach cobbler waiting for me, like she always does.

I go to bed with this thought: My road to bliss is not perfectly paved.

JULY 1, MONDAY/LOUISVILLE, KENTUCKY

I'm sad for Al Geiberger, who didn't win yesterday, but I'm happy for Jim Colbert, who did. It's Jimmy's first Senior Tour victory after three second-place finishes. It's a great thing for Kansas City, too, because Kansas City is where Jimmy grew up and played most of his amateur golf. His eighty-four-year-old dad, Jim Colbert, Sr., was there, and I'm sure that added to the thrill.

I guess we never grow up in the eyes of our parents, and we never stop trying to please them. I've felt a real void since Pro died. I think constantly of the joy my return to tournament golf would have given him.

It's the same with my mom. My mother has always been the driving force in my life, and my own gray hair hasn't changed things much. Last year, right after I won the Murata in Dallas, I made a detour on my way to the press tent to call two people: my wife and my mother. Susie had gone out for a minute and had left a message to call back in an hour, but I got my mother after a couple of rings.

I said, "Mom, I did it!"

She said, "What'd you do?"

"I won!"

She said, "What'd you shoot today?"

"Seventy-four."

There was a little pause. "And you still won?"

The breath about went out of me. She didn't mean it in a harsh way, she was thrilled for me. But that was her knee-jerk reaction: I'd had a poor last round.

This was a conversation between a mother and her little boy, who just happened to be fifty-one.

JULY 2, TUESDAY/CINCINNATI, OHIO

I got up early this morning, had breakfast with Mom, and then drove here in time to warm up for the Tuesday Shoot-Out. I only found out last week that I was invited. They take three guys off the all-time money list, three off last year's money list, two or three of this year's top winners, and then the sponsor gets to pick two guys out of the air. Most of the

Shoot-Outs are sponsored by Merrill Lynch, but this one was a Procter & Gamble production. I got invited because I'm "local"—I've got a following in the Louisville-Cincinnati area.

The rules are simple. You start with ten guys and play nine holes, eliminating one player per hole. The player with the highest score on a hole is out. If several players tie for high score, and this is often the case, you have a shoot-off, usually a chip, pitch, or bunker shot. Whoever winds up farthest from the pin is eliminated, and the game moves on to the next hole. The more holes you survive, the more money you get. The total purse is $10,000. First prize is $5,000 and second prize is $2,500.

This is my fifth or sixth Shoot-Out, and they haven't been as much fun to play in as I expected. For one thing, they're kind of pokey—more than three hours, if you play the full nine holes. And there's a lot more pressure than I ever dreamed. When you're eliminated, you have to shake everybody's hand, wave to the crowd, and then ride back to the clubhouse. You're like a relief pitcher who's been shelled.

And it doesn't get much better as the holes go by. It's hole after hole of sudden-death pressure.

We went off on the back side with a couple of thousand people following us, and the first guy eliminated was the South African, Simon Hobday, who three-putted from the back of the green. That was nice because it eliminated the need for one of those eight-man chip-offs that take about ten minutes. The second guy out was Jim Ferree, who lost a sand-bunker blast-off with Bruce Crampton, Walt Zembriski, and John Paul Cain. Jim just hit a bad blast, didn't even get on the green. I made a thirty-foot birdie putt there to avoid the blast-off. That's how you keep your sanity in these things—get the ball down early and watch the other players sweat it out.

The next three holes were easy because only one guy made bogey. Jim Dent three-putted No. 12. Jim Colbert did the same thing on thirteen. He had a little birdie putt of about ten feet, ran it past the hole four feet, and missed coming back, one of those weird things that happen. If he had made his par we all would have been in a six-way chip-off, because no one made birdie. Then on No. 14 we lost my old buddy Charlie Coody. He hit one over the green, chipped back long, and missed about a twenty-foot putt.

With half the players gone, I began to look at the Shoot-Out a little differently. The first few holes, you're just trying not to embarrass yourself. The rest of the way, you're playing for money. It's not a lot of money, not by tournament standards, but $5,000 is good pay for three hours' work, I don't care what you do.

On No. 15, I made a twenty-five-footer for birdie. That kept me out of another blast-off, this time between Crampton, Cain, and Zembriski. Zembriski lost—if you call a check for $1,000 "losing." Then Cain hit it way right on No. 16 and was out of the hole before we reached the green. One, two, three little Indians left—Beard, Crampton, and Dale Douglass.

I'd had a pretty easy run. No chip-offs, no blast-offs, and no pressure putts to stay alive. That ended on No. 17. All three of us hit pretty good iron shots into the green. Crampton had about twenty feet for birdie, Douglass about the same distance, and I had fifteen feet. Crampton put the heat on by making his putt, getting a good roar from the crowd for his effort. Dale then stepped up and missed his.

Now I'm getting excited. If I make my putt, I go to the eighteenth hole with a guarantee of at least $2,500. If I miss, it's either Douglass or me in a chip-off. I gave the putt a hard look, consulted with my caddy, and finally gave the ball a good firm roll, right into the cup.

So it came down to Crampton and me on the last hole. And I have to say, I wanted to win. I mean, I really wanted to win. This year, 1991, has been a dry one for me. Winning an event, even something as insignificant as a Shoot-Out, might give me just the kick-start I need to turn things around.

No. 18 is a par-5 where you have to lay up. Neither of us hit very good 9-irons to the green. I had twenty-five feet for birdie, he had about fifteen. I missed mine. He missed his.

So we got into a chip-off. Actually, it was more of a pitch-off, because the guy from Procter & Gamble led us to a spot about thirty yards from the pin.

Bruce ambled up to me and said, "What do you say, Frank—want to split?"

He kind of caught me by surprise. It used to be common practice on the big tour for playoff participants to privately cut a deal before going to sudden-death. The tour's tournament policy board took a dim view of the practice and banned it. So my first reaction was to think, "We have rules about splitting." But then I remembered that the ban does not extend to side competitions like the Shoot-Outs, what we call our "funny money" events.

I said, "How much is involved?"

"The difference between five and two-and-a-half."

Twenty-five hundred dollars seemed like a lot to lose on just one shot. I said, "Okay, sure. Let's split."

Bruce turned out to be a pretty smart guy, because he flubbed his pitch. He flat-out chunked it and didn't even reach the green. I turned to the official and was about to ask, "Do I just have to get on the green?" Because I wasn't sure if they went strictly by distance or whether on-the-green always beat off-the-green. I caught myself, though. Goodness gracious, I thought, he's forty feet from the pin. If I can't hit it closer than that, I don't deserve to win.

I was a little tense over the ball, but I pitched it safely to about eight feet. I had won the Shoot-Out. The crowd gave me the local-favorite treatment, a nice ovation.

But during the awards ceremony, which took place right there on the eighteenth green, my mind was turning over the deal I had made with Crampton. It dawned on me that if I paid him $1,250 out of my winner's check, I'd have to send him the 1099 form and do all the federal and state paperwork. I was thinking about this as I took the microphone. I made the appropriate and gracious remarks to the people gathered around the green, but I was thinking, "That crafty Crampton has outsmarted me."

I fooled him. I went to the sponsor afterward and said I'd agreed to a split with Bruce. He said, "No problem," and wrote each of us a check for $3,750.

It was just a little paperwork, but I felt like I'd dodged a bullet.

JULY 3, WEDNESDAY/CINCINNATI

You may not believe this, but we're playing a Jack Nicklaus–designed golf course this week, and no one minds. It's called the Grizzly Course, and it's one of his early efforts. We played on it in the seventies, and it's a pretty good golf course. It doesn't have the harsh features we complain about today. Whether that's what the clients wanted or that's just the way he designed back then, I don't know. The Jack Nicklaus Sports Center is right across the interstate from the Kings Island amusement park, so they probably wanted a layout the average golfer could get around without losing a dozen balls and his temper.

I won about two hundred bucks in today's pro-am, and it's one of those lessons that I seem to keep relearning. We shot 6-under on the front side and we were out of it, no chance. I didn't give up on my guys, but I lost some of my energy. When you're in contention, you're lining up putts for them, you're helping with club selection. When you're out of contention, you start giving lessons and asking about their families. That's what I was doing on the back nine when they started holing chip shots and long putts. We shot 12-under on the back side, and this is a team that should have trouble shooting 12-under for thirty-six holes.

One of the guys in the pro-am sidled up to me while we were waiting on the tee at a par-3. "Frank, I notice you use perimeter-weighted irons. Do you really think they make a difference?"

My answer was kind of long-winded, but the gist of it was, yes, they help.

For those who don't know what I'm talking about, perimeter weighting is a design option in which the back of the clubhead is hollowed out and the weight distributed more around the edges. This enlarges the sweet spot and makes the club more forgiving on off-center hits. The traditional forged blade, by way of contrast, is basically a slab of steel that has been shaped and scored to make a clubhead. The sweet spot is smaller, but good players have historically preferred the forged club's superior feel.

I preferred the forged blade myself until 1988. That's when H&B sent me a set of investment-cast, perimeter-weighted irons to evaluate. They send me new clubs every year, just to check out, and I send them back a letter saying "They're great" or "They're terrible," whatever I think. And when I got these clubs out of the shipping carton, I kind of wrinkled my nose. I had the typical macho-male golfer's aversion to the concept. I thought they were for women and old men.

But I took them out on the range to make an appraisal, and I had to admit, they felt pretty good. They were nothing like the cast metal clubs of the seventies, which had a hard feel and fired the ball all over the place. These were beryllium or some other exotic alloy, and they had a soft comfortable feel.

I took them out for a few practice rounds, and some fat shots I hit, which should have gone in the water, were reaching the green. Some heel shots that should have landed in bunkers were also getting to the green. But I found that I could still control the ball and maneuver it the way I was accustomed.

I wrote back to H&B: "I'm using 'em."

I've since reached the conclusion that anyone who plays golf, even the world's best tournament players, can use the help these clubs provide. And that's why I get a kick out of it when I look in the bags of my pro-am partners and see all these classic forged irons. It's ego, pure and simple.

JULY 4, THURSDAY/CINCINNATI

When they weren't waving their Fourth of July flags this morning, some of the guys were in the locker room, talking about the Ryder Cup. Dave Stockton is the captain of the American team this time around, and he's getting all kinds of unsolicited advice on who he should take with his captain's choices. (The first ten guys on the big tour's money list are automatically on the team; the captain gets to choose the final two.) The names being tossed about are Ray Floyd, Tom Kite, Tom Watson, and Jack Nicklaus.

From what I read in the papers, Stockton has pretty much ruled out Nicklaus. He says, "Jack doesn't play enough, and I'm not sure you can come off the Senior Tour and have the chemistry with the other guys."

Stockton's studied this thing for two years and I've studied it for two minutes, but I wouldn't dismiss Nicklaus so quickly. We haven't done too well in the last three Ryder Cups—two losses and a tie—so maybe it's time to try something different. Let's choose a guy who doesn't qualify on points and let it be known that we're choosing him because, by God, he's the greatest player in the world and we want the inspiration.

And then, if you've got him, I say *use* him. First, he still plays well enough. The Ryder Cup is match play, basically—best-ball, alternate shot, individual, it's all match play—and that means you can hit the occasional bad shot and still beat the pants off somebody. And that's the only difference in Jack Nicklaus now and Jack Nicklaus twenty years ago—he just hits a few more bad shots. He hits as many *good* shots as he ever did.

I'm not saying Stockton is insane if he passes on Jack. But I'd pick him.

The choice that's already been made—Stockton as captain—is a good one. I know Dave pretty well, and I think he'll do a great job, as long as he doesn't overcoach. He's a rah-rah, gung ho type guy, and he's a competitor beyond all boundaries. So it may be hard for Dave not to get too involved. In other sports, I find that the most successful coaches are those who condition and train their players and teach them a system, but when game time comes they let the players play. I don't know if that holds true for golf, but I suspect it does.

God knows, Stockton won't have to motivate his guys. My first year on the Ryder Cup team, 1969, I couldn't believe the intensity of my teammates, the screaming and hollering. It was still just Great Britain at that time, not all of Europe, and the British had just begun to field some very good players, Tony Jacklin and the like. I had never followed a golf pro in a tournament round in my life, but we were all out there with the galleries at Royal Birkdale, cheering for one another and yelling support. As I recall, Dave Hill practically got into a fistfight with one of the Brits, and then one of their guys, Bernard Gallacher, had to be pulled off one of ours. Feelings ran so high that players were getting into arguments with their own teammates. Davey and I had a few words over something, I don't remember what. It was that intense.

Sam Snead was the captain that year, and he took it seriously. He did a good job of preparing us, and he was wonderful about including us in the decision-making process. He even let us vote on who we wanted to play with—secret ballot, of course.

What I remember most about my first Ryder Cup was the opening ceremony. They ran up the Stars and Stripes and began to play the "Star Spangled Banner," and it hit me that I wasn't playing for Frank Beard anymore. I had my teammates and the whole country counting on me.

I don't mind telling you, I cried.

JULY 5, FRIDAY/CINCINNATI

You wouldn't believe the traffic jam this morning. There were cars backed up over a mile on the freeway. Everybody was trying to get in to see today's pairing of Jack Nicklaus, Arnold Palmer, and Lee Trevino.

Usually our Friday pairings come out of a hat, but they must have kept shaking the hat to get those three guys together. The gallery today was estimated at forty thousand people, which is by far the largest I've ever seen on the Senior Tour. It was just extraordinary.

The star attractions didn't play that well. Trevino shot 68, which was not bad, but Nicklaus was at 1-under-par 70 and Arnie double bogeyed the first hole and shot a 76. There were a bunch of rounds in the 60s, including 66s by Dale Douglass, Al Geiberger, Terry Dill, and Dudley Wysong. I could be wrong, but I bet the newspapers tomorrow will have in big headlines: DREAM PAIRING THRILLS SPECTATORS. And down there in small type it'll say, "Four Lead Kroger Classic." Which is just great, from my perspective. Those guys deserve the ink.

If any of those forty thousand spectators came to see Frank Beard play, they didn't hang around for long. I scraped around in 73 and didn't scare a soul, except for a few innocents who had to jump out of the way of my tee shots. My game has shown very few vital signs these last weeks, and I'm getting a little desperate. I continue to feel that I'm *almost* ready to play good golf. I have this feeling that good golf is right around the corner, but I keep turning the corner. There's nothing there but another corner.

I don't drink, so I can't anesthetize myself. The best I can do is run and hide in my room, which I've done quite a bit the last three years.

Trevino's another guy who's fighting it. He shot a good score today, but he was really dragging in the locker room yesterday. Walt Zembriski and I spent a few minutes with him, and Lee said he was ready to chuck everything. "I've just got to get me some rest," he said. "I've got to get rid of something, and the flatbellies tour may be the place to start. If you ask me today, I don't think I'll play in Indianapolis."

He meant the PGA Championship at Crooked Stick in August. If Lee's thinking of skipping a major, he *must* be tired.

Some of the guys say the locker room seems spooky without Rives McBee. Since he turned fifty a couple of years ago, Rives had played in sixty-seven straight tournaments. That blows everyone's mind. He's won three of them and made about $800,000 in official prize money, which kind of supports my notion that you play better when you play a lot. But Rives's daughter is getting married this week, so he's taking the week off. He told me in K.C. that he'll probably take *two* weeks off because he's got a hand injury that won't heal. I kidded him about taking so much time off, and he smiled. "It's no good," he said. "I'm just gonna have to give it a rest."

Rives and I didn't get along on the other tour, a long time ago. One of us drove a tec ball into the other somewhere, and to show how dumb it was, neither of us can remember which one of us it was or where it happened. We had some words over it, and then we didn't speak for twenty years.

The Senior Tour brought us back together. We went to Japan on a junket in '89, and I approached him at the outset. I said, "Look, Rives, I don't even remember what happened years ago, but it's time to get things straightened out between us."

He kind of hung his head and said, "You know, I don't remember what it was about either. Let's be friends."

We shook hands, and we've been real good buddies ever since. What a waste, though, that it took us twenty years to come around.

JULY 6, SATURDAY/CINCINNATI

It rained this morning, so we had to juggle the tee times, and I wound up playing the back nine first. I went out playing like a dog, and after a few holes I was looking for a way to escape. I was 2-over when I teed it up on No. 15 (my sixth), and when I went OB with my drive, I said, "That's it. I'm outta here." I turned to Jimmy Powell and said, "What do I have to do to withdraw? Get a doctor's note? Write a letter to Deane Beman?"

Jimmy said, "No, you've just got to tell a tournament official."

I decided I would wait till the turn and just slink out of there. There was no gallery to speak of. I was playing with Jimmy and Bruce Crampton, and I wasn't worried that I would disappoint anyone by leaving. I was just going to quit and get some distance between me and golf as fast as I could.

It's funny, though. I'm always setting goals. I was going to quit, but I told myself, "if I play the last three holes in 1-under, maybe I'll go on and play the other nine." I put some effort into the last three and a half holes. I parred No. 16 and No. 17, and then I birdied No. 18, a par-5, by knocking it on with a driver and a 3-wood and two-putting.

Having met that little goal, I decided to keep going. I said to myself, "If we're gonna do this, let's really *do* it. Let's put some intensity into it." I put the airport out of my mind and went at the golf course as if I had a job to do. It was like scouring windows or washing dishes, but I really buckled down and played some golf. I shot 4-under on the back side and got back to where I could make some money.

I talked with Susie and the kids after dinner, and Susie said she might caddy for me at the Northville Long Island Classic, the week after the Senior Open. It's a course the ladies played on, so she knows it well. I lost in a playoff there two years ago, and I led the tournament till the last hole last year.

Michael came on the line and acted as her agent. "Oh, Daddy, have her caddy for you. She's *good*. She'll calm you down, Daddy."

Susan explained that she'd been working with Michael at home, little things with his swing. "He forgets that I played the tour and that I'm more than just his mother."

I didn't need to be sold on the idea on Susan caddying. I've been crying in my beer ever since she quit me at the Vintage.

JULY 7, SUNDAY/CINCINNATI

I was paired with Rocky Thompson today, and Rocky shot a marvelous 65. I hadn't played with him in twenty years, and I was shocked at how well he played. I mean, I played a fair amount with him back on the old tour, and he didn't hit it anywhere near where he hits it now. I'd have asked him about it, but I don't know how you broach the subject. Do you just walk up and say, "Rocky, why is it that you couldn't hit your ass for twenty years, and now you play so well?"

So I just said, "Nice shot," a couple of dozen times and admired his play.

He could have shot 62 or 63. He lipped a few putts, he made a bogey. He's obviously one of those guys who finds his game as a senior, and what I saw today proves that his win at Syracuse was no fluke.

I shot 72 and made somewhere between $3,000 and $4,000. Not a great result, but better than I was going to do. If I'd walked off the course on Friday I wouldn't have made a cent.

I collared Rocky after our round and said, "Rock, you used to play golf with me. What's it look like, what's the trouble?"

He said, "The Frank Beard I used to know had tempo. It looked like it took him forever and ever to complete his swing." He gave me a pat on the back. "The Frank today is just too fast."

JULY 8, MONDAY/PALM DESERT, CALIFORNIA

I'm not going to lay my poor play on my family. The bad shots I'm hitting this year, I hit last year. I just feel better when they're with me. Vegas was a wonderful weekend, the Tournament of Champions was great. And I'm really looking forward to this stretch starting with the U.S. Senior Open in Detroit. Susie and the kids will be with me the whole week, and then we're taking a float trip together in August, the week before Albuquerque.

If Susie caddies for me at Northville, it should be a great month.

JULY 11, THURSDAY/PALM DESERT

We're having a real mild summer in the Valley. Of course, a mild summer to us is anywhere from 100 to 108 degrees. The gnats come out in the afternoon, so I do all my playing and practicing in the morning. Today I just went out and hit balls for a couple of hours and then got a haircut.

Before the heat closed in, I spent a half-hour or so on the putting green. I really ought to do my putting at night, because my putting technique is like catnip to kibitzers. Someone's sure to come up and say, "What the hell are you doing, Beard? Can't you putt like a man?"

The putter I use is a forty-one-inch Slotline. It's not quite a long putter, it's more midsize. When I joined the Senior Tour, I had a conventional Ping putter, and I did well with it. I finished second three times and made $190,000 in an abbreviated year. But somewhere along the line it occurred to me that I might putt better if I made a change. I'd seen the guys with the long putters, and while some, like Orville Moody, had been terrible putters before, other guys, like Charlie Coody, had been great putters on the big tour.

Suddenly, in October of '89, I had some trouble finding the line. My stroke was good, the ball was rolling okay, but I couldn't start it where I was looking. The week before I left for Florida in 1990, it got worse. I played a couple of practice rounds at Key Biscayne, and I putted terribly.

Larry Mowry said, "You gotta do something."

So I walked right over to the putting green and picked up the putter I have now. Not this actual one—an airline broke the first one—but the same putter, a Slotline.

The Slotline tour rep was a guy named Don Schvorski, and he had a good sales technique. He'd just leave a few of his putters out and walk away. This is smart, because nobody wants to fool with the reps who hang around.

I picked up the midsize one because I didn't want the longer ones. I had tried to hit a couple of putts before using Orville's under-the-chin technique, and I just couldn't get comfortable with my left hand upside down and my thumb on top the putter. So I picked up the midlength and hit about two putts with it.

I said, "This is it."

I went and got Don and said, "Show me how to set up with this thing." He spent two or three hours with me, and I put it in my bag before the pro-am the next day. I've never been without it since.

I've had days where I've thought maybe I should go back to my old Ping. But, as with most things in my life, change has meant growth and improvement. That's why I've got graphite shafts on my metal woods, perimeter-weighted irons, and this crazy putter. The only remnant of my past is my old brown sand wedge, my Wilson R-90, and I suspect it's on its last legs. I've had it refaced once, and I don't know if I can find the guy to reface it again.

Maybe it's just time to cut the last tie and get on down the road.

JULY 16, TUESDAY/AURORA, ILLINOIS

I've been out here two years, and I'm still trying to figure out how our pro-ams are put together. It's too intricate to explain, but it has to do with last year's money list. If you were in the top thirty-one, you don't have to play in the Wednesday pro-am, just the one on Thursday. But if you volunteer for Wednesday, they have to put you in. And they're happy to, because it pleases the sponsors.

Sometimes you *have* to play on Wednesday, if they need you to fill the field. They start with number thirty-one and work down, thirty, twenty-nine, twenty-eight . . . I was number sixteen on last year's money list, and I may be asked to play a few Wednesdays this year. But you're never quite sure if they're going to fill to your number until you get there. That's why I sometimes volunteer to play on Wednesday. I use the extra pro-am as a practice round. That allows me to stay home with my family and fly in on Tuesday night.

I got to the golf course this afternoon, and the first thing I did was check tomorrow's tee times. And I'm not on the list. This is a new golf course, I've never seen it, and now I'm only going to get one practice round. I went and raised some hell, and they're going to see what they can do.

Back at the hotel, I had a phone conversation with Larry Mowry, and he's hoping to play next week in the Senior Open. "It turns out I was misdiagnosed," he said. "I don't have Meniere's disease."

"You're kidding."

"No. I was getting real discouraged with my progress, and this doctor I know sent me to the fellow who's supposed to be the best in town. I went to this guy and took the same tests over again. Which are miserable, they turn you upside down. But he came up with a different diagnosis. He says it's neuritis, and he says it's 99 percent treatable with medication."

I told him I was just getting to where I could pronounce Meniere. "What does the new doctor say about that?"

Larry laughed. "He said Meniere's disease is what the doctors tell you if they don't know what the hell's wrong with you."

JULY 17, WEDNESDAY/CHICAGO, ILLINOIS

I don't know Tom Fazio well, but I sure like his golf courses. This week's course, Stonebridge Country Club, is just marvelous, one of the best courses I've played in a long time. It's not easy, but when you miss a shot you feel like you can recover. On most new courses you have this ominous feeling that you're going to hit the best shot of your life and still make triple bogey.

I can wax so eloquent on the merits of Stonebridge because I got into the pro-am after all. Another pro dropped out, and I got his spot. Amazing what you can accomplish if you're willing to cry on someone's shoulder.

My pro-am partners all had the same question for me today: "What's with Gary Player?"

It's in the papers that Player has a new book out, an autobiography. There's a whole chapter devoted to Tom Watson. Player rips him. He says Watson is cold and distant and he accuses him of dishonesty because Watson won the 1977 British Open and Masters with golf clubs that were subsequently ruled as nonconforming.

Frankly, I'm shocked. Shocked that after all these years Player would bring this up. Watson, in my opinion, is truly beyond reproach. He is unsurpassed in his personal ethics and his devotion to the game of golf. Joe Golfer has nothing but respect for both Tom Watson and Gary Player, and now one of them is calling the other a cheat and a liar. Joe Golfer is the loser.

The Ram clubs that Player refers to had grooves and facings that didn't conform to the rules of golf. That happened, there's no doubt about that. But what Player doesn't mention is that Watson didn't know the clubs were nonconforming until months later. Neither did the many other players who used the same clubs. Gary's book makes it sound like Watson did something underhanded, which is absurd. If I win the U.S. Open with Titleist Tour 100s, and a year later they test them and decide the ball is now nonconforming, do you take my title away from me? Of course you don't.

You can't even say that the clubs helped Watson win. I mean, Tom Watson in his prime could win with broomsticks.

Player obviously nurses a grudge from the 1983 Skins Game. I had totally forgotten about the incident, but the newspaper stories jogged my memory. Watson confronted Player after that match and accused him of improving his lie for a chip shot by uprooting a plant or something. Their argument got overheard by some reporters, and the whole thing wound up splashed across the sports pages. Gary was hurt by the publicity, and he must feel a need to vindicate himself. But this just looks like a sad attempt to bring Watson down a peg.

Whoever wrote Gary's book for him has served him badly. Gary Player worked very hard to attain the enormous prestige he enjoys. This will do nothing but detract from that.

JULY 18, THURSDAY/CHICAGO

They had the first round of the British Open on the TV in the locker room this morning. They're playing at Royal Birkdale, outside Liverpool.

It brought back some memories. I first played at Birkdale in the old Alcan tournament in 1967. I shot 88 or 89 in the first round. It was absolutely the most insane weather I'd ever seen, an absolute hurricane. They don't cancel golf rounds over there, so we were all out there playing in the hurricane. By the sixth hole, I was drenched and disgusted, and I just gave up. I couldn't leave the course because we were all over there as a contingent and our tickets were paid for. But I just swam home.

I can't say I love the old golf courses. I go over and play this Birkdale course, and they've got blind shots all over the place, bunkers you can't find, upside-down greens . . . and I'm looking at these things, and I'm saying, "If I duplicate this course in America today, they won't pay me. They'll say it's crap."

And then I hear the rationalization: "They didn't have the earth-moving equipment in the old days."

Well, fine. We've got a dippy course here because they didn't have the equipment in the old days.

I'm not knocking tradition. I'm not saying that great tournaments and Old Tom Morris and two hundred years of lore don't count for something. And I'm not saying I don't want to play, either. But great golf courses? I can't see it.

I did have my share of fun at Royal Birkdale: the British Open a couple of times, the Ryder Cup in '69. My best memories are of the Ryder Cup. That was the year of the famous "gimmee" by Jack Nicklaus. I remember sitting with Kenny Still by the eighteenth green, watching the final match. Nicklaus made his putt, and then Tony Jacklin had to make a putt for the British to tie.

I've heard people say that it was a very short putt, something in the one- or two-foot range. The putt was actually no less than four feet, and my guess at the time was five. Kenny and I were sitting there with our fingers crossed, hoping Jacklin would miss it.

Nicklaus picked up Jacklin's marker and handed it to him.

I looked at Kenny. "What did he do?"

Kenny's mouth was open. "He gave him the putt."

Oh, we were irate. I was, for sure. It may have been a great gesture for Jack Nicklaus, but the other eleven of us had worked very hard and we wanted to win. He just arrogantly assumed that the team and the country, individually and together, would want him to make this sporting gesture.

I don't know why I was shocked. I can't conceive of Jack Nicklaus making a decision based on anything other than what he thinks. I just can't. If he'd asked us, we'd have told him no, and he'd probably have done it anyway. I don't mean that in a belligerent or angry way. That's just Jack's makeup. He's a very independent, dynamic person who lives in his own world. That's why he's number one, that's why he's the best golfer who ever lived.

Looking back, I recognize the conceded putt as the act of a man of considerable class and sophistication. But I guarantee you, if I'd had the same decision to make, Tony Jacklin would have had to show us he could make a four-footer with the weight of a whole nation on his shoulders.

JULY 19, FRIDAY/CHICAGO

The man in the Panama hat grabbed my hand on the first tee today. "I'm playing with Frank Beard again," Chi Chi said. "Last time I played with him, I won in Dallas."

He was thrilled to see me. His lucky rabbit's foot.

Unfortunately, the luck didn't run to the rabbit. I shot a 77 and sort of embarrassed myself in front of Chi Chi's big gallery. I hit balls on the range for a while, drove back to the Holiday Inn, and showered. Brooded.

I called home tonight, and Mikey was back from San Diego. He told me he hadn't done as well as he wanted to in the Junior Worlds. He'd tried to concentrate real hard, tried to stay intense and focused, but it hadn't worked. He said, "Dad, I think when I talk to my partners, kid around and all that, it takes some of the pressure off and I play better."

I said, "That's right, Mikey. You're absolutely right."

He said, "But you don't hardly do that at all."

Wham. You go back to the Bible, where it says, "And a little child shall lead them." Sometimes Mikey just shocks me with his powers of observation.

We finally hashed it out that there is probably a happy medium that each of us needs to find, a point somewhere between Ben Hogan–type dourness and excessive garrulousness.

It's amazing how often we need somebody to shock us out of our hurtful ways. Just this morning, Charlie Coody took me aside in the locker room and played the Dutch uncle. He knows I've been struggling with my schedule, but he said I have to get my head out of my butt. "You won't be out here twenty-five years like the other tour, Frank. You've got to get your mind off your family and get out here and play. Then you can go home and get your mind off golf."

There was a phone call and he never got to finish, but I got the point. I'm lucky to have a good friend like Charlie.

JULY 20, SATURDAY/CHICAGO

Hot and windy today, same as yesterday. I played with Dick Hendrickson, and he shot a marvelous round, a 64, after a first-round 78.

The gallery that followed us was pretty small, but I was acutely aware of one little pocket of Beard supporters: my son Danny and his new wife and in-laws from Wisconsin.

Danny will be twenty-five in August. He still harbors some anger and resentment about my divorce from his mother, and there's even some anger that I don't play as well as I used to. That may sound strange, but he put me on a pedestal when he was little. Danny found this little niche—"son of Frank Beard, pro golfer"—and built his priorities around that. So his world was shattered when I stopped playing well and fell off the tour. It's not something that he's worked on, he's had no therapy. But we've gotten at it over the years through trial and error—loud words, hanging up the phone, that sort of thing. He reminds me a lot of Michael. He could be a scratch player himself.

Homero Blancas came up to me before today's round and said, "You remember when Tommy bit Danny?" His son Tommy was standing there with Homero's golf bag; he's caddying for his dad this week.

I said, "Jesus Christ, yes." It happened on the old tour, when the kids were about three. Tommy bit Danny on the cheek, right under the eye. They had to take stitches.

I said, "That's a shocker. They're twenty-five, and here we are with our big guts, lookin' at 'em."

Danny had told me that he had a real important fishing trip scheduled for Sunday. So I was surprised at the end of today's round when he said, "Dad, I'm going to follow you again tomorrow." It really touched me that he would cancel his fishing to see me play. I'm not playing that well—I shot 71 today, I'm fifteen shots out—so it tells me that he isn't as tied to the celebrity thing as he was. He just wants to spend some time with his old man.

JULY 21, SUNDAY/CHICAGO

I eagled the eighteenth hole today, but it wasn't enough to keep me out of the 500 Club. I made the 500 Club only once in my first two seasons. Now I've done it three times in one season. The trend is ominous.

J. C. Snead made some pretty strong statements in the newspapers this week. He said when he came out on the Senior Tour last fall he expected it to be a big party. "It is—" he said "—a big crybaby party. Everything bothers these guys. They complain about the birds chirping, the color of your shoes, the coin you use to mark your ball, the side of the fairway you drive the cart. It's just ridiculous. It takes the fun out of it."

He went on: "Some of these guys are almost mean. There's been more fights out here than in the last fifteen years on the other tour. We've had guys almost get into fistfights. They're like old dogs fighting over a bone."

Right off, I should say that I'm leery of what I read in the paper, especially caustic remarks. There's so much that's said rhetorically, tongue in cheek. I've been misquoted often enough to know that.

But I haven't seen much of the gamesmanship Snead complains of. The fistfights, I don't know—maybe he's referring to the little altercation Jerry Barber told me about at the PGA, the misunderstanding he had with Mike Fetchick.

My guess is that J.C. just doesn't feel welcome yet. He's never been a joiner or an overly friendly person. Maybe he made some enemies before and they were here waiting for him. Or maybe he just can't accept the fact that he's on the Senior Tour. J.C.'s one of those guys who played the other tour until he was fifty, and maybe he just can't accept that he's not around the big action anymore. He hasn't had much success in his months out here, and that has to be gnawing at him, too—as my recent failures gnaw at me.

JULY 22, MONDAY/LOUISVILLE, KENTUCKY

It has not been a good year for the golf industry. In fact, it's been pitiful. Hillerich & Bradsby, the company I've been with for thirty years, has enough history and financial power to ride out the recession, but a lot of the smaller companies are going under.

The mood today at H&B's national sales meeting was not "down," exactly. But you could feel the uncertainty.

The day went like a normal Monday thing. H&B brought in thirty or forty sales reps, and I shot the bull with them for about an hour and had lunch. Bill Kratzert was there, one of the regular tour guys, and we put on a clinic. Hit golf balls. Then we went out on the course for a shotgun start. I played with nine groups, two holes each. A local radio station sent a mobile unit out and did a call-in show with us during the cocktail hour. The normal Monday thing, except this one is included in my contract and there's no extra compensation.

I'm not complaining. H&B passes enough money my way that two or three appearances a year is more than reasonable.

We had a dinner, followed by some presentations. I said a few words. I'm not a great speaker, but you don't have to be. You tell a few stories about the tour, shake hands, and go home.

A fairly routine late weekend in the life of a pro. Tomorrow morning, I'll get up at five to catch a 7:10 flight to Detroit.

The rest of the week won't seem so routine. There's nothing routine about Open week.

TEN

JULY 23, TUESDAY/BIRMINGHAM, MICHIGAN

The U.S. Open is absolutely six days of misery. We're talking rough up to your butt, greens you can't putt on, bunkers you can't get out of, fairways you can't hit, and twice the pressure of any other tournament. That's a pretty dire picture, coming from a guy who's played in every Open he could get in, but it's how I feel.

I've always had a love/hate relationship with the Open. I can't deny the Open's mystique—it's *not* just another tournament, it's very, very special—but I often wonder if the reward is worth the agony. The closest I ever came to winning the U.S. Open was at Medinah in 1975, when I led after three rounds and missed the playoff by a stroke. This one, the Senior Open, I nearly won two years ago at Laurel Valley, but Orville Moody was too good for me. That's the tournament that announced to the world that Frank Beard was back. I was pretty shaky. Happy to be back, thrilled to be in the hunt, but scared.

The Open is a myth. Everyone says, "You've *got* to play in the Open." Well, I've got news for you. Unless you can win the U.S. Open, there's no reason to play. All right, maybe second, third, or fourth place you can justify from the standpoint of prize money. But below that, the money dive-bombs.

A guy like me, a guy like Jim Ferree—we're forty-to-one shots, we win one tournament a year. Why endure a week of misery for a forty-to-one shot?

But I'm here. I'm here, first of all, because I would dearly love to win an Open. And I see myself as better than forty-to-one on a U.S. Open course. If you look back at my career, you'll find that I've won 75 percent of my prize money on the most difficult courses. I've never been a birdie machine, but I've usually been able to hold my game together when other guys are going down in flames.

But Lord, it's a tough week.

Anybody who travels can appreciate this. It took me one hour this morning to fly from Louisville to Detroit, which is four hundred miles. It took me *two* hours to go from the Detroit airport to Oakland Hills Country Club, which is about thirty miles north. I had to pick up a car, get some instructions, fight the traffic, and get instructions twice more because the first instructions were wrong.

I wanted to make sure I got my practice round in, so I came straight to the golf course. Eddie Terrell was out by the putting clock, waiting for me. He's my caddy this week—"Fast Eddie" Terrell. I've known Eddie for ages, although we've never worked together. His regular bag is Homero Blancas, but Homero isn't playing this week.

My having to rush I blame on the United States Golf Association. They're the people who put on the U.S. Senior Open, the U.S. Open, the U.S. Amateur, the U.S. Women's Open, and a bunch of amateur tournaments. They're also the governing body and rules maker for golf in North America.

I've never been a fan of the USGA. There is a definite need in golf for a governing body, but I see the USGA as a typical bloated bureaucracy. Too many of its officials are pompous and self-important. They do things their way, and you'd better do it their way too, or else.

A typical example: my having to rush this morning. They have 150 entrants here, and the PGA Tour will have 150 entrants this week at its tournament in Hartford, Connecticut. The first tee at Hartford will be wide open, and anybody who wants a practice round will get one. You just show up and wait your turn. The USGA, on the other hand, insists on having tee times for practice rounds. So we've got chaos on the first tee—players not showing up on time, other guys waiting for hours, everybody with upset nerves. We've suffered through it for years at the U.S. Open, and it's the same big mess at the Senior Open.

The players complain, but no one listens. It's always, "This is how we do it."

Today I was lucky. I missed my 11:05 tee time, but somebody else didn't show and I was off the tee in four minutes. But I could just as easily sat on my duff for three hours.

I will say this in defense of the USGA: They take some pity on us old men. The golf course is not set up too difficult. The rough is penalizing, about three inches deep, but it's not "U.S. Open rough." The greens aren't that firm, either. Of course, it's only Tuesday. They'll stop watering them, and they'll get firmer.

What the course is, is *long*. It's right at 6,800 yards on the scorecard, but that doesn't tell the story. We're playing it as a par-70. That means instead of four par-5s we've got two, and one of the par-5s isn't that long, maybe 490 yards. That allows them, at 6,800 yards, to make a whole bunch of 4-pars that are about 440 yards long. And that's long. You could take the same yardage and make two 5-pars of 600 yards and a bunch of 375-yard par-4s . . . but then it wouldn't be an Open course.

The eighteenth hole is the best example. The members play it as a par-5, but we're playing it as a 447-yard par-4. That's 447 yards around a slight dogleg-right and up a hill to a green guarded by deep bunkers. The best play is to drive over the sand bunker in the right rough, but if you don't reach the fairway, you're dead. Anything left, you're also dead. You just can't hit a 2-iron or a 3-wood out of this rough.

From the tee today, I pulled one way left behind a sand bunker. That didn't tell me a thing, so I took another ball and tried again. This time, I pushed it into the trees on the right.

"Gimmee that last ball," I said to Eddie. I turned to Joe McDermott, one of the guys I was playing with. "We're gonna go down in flames, Joe."

Drive number three wasn't real pretty, either, kind of a flat hook, and I had to laugh. "Give me a small bucket, Joe." But that drive was effectively long and in the fairway, and from there I hit a 2-iron about as good as I've hit in twenty years, and it landed right in the middle of the green.

So we're talking big holes here, *big* holes. And the eighteenth green, when I got up there, was a terror. It's pitched steeply back toward the fairway, so anything behind the hole—a putt, a chip—you've got no chance of stopping coming back. You can't hold a shot from the fairway, either, because the green was designed to receive par-5 wedge shots, not low 2-irons.

I've been playing Opens since '63 or '64, so it's no surprise that the greens are fast. But these greens, quite frankly, are *insane*. They've got elephants buried in them, unbelievable slopes. If they get to ten on the Stimp-meter, we won't finish. We absolutely will not finish. Jack Nicklaus was in the locker room, commenting on his play last week in the British Open, and he said it was tough going from the world's flattest greens to the greens here. He said, "I've always thought the greens at Augusta were the toughest, but these are tougher."

You won't hear me criticizing the course, though. Not publicly, anyway. I've always tried to keep my mouth shut when we play the hallowed golf courses, places like Baltusrol, Merion, Medinah, Winged Foot, and Oakland Hills. The whole world looks at Oakland Hills and says, "What a great golf course!" And the design is fine. The bunkers are good, the routing of the holes is tough. But greens amount to more than half the playability of a golf course, and if you apply the "two putts per hole" standard to this golf course, it falls short. If you went out today and took the normal $20 million to design a golf course for somebody, and you put these greens on that golf course, they'd run you out of town. Just like we run Nicklaus out of town, figuratively speaking.

But *this* is a great golf course. I say that with tongue in cheek.

Before I left the club, I asked Fast Eddie if he needed some cash for the week. He said he did, so I gave him his week's pay in advance. He's never carried for me before, but I know him well enough to give him the money. He's responsible. And loyal, too. He's caddied for Mike Hill when Homero didn't need him and he's won about $700,000 with Hill—a $400,000 tournament in Puerto Rico and a couple of other tournament wins. He says Mike would like to use him more, but he's been with Homero a long time and doesn't want to leave. He's a good caddy, and I'm lucky to have him this week.

But still no word on what happened to Seemore. There may be a body in some river, I just don't know.

JULY 24, WEDNESDAY/BIRMINGHAM

I was upstairs in the clubhouse before today's practice round, changing shoes, when I spotted Jim Albus sitting at his locker. I went over.

"Jim, I haven't seen you since you won the TPC, and I just wanted to say how pleased I am that you won. You're a good player and you deserve a lot of credit."

He said, "Well, thank you, Frank." He looked up. "I read your article a while back, and that's not what you said in that article. You wanted to shut us out of these things."

Ouch. I said, "Jim, you must not have read the article. That's not what I said at all."

So I sat down and talked with him. I had promised myself that I wouldn't defend myself anymore, but I keep running into people, four months later, who are still ticked off. Albus has always been opinionated, kind of a hard guy, and he's been caught up in the club pro/touring pro controversy for years. He's very much on the side of those who feel they're kept on the outside by the tour's exemption policy.

We talked for about ten minutes, and I tried to explain my position—that I wasn't trying to keep the good players out, I was just trying to keep the stars of yesteryear *in*. Mike Joyce, who's a club pro, was sitting there, and he nodded whenever Albus said something and shook his head whenever I said something.

In the end, Albus said, "Well, I think I understand what you were saying a bit more." But it was clear that he wasn't convinced. When I walked off, Joyce just smiled and shook his head.

I guess the battle lines are drawn, and no one wants peace.

The other issue we have here, which we have at all the Senior Opens, is the cart business. The USGA won't allow golf carts for the players, and some of us just *need* golf carts to play. Golf carts are as much a part of the Senior Tour as long putters, paunchy bellies, and gray hair, but the USGA insists that we perform like we're still twenty-six years old.

Homero Blancas has had some knee operations, so he can't walk seventy-two holes. I played with him a couple of weeks ago, and he walked about nine holes and rode the rest. Jim Ferree, Gene Littler—they're not here either. Without a cart, they can't play. Sam Snead! Wouldn't you give anything to see Sam Snead play Oakland Hills one last time?

George Archer was talking about it last week at the Ameritech. "No carts, no Archer," he said. "If I stand up for five minutes in the same place I'm in trouble. My back goes bad. Last year there were six-hour rounds at the Open and no benches on the tees."

I think it's outrageous. Any man who wants a cart should have a cart.

JULY 25, THURSDAY/BIRMINGHAM

You know a course is tough if a player is ready to quit after one hole. We were on the second green today, the par-5, and

Dave Hill turned to Dale Douglass and said, "You may be a twosome in a few holes."

Davey makes no bones about it, he hates this course. "I guess I've played here twenty or thirty times," he told me on the first tee, "and I've never broken 75. I just can't handle it."

That's Davey. He runs hot and cold, as a golfer and as a person. He three-putted the first green today, and when his little par putt lipped out he just walked by and angrily back-handed the tap-in. Which shocked me. First of all, it was the worst-looking backhand I've ever seen. He kind of dropped his putter on the ball while he was walking by, and the ball jumped in the air and fell straight in the hole. But more than that, he had seventy-one holes to play. He just wasn't giving himself a chance. I don't think Davey realizes how good a player he is, and so he starts out with kind of a negative attitude.

But I'm a fine one to talk. This morning at breakfast I was telling Susan that I just had no confidence. I felt I was letting down H&B and Phil Armbruster and President Bush and the pope and a bunch of people whose names I don't even know. She looked exasperated and said, "Frank, you're better than 80 percent of this field at your *worst*."

She's right, of course. I took that with me to the first tee, and I got off to a good start. The first hole is a fairly short par-4. I hit a pretty good drive, threw a pitching wedge to five or six feet, and made birdie. That made Eddie smile. On the next hole, a reachable par-5, I had maybe twelve feet for an-other birdie, but the putt turned right at the very last and went by.

Mikey ran up to me as Eddie and I went through the crowd to the third tee. "Dad, on that putt, did you read it going left?"

"Yeah, did you read it going right?"

"Yeah."

"Well, I must need you on the bag."

Mikey beamed, and so did Eddie.

It felt good to be out there on a gorgeous sunny day with my family behind the ropes and a caddy I'm comfortable with at my side. It eased the pressure some. Susan told me that Bridget was doing handstands against a tree while I was hitting my tee shot on No. 4. "She's my *yogini*," Susan said. Mine too, I guess. I birdied that hole from five feet and was 2-under.

No. 5 is 426 yards and played with a crosswind today, and I drew my drive a little too much and wound up in the rough with some tree branches in the way. But I played a nice run-up shot that left me with eighteen feet for birdie, and I almost made the putt. It died inches from the hole, right in the jaws. The same thing happened on No. 6—my birdie putt from six feet died right on the edge.

Somewhere along there I looked up at a leader board and saw that I was the coleader at 2-under with J. C. Snead and John Paul Cain. Nicklaus, playing right behind me, was a stroke back. People are always asking us if we peek at the leader boards. Some of us do, some of us don't. I like watching the scoreboard. Not looking would be like playing in a baseball game and not knowing the score.

The seventh hole, I hit my second behind the green but made a great up and down to save par. And then I missed a twelve-footer for birdie on No. 8, a putt that would have put me in the lead.

That brought us to the ninth hole, a tough par-3 that finishes just below the clubhouse. We had to wait on the tee, and while I was standing there visiting with Dale and Davey, both Snead and Cain made bogeys somewhere and left me alone with the tournament lead. Which, of course, meant absolutely nothing at that stage.

When we finally got to hit, I drilled one right at the flag, but it came down a little long, which you just can't do on that hole. I had a very fast downhill fifteen-footer for birdie, and I couldn't keep it from rolling six feet past the hole. I missed the comebacker, and that gave me my first bogey of the tournament.

Bridget ran up at me as I walked to the tenth tee. "Daddy," she said breathlessly, "you were winning!"

"Honey," I said, "I'm still going to win."

Dale was playing pretty well, but Davey looked like he wanted to break his clubs. He was 5-over after eight, and when he double bogeyed No. 11 I knew he was done. He didn't walk off the course, but his mind was already taking a fishing trip in the north woods.

I continued to do pretty well until the fourteenth hole, a long dogleg par-4. I hit an enormous drive there and only had a little pitching wedge left, but I caught the fringe instead of the green with it and ran off onto the back collar.

Then I had one of those episodes I've talked about. I was stepping up to chip the ball, I was focused. And then there was a tenth of a second when I wasn't there. I looked up and the ball was gone. I was chipping uphill, I should have left it short, but I hit it and immediately yelled, "Whoa! Whoa!"

Just not good thinking. I missed the six-footer coming back, and it kind of ticked me off. I made a good fifteen-footer to save par on the next hole, but it almost didn't help. The closing holes are so difficult that you have to be very, very confident.

I dropped a couple more strokes coming in and then bogeyed the eighteenth, playing it like the par-5 it normally is. I finished 3-over, which is not that bad. I kept looking at the leader boards, and everybody else was having trouble, too. You don't feel like a complete jerk when the scores are uniformly high.

When we finished, Davey grabbed his scorecard and signed it without looking. He practically ran out of the scorer's room. Dale found a mistake on the card—Davey was down for a 4 instead of a 5 on the fourth hole—but it was too late to correct because Davey had already signed it. That means Davey is disqualified. Not that he'll care. He shot 82, and the way he hates this golf course he's probably on some lake already. The scorecard mistake just saved him the trouble of having to call somebody to withdraw.

How's this for irony? The leader of the tournament, after one round, is Mike Hill, Davey's brother. Mike shot 68, a stroke better than Gary Player and two shots better than Lee Trevino. Mike won last week in Chicago, so you'd have to say he's our hottest golfer.

JULY 26, FRIDAY/BIRMINGHAM

Trevino was out this morning, working on his putting. His nickname is "Fork" this week. He's started gripping his putter with the shaft running down between the index and middle fingers of his right hand. He didn't like how he was putting in Cincinnati, so he decided to try something different last week in Liverpool. "I was watching the guys putt with that long putter," he said, "and their hands worked very well back and forth. So I said, 'I'm going to try that.' I did it in all the practice rounds over there, and I drove Tom Watson and Freddie Couples crazy with it. I was holing putts from everywhere."

Lee calls it "the fork," but the guys who use the long putter call it "the claw." He'll probably get some criticism for fooling with a putting stroke that's served him well for so long, but it tells me that he's adaptable, that he's open to change.

It looks like par might win this tournament. Today was another cool sunny day, perfect golf weather, but the greens get faster every day we go without rain. The craziest green on the course is probably the eleventh, which is up in the air between two hills. The two sides are turned up like the brim of a cowboy hat, and the front falls off like one of those melted watches Salvador Dali used to paint. You can hardly walk on it, much less putt on it.

John Paul Cain was shaking his head in the locker room. He said he skulled a chip shot on No. 11, just plain bladed it twenty-five feet past the pin. The ball turned around and rolled all the way back to the cup, and he had a tap-in of inches for his par.

"That was nothing," he said. "You get the windmill and the clown's mouth at eighteen."

I know the course is tough, because I've played about as badly as I can play for two days, and I still have a representative score. I shot 74 today and came off the course feeling very frustrated, but I still finished in the top third of the field. The one thing I have that is so critical to playing a U.S. Open course is patience. No matter how hard I whip on myself, I keep plugging. I try to make 6s into 5s. I work real hard on those little one- and two-foot putts. That's where you throw the strokes away on this course—right around the hole.

The leader after two rounds is J. C. Snead at even par, but he can't be comfortable with the four guys who are a stroke behind him—Chi Chi, Trevino, Al Geiberger, and Nicklaus.

J.C. is Sam Snead's nephew, if you didn't know. A good ball striker. He won a few times on the regular tour, and his name still popped up now and then as he neared fifty. But he hasn't done a thing since he came out on the Senior Tour last year. We all know he can play, but he still has to prove to himself that he can. Until he does, he's a big question mark.

I know the Open isn't the time for it, but I've been rethinking my caddy situation. Eddie's good. He's a hard worker and a good influence. He's not beating on me to do better, and he doesn't get upset when I hit a bad shot. Susan says that I should look at him as someone to use on a semiregular basis. It turns out he's no longer with Homero Blancas, and he's looking for a steady bag.

Susan planned to caddy for me next week on Long Island, but she asked me to reconsider. "My feelings won't be hurt," she said, "and this is business. If you've got a chance to win, Eddie can help you more than I can. You know that's true."

Actually, I *don't* know that's true, although I agree with her about Eddie. I've won, up to this week, about $120,000. That's not much, but I won about $80,000 of it in just three tournaments. One was the Tournament of Champions, where my caddy was Gary Colvin, who can't hit a bull in the ass with a bass fiddle. The second was the Tradition, where I had

Jennifer, who knows even less. And the other was the TPC, where I just picked up some kid, gave him the bag, and told him to stay out of the way.

What I'm saying is, I've made most of my money with three caddies who weren't professionals. It may or may not be coincidental.

I go off on tangents. If something doesn't work, I try something else. It's the compulsive-obsessive thing. If zero's not working, let's go to 180.

I suspect if I do go to a professional caddy, it will be somebody like Eddie. I trust Susie on these things.

JULY 27, SATURDAY/BIRMINGHAM

Tempers are getting short. I saw in the paper this morning that a reporter tried to talk to Bob Charles after his round yesterday, and Charles bit his head off. "I hate these greens," Bob told the guy. "I hate this golf course. I hate everything about it! I missed so many short putts it's not funny, and I'm not laughing."

Charles must have shot 80, right? Nope. He shot a 70 and is just two strokes out of the lead. That just goes to show how this golf course and the Open pressure wear on you. A USGA guy tried to get Bob to go to the press tent, and Bob said, "Not going," and walked off to hit balls on the range.

Eddie and I were a tired team after today's round. "My feet's killing me," he said. "I haven't walked in so long. Jesus Christ, this ground is soft."

The fairways maybe, not the greens. Another day of good weather and no rain had them putting like linoleum. I bogeyed No. 1 from the bunker and then three-putted two and three for par and bogey. Then I bogeyed No. 4.

As so often happens, I played well after that—after I'd killed my chances of doing anything. I hit a hell of a good golf shot on No. 11, a flyer from the rough that landed a third of the way up the green and rolled to about three feet from the hole. It came at a good time, because I was still at 4-over for the round. The birdie there made me think I could shoot 71 or 72. I parred the next hole, and then hit an 8-iron to about three feet on the thirteenth hole, the par-3, and made that for birdie. Suddenly I was 2-over, I was all right. I still had the hard holes to play, but Christ, I should have been 8-over.

But I lost it coming home. I hit a bad tee ball on No. 16 and then tried to recover with a big hook around a tree from the left rough. It was a dumb shot. I started thinking about the money. At the Open, all the places below tenth place are just a few hundred dollars apart. Where I'm placed in the field, a bogey doesn't hurt as much as a birdie helps, so I decided to take a chance. And of course I hit the tree and made bogey.

And then I made what I thought was a perfect drive on No. 18, right over the bunker, but it didn't make the fairway. So I hit what I thought was a perfect second shot from the rough, and it wound up over the green. I was lucky to make bogey from there.

I hate to repeat myself, but the greens here are insane, absolutely unplayable. Maybe I'm the only person that feels that way, I don't know.

Kenny Still was my partner today, and he played well. Played within himself, kept the ball on the fairway, made a lot of good puts, and shot 72. He was dressed like Father Christmas in red slacks and a red and white striped shirt, and he seemed to be enjoying himself. The only time he got upset was on No. 16, where he had a delicate little greenside pitch over a bunker. Some character behind him didn't know Kenny's brother—Stan Still—and yelled to somebody while Kenny was swinging. Kenny's pitch just cleared the bunker and the ball got caught in the long fringe grass, fifty or sixty feet short of the hole.

"Asshole yells right on my backswing," Kenny said on the seventeenth tee. "Right on my *backswing!*"

The Fork made his move today, shot a 68 and took a one-stroke lead on Chi Chi, Nicklaus, and J. C. Snead. Trevino said he made yet another change in his putting stroke, and it worked for him. "All I did was move the ball back in my stance about four inches so I can hit down on it more. I'm doing exactly what Chi Chi does."

You can hear Lee as he walks around the clubhouse. He keeps chirping, "The Fork!"

Snead hung in there and shot 71. He could win this tournament. Today was really his critical round. This is his first real pressure on the Senior Tour, and if he was going to fold, it would have been today. If he can get it under par tomorrow, he'll prove to himself that he can handle the pressure and he'll probably go on and win.

In the locker room, though, the man of the hour is Jerry Barber. He's seventy-five years old, and he's shot two 74s and a 75 here. In other words, he's shot his age or better three times. And remember, we're playing Oakland Hills. At 75, just *walking* these hills is an accomplishment, and he's beaten about 90 percent of the golfers in the field. To me, this is the most amazing story of the week.

He has to be doing it with his putter. He can't hit it far enough to beat anyone with the other clubs.

JULY 28, SUNDAY/BIRMINGHAM

I had a bad day yesterday. I don't want to go into it, but I had a bad day *off* the golf course as well as on. I woke up with one of those dry drunks, one of those periods of anger and anxiety. It happens when I feel out of control, and my golf game felt out of control. That's what triggered it, I'm sure.

First off, I got on the kids. I was on them to wake up faster, to get dressed and go to breakfast. Let's do this, let's do that, "Why aren't we organized?" I wasn't a very nice person to be around.

We stopped at a supermarket to get some stuff for the kids

to snack on as they walked around—granola bars, something cheaper than the outrageous $9.50 they're charging for a turkey sandwich in the clubhouse—and I had a run-in with a lady at the checkout counter. This lady thought I was cutting in front of her—which I was—and she started telling me where to get off. The kids were annoying me, too. They wanted to buy this, they wanted to buy that.

I had to walk away from the checkout line. I tried to deal with it by going over and cooling off, collecting my thoughts. But apparently I didn't do a good-enough job. I took it to the golf course, and it didn't help with my round at all.

And then I embarrassed Susan in front of Phil Armbruster. She was consoling me, saying, "You didn't do that bad." And I sort of snapped at her: "You *enjoy* watching me play like that?"

So Susan and I had quite a set-to back at the Embassy Suites. She worked me over real good about my attitude. She said, "I don't want to follow you around if you're going to be like this." Of course, I took that as an assault on my unblemished character.

I got off by myself last night and began to look at what had happened. I finally decided, "Hey, it's not that important. Golf is important, but it's not *that* important." Getting the kids organized, beating the lady to the cash register, none of that stuff is important. Life unfolds. It doesn't need Frank Beard's help.

So I woke up this morning with a little better outlook. I came out early, hit some balls, smelled the flowers. Even Michael said, "Jeez, Dad, you've got a better attitude this morning." I don't know whether his mother told him to say that, but I suspect not. Michael is getting pretty perceptive.

The net result is that I enjoyed myself more. I enjoyed the round, I enjoyed the people, I enjoyed the sky. My golf game, up until the tenth hole, was not any better—I hit some bad shots and was 2-over making the turn—but my attitude gave me a chance to be open, to hear and to see.

I bogeyed No. 9, and it looked like I was going to have a

bad round. You really need to shoot par on the front side because the back side is so hard.

On No. 10, I hit what I thought was a good drive, but when I got to the ball it was in an almost unplayable lie in the rough. I had only a 9-iron to the green, but I didn't concentrate well and missed the green completely. And then I hit a pitch shot the same way—thoughtlessly.

I was fifteen feet from the hole and losing it. But I made that putt. And it woke me up.

As we were walking to the next tee, I said, "Eddie, I don't know why the good Lord let me make that putt, but I'm going to bust my butt these next eight holes and I'm going to concentrate. We're going to make some money."

It was like Cincinnati, a few weeks back—that Saturday round where I was playing so badly I wanted to quit. I suddenly had a goal: score, make birdies, do whatever you have to do to get it done. I hit a great drive on No. 11, one of the best drives I've hit all week, and then hit a 9-iron to about six feet. Missed the putt. Hit a killer drive and a 2-wood on the par-5 twelfth, and then hit a pitch that I thought was right against the hole. It ran off the green and I had to settle for another par.

No. 13 and No. 14 were two-putt pars, but I hit a humongous drive around the corner of fifteen, hit a sand wedge to about five feet and made that for birdie. Sixteen, I had a twisting five-footer for par, a putt I've been missing all week, but I made it. And then on No. 17, a long par-3, I hit a wonderful 6-iron and almost carried it home. I made the putt from fifteen feet for another birdie, and I was back to even par for the round.

I was playing golf again. I was *playing* golf, and it felt great.

I came to No. 18, which I'd bogeyed all three days, and hit a drive across the corner. Unlike yesterday, it bounced straight, leaving me just an 8-iron to the green. I was thinking birdie, but the flag was left front, behind the guarding bunker, tough to get at. I kind of pulled one into the lefthand fringe and had to settle for a two-putt par.

But I really played golf. I was 2-under for the last eight holes, and they are hard holes. If I hadn't missed some pretty good putts, I could have shot 30 on the back nine. I passed a bunch of guys and finished seventeenth. Made $7,688 and salvaged some pride. In fact, I finished just a stroke behind J. C. Snead, who shot 79 today. I made up nine strokes on a guy who was just one off the lead when he teed off today.

I may want to read my own book. Because this is the crux of tournament golf—getting away from golf swings, abstracts and hypotheticals, and playing in the here and now.

Why today? Why not on Thursday or Friday? Why not on the front nine on Saturday? I don't know.

Susie and the kids were happy for me. I know they'd be happier if I could walk a straighter line in life and control my mood swings better. That's something I have to work on. But I got some nice smiles and hugs under the trees behind the eighteenth green.

I had a brief conversation with Fast Eddie and gave him a check for 5 percent of my winnings, based on a twentieth-place finish. "I may finish a little higher," I told him, "and I'll catch up with you down the road and give you a little more." And we talked about maybe working together again, maybe in the fall. Susan is hard on me to get together with Eddie, and I think she's probably on the money. He showed me an intensity I hadn't seen in a while, but without putting any pressure on me. I hit some godawful shots this week and I made some double bogeys, and I didn't see him slinking around and slamming the pins down. I've got a feeling we'll team up again, maybe on a permanent basis.

On the way to the airport, we stopped for something to eat. The restaurant had a lounge with a TV going, so we went in there and watched the leaders finish up back at Oakland Hills.

We picked up the action with Nicklaus and Trevino at the seventeenth hole. It was a four-way tie at 3-over-par between Al Geiberger, Trevino, Nicklaus, and Rodriguez, with Geiberger already in the clubhouse.

Jack and Lee needed birdies to grab the lead. The seventeenth is a 185-yard par-3, and the pin today was in a hard-to-reach spot behind a bunker. Trevino tried one of his low-trajectory 5-irons, but he must have flat-out scuffed it because the ball landed left and way short of the green. It was one of the worst shots I've ever seen Lee hit under pressure. Nicklaus then took *his* 5-iron and hit one of those high shots that he's famous for. He cleared the bunker and put the ball down five feet from the hole. He made the putt for his birdie and the lead.

But the shot I'll always remember was Chi Chi's. Rodriguez was in the eighteenth fairway—downhill lie, 167 yards uphill to the hole, and absolutely no way to attack the pin. The green was so hard today that any shot flown over the front bunker bounced to the back edge, a horrible place to be.

Chi Chi took a 6-iron, aimed way right, and hit the damndest snap hook you ever saw. When he first hit it, I thought . . . well, I didn't know what to think. The ball curved back to the open part of the green, landed well right of the flag, hopped left— it had incredible English on it—and then fed back toward the pin. When the ball finally stopped rolling, it was two feet from the hole. The gallery went crazy.

The shot took my breath away. I turned to Susan. "You know what? Nobody's gonna believe it, but he knew exactly what he was doing."

There's not another player in the world that could have hit that shot under pressure. Chi Chi has marvelous, marvelous hands.

But it was more than technique. It was almost like Shivas Irons and the ray of light from the book *Golf in the Kingdom*. It was as if there was a ray of light from the hole back to Chi Chi and all he had to do was follow the light home.

A shot like that comes from the spirit. Chi Chi hit it with his hands and through his spirit, and the ball flew as if shaped in flight by his mind.

I would love to hit one shot like that in my life.

EPILOGUE

NOVEMBER 1, FRIDAY/PALM DESERT, CALIFORNIA

I recently read back over my journal entries, through the Senior Open. I was appalled at how negative I sound. Even at the Tournament of Champions, where I played very well, nervousness and fear jump off the pages.

I had the exact same reaction twenty years ago when I read the manuscript of *Pro*. "I sure don't sound like the leading money winner," I told my wife. "I sound like the leading money loser."

For someone as concerned with personal growth as I am, the gloomy outlook of both books serves as a rebuke. I clearly haven't made the progress I thought I had.

The truth is, 1991 has been a wonderful year for me. My wife and I are on better terms than ever. I've got good friends who care about me and enrich my life. I've been a good father to my little kids. My older children and I are re-forming our relationships and have spent quality time together. And I've written this book. Everything about this year has been exceptional and rewarding . . . except the golf.

There's no way to get around the fact that I had a poor tournament year. My Sunday round at Oakland Hills didn't carry over. I played badly the next week at Long Island and most

252

every week after that. I only had one top-ten finish after the Senior Open—a seventh place at the Digital Seniors Classic in Concord, Massachusetts.

My 1991 numbers are dismal. I played twenty-three tournaments and made about $150,000 (counting the Legends, which is unofficial money). I made about $80,000 of that in three tournaments, which means I only made about $70,000 in the other twenty tournaments. That's very poor.

As I write this, my clubs are locked away. I'm taking the month of November off—no tournaments, no outings, no practice, nothing. I need some time to reevaluate my golf and where I'm going with it.

I've clearly begun to make the mistake I made on the old tour—putting too much pressure on my golf game. What I read in these pages is that I am still too much Frank, the golfer. I need to be Frank, a golfer.

The publisher's deadline dictated a late-summer conclusion to this journal, but I won't leave the reader hanging. Nicklaus beat Chi Chi in the Senior Open playoff, dodging thunderstorms all day Monday. I was back home and missed it, but my coauthor was at Oakland Hills. He tells me that Jack was magnificent, mastering that impossible golf course with a 65, the course record. Jack himself said he ranked it among his greatest tournament rounds, and Chi Chi said, "It was the best golf I've seen Jack play in fifteen years."

Having proved again that he is the greatest golfer who ever lived, Jack went back to designing golf courses and running his business empire. His final Senior Tour numbers for 1991: five tournaments, three wins, and $343,734 in official prize money. That, of course, doesn't count the $285,000 he won in the Senior Skins or the money he won on the big tour.

I can't follow up on everybody who appeared in this book, but a few deserve special mention. Rocky Thompson, who waited his whole life to win his first golf tournament, had to wait only three months to win his second. He sank an eight-foot putt for birdie on the final hole at Concord and beat

Bruce Crampton by a stroke. I didn't know what to think when Rocky won at Syracuse, whether he was lucky or what. But I've played enough with him since then to accept that he's become a complete player. He's going to be a real force for years to come.

A few weeks later, John Brodie beat Chi Chi and George Archer in a playoff to win *his* first tournament, the Security Pacific Senior Classic. (John hit a 9-iron to within four inches on the first hole of sudden death.) I said earlier the odds were long that John would ever win, so I have to eat a little crow. It took courage for him to stick to it all these years, and I take my hat off to him.

I'm not the only guy to make a bad prediction. Some pages back, Al "Mr. 59" Geiberger predicted that nobody would break 60 with that million dollars of Hilton Hotel money up for grabs. So what happens? Chip Beck, one of the big-tour youngsters, birdies the last three holes and shoots a 59 in the Las Vegas Invitational. From the reports I've had, the golf course in Vegas was not as tough as the course Geiberger played in Memphis. But, hey, a 59 is a 59.

Some other updates:

Charlie Coody had a three-stroke lead with two holes to play at Park City, Utah, but finished double bogey, triple bogey, and wound up fourth. Charlie's not a choker by any stretch, but he's at the level now where nothing matters to him but winning. He was not a prolific winner on the big tour—he won three times—and now he wants to win so desperately that it probably gets in his way. He came right back in October, though, and won the Transamerica in Napa, California. With two wins and about a half million dollars in prize money this year, Charlie has to rate 1991 as the best year of his career.

Lee Trevino, our burnout case, *did* skip the PGA Championship at Crooked Stick. The layoff must have done him some good, because he won at Albuquerque a couple of weeks later. Lee won't be the leading money winner this year, but he's in the top five, which is pretty good for an off-year. He's still a marvelous golfer.

The three hottest seniors down the stretch were Mike Hill, George Archer, and Jim Colbert. Hill won at Seattle and Atlanta and leads the money list with $748,689. Archer has won three tournaments since the Senior Open and is second in money with $739,205. And Colbert capped his magnificent rookie season by winning our biggest money tournament, the $1.5 million Vantage Championship. I marvel at the Hills and Archers and Colberts. I play with them daily, and they continue to amaze me.

Larry Mowry, I'm happy to report, is restored to good health. His last doctor, the one who said he didn't have Meniere's disease but merely a pesky ear infection, turned out to be right. Larry took some pills and was back out on tour by late August. He shot a tournament-record 64 in Indianapolis, and when I saw him later in Los Angeles he said he was making putts from everywhere with that long putter I talked him into using. "Some mornings I wake up and feel a little funky," he said, "but I'm having no problem on the golf course."

That was great news, and so is the latest on Jim Yancey: His cancer has disappeared. The chemotherapy worked, and the tumor in his throat is gone. I talked to his mom at the Vantage, and she said his hair is growing back and he's happy as can be. I can't wait to see him next February when we swing through Florida.

Seemore? I haven't seen hide nor hair of him. I came home one afternoon a few weeks ago, and Susan said, "Seemore called. He left a number."

I didn't call Seemore. I didn't even look at the area code to see where he was calling from.

Jimmy Colbert and I flew out of North Carolina on the same plane a few weeks ago. He had just won the Vantage Championship, and everybody up front was toasting him and shaking his hand.

About an hour into the flight, he came back and sat beside me. "Frank," he said, "I want to talk to you about a couple of things."

"Okay, pal. Shoot."

"First of all, you can still play."

He had that intense look he gets, a look that says he doesn't expect to be contradicted.

He went on to say some things about dedication and working hard, but I mostly heard those first words: "You can still play." He was obviously aware of the tournament I'd just had, which was very poor, and of my whole second half, which was awful. He was stepping out of his own glory and exultation to invest some time and energy in me.

"I'll tell you why I'm telling you this," he went on. "These are things that I've lived on, and I got them from a guy who talked to me twenty-five years ago. You probably won't remember this, but you sat me down at Hartford one night and kicked me in the ass for about three hours. About the talent I had and what I had to do to get it done.

"I still live on a lot of the words that you told me that night, and I'm forever grateful. I became a better player as a result of that."

I was never Jimmy's mentor; we'd just played a lot of bridge together on the old tour. So this conversation in the back of the plane, with Jim at the top of his career, struck me as extraordinary. It spoke to the role that friendship and caring play in life. And it reminded me how lucky I am to have gotten a second chance . . . in golf and in life.

INDEX

257